Maintenance of Knowledge-Based Systems
Theory, Techniques and Tools

The A.P.I.C. SERIES
General Editors: M. J. R. SHAVE and I. C. WAND

1. Some Commercial Autocodes. A Comparative Study*
E. L. Willey, A. d'Agapeyeff, Marion Tribe, B. J. Gibbens and Michelle Clarke
2. A Primer of ALGOL 60 Programming*
E. L. Dijkstra
3. Input Language for Automatic Programming*
A. P. Yershov, G. I. Kozhukhin and U. Voloshin
4. Introduction to System Programming*
Edited by Peter Wegner
5. ALGOL 60 Implementation. The Translation and Use of ALGOL 60 Programs on Computer
B. Randall and L. J. Russell
6. Dictionary for Computer Languages*
Hans Breuer
7. The Alpha Automatic Programming System*
Edited by A. P. Yershov
8. Structured Programming†
O.-J. Dahl, E. W. Dijkstra and C. A. R. Hoare
9. Operating Systems Techniques
Edited by C. A. R Hoare and R. H. Perrott
10. ALGOL 60 Compilation and Assessment
B. A. Wichmann
11. Definition of Programming Languages by Interpreting Automata*
Alexander Ollongen
12. Principles of Programme Design†
M. A. Jackson
13. Studies in Operating Systems
R. M. McKeag and R. Wilson
14. Software Engineering
R. J. Perrott
15. Computer Architecture: A Structured Approach
R. W. Doran
16. Logic Programming
Edited by K. L. Clark and S.-A. Tärnlund
17. Fortran Optimization*
Michael Metcalf
18. Multi-microprocessor Systems
Y. Paker
19. Introduction to the Graphical Kernel System (GKS)*
F. R. A. Hopgood, D. A. Duce, J. R. Gallop and D. C. Sutcliffe
20. Distributed Computing
Edited by Fred B. Chambers, David A. Duce and Gillian P. Jones
21. Introduction to Logic Programming
Christopher John Hogger
22. Lucid, the Dataflow Programming Language
William W. Wadge and Edward A. Ashcroft
23. Foundations of Programming
Jacques Arsac
24. Prolog for Programmers
Feliks Kluźniak and Stanislaw Szpakowicz
25. Fortran Optimization, Revised Edition
Michael Metcalf
26. PULSE: An Ada-based Distributed Operating System
D. Keeffe, G. M. Tomlinson, I. C. Wand and A. J. Wellings
27. Program Evolution: Process of Software Change
M. Lehman and L. A. Belady
28. Introduction to the Graphical Kernel system (GKS): Second Edition. Revised for the International Standard
F. R. A. Hopgood, D. A. Duce, J.R. Gallop and D. C. Sutcliffe
29. The Complexity of Boolean Networks
P. E. Dunne
30. Advanced Programming Methodologies
Edited by Gianna Cioni and Andrzej Salwicki
31. Logic and Computer Science
Edited by P. Odifreddi
32. Knowledge Representation: An Approach to Artificial Intelligence
T. J. M. Bench-Capon
33. Integrated Project Support Environments: The Aspect Project
Edited by Allan W. Brown
34. Object-oriented Languages
G. Masini, A. Napoli, D. Colnet, D. Leonard and K. Tombre
35. An Introduction to Programming with Specifications: A Mathematical Approach
R. Kubiak, R. Rudziński and S. Sokołowski
36. Knowledge-based Systems and Legal Applications
Edited by T. J. M. Bench-Capon
37. Fundamentals of Spatial Information Systems
R. Laurini and D. Thompson
38. Inductive Logic Programming
S. Muggleton
39. Expert Database Systems
Edited by Keith Jeffery

* Out of Print
† Now published in the Computer Science Classic Series

The A.P.I.C. Series
Number 40

Maintenance of Knowledge-Based Systems
Theory, Techniques and Tools

Frans Coenen and Trevor Bench-Capon
The University of Liverpool, UK

ACADEMIC PRESS
Harcourt Brace Jovanovich, Publishers
London San Diego New York
Boston Sydney Tokyo Toronto

ACADEMIC PRESS LIMITED
24–28 Oval Road
London NW1 7DX

United States Edition published by
ACADEMIC PRESS INC.
San Diego, CA 92101

This book is printed on acid-free paper

A catalogue record for this book is available from the British Library
ISBN 0-12-178120-8

Printed in Great Britain by Hartnolls Ltd, Bodmin, Cornwall.

CONTENTS.

Preface

In the 1970s Knowledge Based Systems (KBSs) started to emerge on the scene accompanied by three bold claims: that it was possible to simulate human expertise by Artificial Intelligence (AI) systems based on a large body of heuristic knowledge, that such systems would be capable of practical application, and that they would have a tremendous impact on future computer systems. Initially the high cost of developing such systems required that they be applied to correspondingly ambitious tasks with a high payoff, but as expert system shells gradually reduced the cost and widened the availability of the technology, more mundane applications became feasible and it seemed indeed as if they might become a routine and useful part of practical computer solutions. Paul Duffin, a prominent member of the UK Central Communications and Telecommunications Agency (CCTA), could write in 1988 that:

> "The UK Civil Service is the largest single user of conventional IT equipment and services in the UK ... The CCTA has a specific responsibility to research and then encourage the use of appropriate IT to assist in the administrative mechanisms of Government. KBS represents one such technology which CCTA has identified as being of particular benefit ... In terms of government administration, KBS may be the single most significant development to emerge since the computer itself, for it offers a means of streamlining and improving decision-making to an unprecedented degree" [Duffin 1988].

However, this has not happened. Whilst the first two claims cited above have been substantiated, KBSs have not in general had the foreseen impact.

Many reasons have been advanced to explain this failure of the technology to take off: these range from claims that the benefits of the technology have been greatly overstated to criticisms of the innate conservatism of those responsible for commissioning systems. There may be some truth in all these positions but we believe that a major factor has been the lack of good methodologies for building and maintaining the systems. Development methodologies, especially KADS, have received a great deal of attention recently, and we agree that without a sound development methodology the enterprise is doomed to failure. The same cannot be said for KBS maintenance. Building a system is not the end of the story: the system must be used, and during its period of use the knowledge on which it relies will change and develop. A KBS that is not to become rapidly obsolete must change and develop with it. In this book we address this neglected area of maintenance.

The book is thus aimed at anyone, whether in a commercial or academic environment, who wishes to build a serious KBS that will continue to be *used* over a period of time. If the system is to have a useful life it is essential that the system be able to adapt to and accommodate the changes in its knowledge domain that will inevitably occur, and if the investment of time and effort spent constructing the original KB is not to be largely wasted, it is essential that changes can be incorporated into the KB smoothly, so that as little as possible needs to be redone. This can only be realised if the need for maintenance is taken seriously at the outset: these future needs must inform the design of the system, and the methods and tools used to encode the KB.

The first three chapters of the book provide introductory material: to software engineering, to KBSs, and the links between these two areas, and to the crucial area of knowledge representation. The next chapter examines the maintenance needs of KBSs. There follow two chapters on the development of KBSs, and how the manner in which they are developed can help or hinder subsequent maintenance. Then there is a chapter on how the area of the system that requires attention can be identified. The next five chapters describe the kinds of things that can go wrong with KBSs, and some of the tools that have been developed to identify and rectify problems. We then have a chapter on testing the system, both to verify and to validate it, before finally examining some of the issues associated with managing change in a system. Thus our overall intention is to move from very general concerns applicable to all systems through to specific techniques and tools designed to address particular problems in particular representations, before concluding with some more general remarks.

The book developed out of a SERC supported project, Maintenance Assistance for Knowledge Engineers (MAKE), which was carried out in collaboration with ICL and British Coal between 1990 and 1992. Several sections of the book describe tools developed on that project. We would like to thank our collaborators, especially Charlie Portman, Nick Perry, Mick Smith and Phil Race of ICL, and Richard Perkin, Matthew Pitt and Andy Marshall of British Coal. Without their considerable efforts in building the tools and putting them to work in a practical application, much of the discussion of this book would have been far less well informed. We would also like to thank the following University of Liverpool staff members: Kenney Chan, who provided us with invaluable technical support on the project, Ray Paton, for material concerning knowledge acquisition, conceptualisation and analysis and Paul Dunne for advice concerning difficulties associated with the camera ready preparation.

Frans Coenen

Trevor Bench-Capon

I would also like to express my special thanks, to my wife Jan and daughter Kate for their enthusiastic support throughout the long days of writing and also to Trevor, mostly for his hard work and dedication as my co-author, but also for planting the initial seed for this book.

Frans Coenen

I too would like to add my personal thanks to my wife, Priscilla, without whose patient support and encouragement I could not contemplate writing a book. Also many warm thanks to Frans, for his stimulating collaboration on this and other projects.

Trevor Bench-Capon

October 1992

CHAPTER 1

Software Engineering

1.1. INTRODUCTION

This book is concerned with the maintenance of Knowledge Based Systems (KBSs). As such its concerns are broadly those of software engineering, although the application of software engineering principles to KBSs is still more a matter of research investigation than widely accepted practice. It is, however, impossible to minimise the importance of the development of these principles. The practical take up of KBSs is usually described as disappointing: one explanation of the reluctance of organisations to make a real commitment to these systems stems from the lack of well defined techniques to engineer them in an acceptable manner. One of the chief manifestations of the lack of these techniques is that it is impossible to say with any assurance that it will be possible to maintain the systems so that their useful life can be extended. Without the assurance of quality that can be given by the use of a proven methodology, the risk of investing substantially in these systems will remain too great to be taken.

In this chapter we will set the scene for the rest of the book by discussing the current practice of software engineering, and make some broad suggestions as to how it might be applied to KBSs. Clearly we cannot provide a complete discussion of conventional software engineering principles and techniques, but we will provide an overview. Those who want or need a detailed introduction to conventional software engineering may find it in one of the many excellent books on the subject, such as Sommerville [1989] or Pressman [1988].

1.1.1. The Origins of Software Engineering

The term "software engineering" was introduced in the late 1960s as a response to the so-called "software crisis". The 1960s had seen rapid developments in computer technology and the production of the first third generation computers. These machines were much cheaper to produce and were several orders of magnitude more powerful than the machines of the previous generations. As a result they made possible a corresponding increase in the power of the software programs that could be run on them, and a whole new range of previously uneconomic applications was opened up. The potential for exploiting this technology in a range of commercial applications meant, of course, that the demand for computer systems rose sharply. Unfortunately understanding of software did not keep pace with hardware developments and software programmers quickly got into difficulty as it became apparent that writing these much larger and more powerful programs was not simply a matter of scaling up the processes used to develop second generation software. In consequence software development costs soared and many projects fell hopelessly behind schedule. By the end of the 1960s a "software crisis" was evident: hardware costs had tumbled while software costs were rising steeply. Further the demand for software was outstripping the ability to supply it. There was thus an urgent need for new techniques and methods which would allow the production of large software systems in an economic manner. The result was the discipline of software engineering.

The software crisis manifested itself in a number of ways. From the point of view of the managers responsible for software developments:

- Major projects were delivered late (sometimes years rather than months late).
- Projects proved far more expensive than had been forecast.
- The resulting systems were unreliable in use, resulting in customer dissatisfaction and loss of confidence in the systems.
- The productivity of programmers was low and could not keep pace with the demand for their services.
- The performance of the systems was poor.
- The systems could not be maintained so as to correct errors, adapt to changes in specification, or to incorporate new facilities.

Viewed from the standpoint of the software professional there were other difficulties:

- The software development process was poorly understood, so that there was no rational basis on which to estimate project development time. Moreover, matrices for measuring productivity were almost non-existent.

- Customer dissatisfaction resulted not just from system unreliability but because systems often failed to perform the tasks anticipated. Often systems were developed on the basis of the vaguest of understandings of requirements and the communication between customer and developer was insufficient to ensure that the right system was produced.
- The quality of systems delivered was unacceptable because of a lack of understanding of systematic and effective testing techniques. Well founded quantitative measures of reliability and performance were in short supply.
- The importance of maintenance was not sufficiently recognised. In practice much of the cost of the system was spent on maintenance, but maintainability received too little emphasis in determining acceptance of a system.

In short we can say that there were deficiencies in the ability to manage and organise large software projects; there were difficulties in ensuring the quality of such projects, and there were difficulties in finding or training staff to carry out the projects. The discipline of software engineering emerged to provide a set of techniques designed to remedy these problems.

Put at its simplest, software engineering can be defined as:

> "The establishment and use of sound engineering principles in order to obtain economically software that is reliable and works efficiently on real machines."

This definition was originally proposed by Fritz Bauer at the first major conference on the subject of software engineering [Naur and Randell 1969].

These principles would aid the management and organisation of projects by making the stages in the development process more visible, so that progress could be monitored and reviewed at appropriate checkpoints. Quality would be enhanced by the use of structured development techniques, frequent reviews against measurable criteria, and better testing methodologies. Finally the training and productivity of staff would be improved by the production of explicit development methodologies which would mean that the process was one which could be taught rather than simply learned on the basis of (often painful) experience.

All of this necessitated something of a culture change in software developers. At the time of the crisis, many of them had received little in the way of formal training. Software development thus had much of the mystique of a "black art" that could only be acquired through experience, and which could not be understood by outsiders - such as managers. This meant that individuals tended to pick up their own tricks and habits, some good, but some bad, and that there was little standardisation, even amongst programmers working quite closely together. In short program development was seen as being a somewhat anarchic art form, rather than an engineering discipline. As a result of the introduction of software engineering practices this culture has been largely replaced in conventional software development. Practitioners in Artificial Intelligence (AI) and KBSs, however, retain many of these attitudes. It is perhaps an inevitable accompaniment of an immature technology. It is instructive to recall a number of "practitioners myths" [Pressman 1988]:

- There are no methods for analysis, design and testing that work - so just write the code.
- The job is just to write the program and get it to work.
- Quality cannot be assessed until there is a running program.
- Maintaining a running program is straightforward and we will fix problems as they arise.

The myths may have been exposed in a conventional setting, but they are still widespread in AI and KBSs. Now that KBSs are starting to emerge from the purely experimental stage, the time has come for them to be taken as seriously as software systems. This means rooting out corresponding myths from this area too, and in what follows we hope to show that this field is now ripe for the application of software engineering principles.

1.2. THE SOFTWARE LIFE-CYCLE

As we saw in the previous section one of the problems with software development in the late 1960s was that the process was something of a "black box". A vague requirement went in, and a (too often unsatisfactory) system emerged after a rather lengthy period. In order to support the notion of a discipline of software engineering as outlined above it was essential to gain some better understanding of the process, and to give some visibility to the stages of the process. This led to the concept of a software life-cycle which would provide a model of the software development process. This idea was derived from other engineering activities, the principal aim being to determine the order of the various stages of development of a system so that:

- Suitable formal methods could be adopted for each development stage to promote correctness and completeness.
- The understandability of the systems could be enhanced and hence the task of future maintenance eased.
- Managers could be given overall visibility of the development process and hence could introduce check points and review the products from each of the stages.
- The entire development process could be speeded up.

Such a model would, like any other model, be something of a simplification, but if would provide the essential framework for software engineering techniques. The earliest example is arguably that proposed by Royce [1970]. After subsequent development this has become known as the waterfall model [Sommerville 1989, Pressman 1988] and is still the most common life-cycle paradigm in use today for traditional software development. Although it is something of an idealisation and has many critics [Gladden 1982, McCracken and Jackson 1982, Boehm 1988], it has proved its worth. The waterfall model is is illustrated in Figure 1.1. The process is not as neat as the diagram makes it appear because the stages are not really mutually exclusive: a certain amount of overlap exists and information can be passed backwards and forwards from one stage to any other, and on occasion some backtracking and iteration through the stages may become necessary. For the purpose of discussing the software development process, however, it is convenient to treat each stage as consisting of specific separable activities. In the rest of this chapter we will consider each of the stages in turn, and attempt to draw some parallels with KBS. Again we must stress that in the space available a complete discussion of the software engineering practices, methodologies and techniques appropriate to each stage is not possible: interested readers are therefore referred to the references cited in the following sections for more detailed discussion.

1.2.1. System Analysis

Conventional computer systems are never introduced into an organisational vacuum. Typically the task or tasks to be computerised will form part of the existing activities of the organisation. If the computer system is to fit into the larger system, investigation must begin with this larger system, so that the various interfaces with hardware, people, databases, other computer systems, the rest of the organisation and other external organisations can be determined. Most importantly of all, at this stage

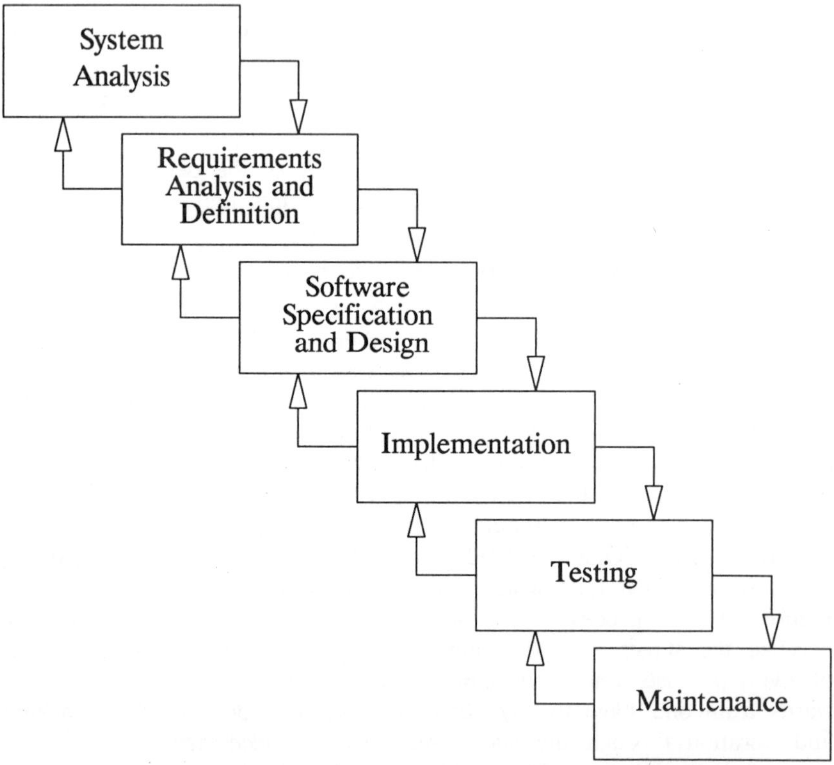

Figure 1.1: The traditional waterfall software life-cycle paradigm.

a boundary should be drawn around the proposed computer system, so that it can be clearly understood what is in, and what is excluded from, the remit of the proposed system. Drawing up this overall picture of the existing system will involve a certain amount of requirements gathering at the top system level and some top-level design and analysis.

To establish an overall system description there are a variety of well established techniques such as the use of Data Flow Diagrams (DFDs) and entity models. DFDs are used for functional system modelling where the system is considered as a set of function transforms with data flowing from one to the other. DFDs form part of several analysis methodologies, such as those proposed by Yourdan and Constantine [1978], De Marco [1979] and Gane and Sarson [1979], as well as SSADM (Structured Systems Analysis and Design Methodology), the methodology now adopted as standard throughout the UK government service. SSADM is a data driven method of system analysis and design and is described in Cutts [1991].

Entity models, or diagrams, represent a user view of the system in which entities are represented by data groups or logical records and the relationships between them by logical access paths. Entity diagrams are also used extensively in several system development methodologies such as DSSD (Data Structure System Development) and are also used in SSADM to provide a complimentary view to DFDs. DSSD [Orr 1977] is essentially a manual analysis technique supported by automated tools used to model systems from a functional viewpoint.

The use of DFDs and entity diagrams as described here may also be incorporated into the subsequent stages of the software development process. Other modelling techniques include Warnier diagrams, hierarchical structured charts, action diagrams and entity life history diagrams.

The aim of the system analysis stage is to produce a *software plan*. This is drawn up in the following manner. Once an overall view of the system into which the new system will fit has been established, a description, or set of alternative descriptions, of the scope of the proposed new system is produced. From this it is possible to estimate the resources that will be required to produce such a system, and to make some predictions as to the costs, production schedule and expected benefits of the system. This allows the feasibility of the project to be examined, any areas of technical risk identified, and a cost benefit analysis of the system to be carried out. Thus a basis can be provided for making selections between alternative possibilities, so that a firm recommendation can be made. All of these elements are then brought together into an initial software plan, to be reviewed by management, and which will give a preliminary indication of the viability of the proposals. After the review it may be that the project is accepted and allowed to proceed, or it may be that the plan is unacceptable, in which case it must be revised, perhaps redrawing the boundaries of the proposal so as to produce greater benefits or fewer costs, or to allow the project to be completed in time to meet external constraints. Once an acceptable plan has been completed and approved, the project is ready to proceed to the next stage of the life-cycle, the stage of detailed requirements analysis and specification.

Systems analysis rarely receives this degree of attention when the proposed system is to be a KBS. These are typically directed at a function performed by a person in the current system, and because of the exploratory nature of such projects, the system is insufficiently well understood at the outset to consider how it will integrate into the organisation as a whole. Moreover, in such projects estimates of time, costs and benefits tend to be extremely unreliable. The neglect of systems analysis in KBSs is thus understandable: it does mean, however, that there are no fixed points of reference against which the subsequent development can be compared. Therefore the valuable aid to project management and evaluation criteria for use throughout the life of a project available in conventional systems through a software plan is not available for KBSs. Finally it should be noted that there have been reports of system analysis methodologies such as SSADM being successfully adapted for KBS development [Threadgold 1991, 1992].

1.2.2. Requirements Analysis and Definition

Once the role of the proposed system has been agreed, and the proposal accepted on the basis of a preliminary software plan, the phase of detailed analysis and specification of user requirements can begin. The importance of this stage cannot be overstated: if the requirements are not properly understood and agreed, all subsequent effort will be directed towards building the wrong system - a system which will not do what the users expect and need of it. At this stage it is very important to separate notions of what the system will do from notions of how the system will do these things: a common fault of requirements specifications is that the method intrudes so that there is a premature commitment to specific implementation details that really should be left to a later stage. Moreover, the "what" part of the requirements can be stated in a language that the users will understand and can therefore commit to with some degree of confidence: once the "how" is reached the users may begin to flounder.

Requirements analysis requires close co-operation with the procurers and the intended end users of the software so that a model of what the intended software system will do, based on information gathered from these meetings, can be developed. The model must represent both the problem area to be addressed (the functional domain) and the data to be processed (the information domain). The model will thus include the manner in which data will flow through the system, the content of this data, its logical structure and the transformations that will be carried out on it. Often a suite of models will be produced arranged in a hierarchical manner to allow the problem domain to be analysed in a top-down manner. The modelling techniques that can be used are similar to those described above for system analysis, such as data flow diagrams and entity diagrams, although in this stage they will be focussed on to smaller operations and thus show a finer grain of detail. The information, or data domain, may also be represented using relational modelling techniques where the logical structure of the data is represented as a set of tables with common keys. In practice several modelling techniques will be used to represent the intended software system.

Once developed the software system model must be analysed from both the logical and physical viewpoints. A number of methodologies and formal analysis techniques exist. These usually consist of a graphical notation, or some structured or formal language, to represent the model coupled with an analysis technique and, in some case, automated tools to produce documents. A structured language, also known as a formatted language, is a semi-formal language based on natural language with a structure and some rules imposed on it. A formal language has a rigorous syntactic and semantic specification and a precise set of rules for its use. Originally many of the analysis methods available were intended to be implemented manually and were designed with particular classes of system in mind. However in more resent years they have been "computerised", given software support and broadened for use on more general applications. Well known examples include PSL/PSA (Problem Statement Language/Problem Statement Analyser) and SADT (Structured Analysis and Design Technique). PSL/PSA [Teichrow and Hershey 1977] is a structured language designed to specify the requirements for information processing systems, a model is developed using PSL which is then analysed using PSA. SADT [Ross 1985], originally designed to specify the requirements for management information systems, consists of a "box-and-arrow" graphical language called SA and a design technique called DT.

Other well documented requirements analysis methodologies include SREM (Software Engineering Requirements Methodology) and TAGS (Technology for the Automated Generation of Systems). SREM [Alford 1985, Scheffer and Rzepka 1985] is an automated requirements analysis tool which uses a specifically designed language, RSL (Requirements Statement Language), to specify the requirements for real time systems. TAGS [Sievert and Mizell 1985] is a self contained specification system consisting of a graphics and tabular specification language called IORL (Input Output Requirements Language) mounted on a graphics work station equipped with appropriate software support tools.

Specifically for data analysis, normalisation techniques [Codd 1970] have been adopted for use in development methodologies such as SSADM, SSA (Structured System Analysis), and others. SSA [Gane and Sarson 1979] is used primarily in traditional data processing environments and uses a graphical language to build models of systems. Normalisation is used in conjunction with relational modelling techniques, and is designed to establish relationships between data items and to identify redundant data that may exist in the data structures and unique keys to access data items. Three levels of normalisation, referred to as first, second and third normal forms, are usually implemented. Further levels of normalisation have been described but these are rarely used in practice.

One of the problems encountered during the software requirements stage is that it is often very difficult to clearly identify the requirements, either because the users are unsure of what their requirements actually are, or because they have not been properly understood by the developers. The use of formal requirements analysis techniques, which combine systematic procedures and unique notations to analyse requirements such as those described above, can alleviate the problem. The problem remains real, however, and dissatisfaction with this stage of the process is one of the major driving forces behind the suggestion of alternative software life-cycles, such as rapid prototyping, discussed later in section 1.3.

Requirements analysis results in a software requirements definition and a software requirements specification. The first is a statement of the services that the customer expects from the software system. It is a user oriented document and is therefore usually set out in natural language. The second is a statement setting out the user's requirements in more detail. It is orientated towards the developers and may be set out using a formal requirements language. One example of such a language is RML (Requirements Modelling Language) which is an object oriented formal requirements specification language which was developed out of AI knowledge representation techniques and can therefore also be used simply to express "knowledge" [Borgida *et al.* 1985].

When the documents have been prepared there must be a critical reviewpoint at which the users accept the requirements definition document as providing a true description of the system that they will accept. Such agreement is essential as it is this document which will determine the system that is developed and will serve as the source of criteria for the validation of the completed system. Such a review must clarify any points of misunderstanding and vagueness, and may result in some iteration within this stage. Only when the users are satisfied can the requirements specification document be passed to the technical developers and the process of software specification and design begin.

Like the systems analysis stage, the requirements stage is often neglected in the development of KBS. Because there is no clear picture of what will be technically feasible it is hard to specify in advance what will be required of the system. Requirements are thus vaguely designed along the lines of "provide support for" some task. This can lead to problems later when the system is finished since the system may not perform as the user expected, and there will be no firm basis for the evaluation of the success or failure of the system. These difficulties led to the early popularity of prototyping life-cycles for KBS: these, however, have their own problems, as we will see in section 1.3.

1.2.3. Software Specification and Design

The process of specification and design takes the *"what is to be done"* of the requirements specification, and transforms it into a specification of how these things are to be done which can be encoded in a suitable programming language. The process may have several stages as the design becomes increasingly specific. Three distinct aspects of the final system must be detailed: the data structures, the software architecture and the algorithms and procedures that will carry out the desired functions. The final output from the software specification and design stage will be a detailed representation of the software that is to be produced which can be checked against the requirements specification and assessed for quality before actual coding begins. The design specification may be written in natural language, using diagrammatic techniques, structured English or using formal methods.

The main impact of software engineering on this stage of the development process is to systemise a process which used to be performed in an unsystematic manner. A number of approaches and methodologies have been proposed. These approaches can be broadly categorised as either top-down or bottom-up. In the top-down approach, as the name suggests, the design starts at the highest level and continues by decomposing the system into smaller and smaller chunks until it cannot be decomposed any further. Bottom-up design is then the reverse of top-down design, in that the lowest level components are designed first and higher level functions constructed from them. The current climate seems strongly in favour of top-down design: it is argued both that top-down design creates more readable and reliable programs, and that bottom-up methods tend to lead to undesirable local optimisations.

There are a number of software specification techniques that may be utilised. These include interface specification, operational specification and formal specification methods. Interface specification provides the most abstract view of the specification. Each component is considered as a "black box" and its function defined in terms of its input and output. Operational specification is the reverse of interface specification and focuses on the internal, "white box", operation of each component. Formal specification techniques use formal languages to express the software specification. These may be classified as either algebraic or model based. Algebraic, or axiomatic, specification is an approach generally used to specify abstract data types but may be used for broader based specifications. This technique is exemplified by OBJ [Futatsugi *et al.* 1985], a structured language for writing software specifications in an algebraic style which can be executed and hence tested. Model based specification is a technique that relies on formulating a model of the system using mathematical entities, such as sets, and some symbolic notation. Examples include VDM (Vienna Development Method) and Z. VDM [Jones 1986] is a formal specification technique based on top-down decomposition which uses set and logic notation to model a description of the system. Z [Hayes 1987] is based on typed set theory and uses schemas to introduce and set out relationships between entities.

Once the software specification is complete the design may be commenced with reference to the specification. Well known software design techniques include functional design, object oriented design and data driven design. In function-oriented design, as the name implies, the system is viewed and decomposed from a functional viewpoint, a process based on ideas about stepwise refinement [Constantine and Yourdon 1979]. In object oriented design, a method which incorporates ideas about information hiding and data abstraction, the system is viewed and decomposed as a collection of objects [Booch 1986, Wiener and Sincovec 1984 and Robson 1981]. Data driven design focuses on either data flow or data structure. The first follows on from the use of DFDs and the second is typified by JSP (Jackson Structured Programming). JSP [Jackson 1975] uses data structure as a basis for program design where by both data and program structures are represented using a diagrammatic notation which has a schematic logic associated with it. An extension of JSP is JSD (Jackson System Development). JSD [Jackson 1983] is a software development technique designed to encompass both the software requirements and the software specification and design stages of the development cycle.

There are also a number of notations that can be used to support the above design methodologies. These include flow charts, DFDs, hierarchical structured charts, Nassi-Shneiderman charts and design description languages or pseudo code.

The overall aim of software design should be that the structure of the resulting system mirrors the structure of the task it is to perform, with the goal that small changes to the requirements specification will result in only small changes to the program. Eventual software maintenance problems can also be limited by suitable design testing to show that (a) the software specification is correct (verification) and (b) it meets the requirements in full (validation). The use of structured and formal languages to specify the design allows for mathematical verification. It should also be noted that both modular and information hiding design concepts tend to result in more maintainable programs because the risk of corrupting sections of code contained in other modules is reduced.

The above remarks on design apply to conventional systems. In the case of KBSs the process is necessarily different. KBSs do not have the same notion of data structures and procedures applied to them, but rather the notion of a Knowledge Base (KB). The design process thus still includes the design of a system architecture, but the other two activities are replaced by the design of the KB, including both a choice of representation for the knowledge and an engine to manipulate the knowledge. This will be discussed further in chapter 2.

1.2.4. Implementation

The implementation phase is where the software design is translated into an executable form. Generally this involves the use of high level languages, which can be automatically compiled into the executable object code. In theory this should be the most straightforward stage of the process: if the design is good, then translation into code should be a fairly mechanical process.

Implementation can proceed in either a top-down or a bottom-up fashion. In a top-down development the highest level modules are implemented first, and tested using stubs to replace the lower level modules. As development proceeds the stubs are replaced by the actual modules they represent, until finally the lowest level modules are implemented. This has the advantage that the global environment in which a given module will operate is always available during its development, that integration testing and module testing are carried out simultaneously, and there is always a partially working system available for customer inspection and feedback. Disadvantages include the need to develop stubs which may need to be quite sophisticated; that when specification deficiencies are not detected until lower levels are reached this may require revision of the higher levels; and that the testing of lower level modules may not be complete, since they will be exercised only in the ways resulting from higher level calls. This last point may present especial problems if their mode of use changes during the maintenance of the system. In bottom-up design the lowest level modules are developed first, independently tested using drivers, and gradually integrated into the system as higher level modules are developed. This has the advantages of allowing for efficient development and thorough testing of the low level modules, and supporting the accumulation of code libraries: but it has the disadvantages of requiring drivers to be built, which may itself be a substantial task; forcing the need for separate integration testing; and delaying the visibility of the working system.

In practice, the best approach has been found to be to adopt a top-down approach, but to try to minimise the number of levels required to reach the bottom. This can be facilitated by building up libraries of code, so that well tested modules can be re-used across applications. If this approach is followed, the system can be designed recognising the existence of these units, so that decomposition is aimed at the modules available in the code library.

When implementing code *standards* should be observed. These standards will concern such things as the choice of variable names, indentation and other layout formats, and the means by which particular design constructs are realised. Standards are important in a large organisation, because they mean that all the members of the organisation will write similar code, and thus it will be very much easier for people to understand the code written by different authors. This is particularly desirable when reviewing and maintaining code, because such actions will normally be carried out by people other than the original author.

Implementation of a KBS can be rather different. Firstly the design - even when an intermediate representation is used - is often far less specific than that produced in the case of a conventional system. This means that the encoding of the design is not the same straightforward, almost mechanical, process. KBSs are normally implemented either in a specialist language, such as LISP or PROLOG, using a commercial shell, or using an "AI Toolkit". In all of these cases, top-down development is usually seen as the most appropriate. It should, however, also be noted that the concept of re-usable code is stressed in all of these, with the exception of the simplest shells. LISP has an extensive range of built-in functions, and programmers can quickly extend this by designing further ones of their own. Similarly PROLOG users will build up a library of procedures, and users of AI Toolkits a library of objects and "mix-ins".

A final problem which must be addressed when implementing KBSs is the lack of widely accepted standards. This can be attributed to the fact that because KBS coding has often been a relatively solitary and self-taught activity. This can make programs - particularly those written in LISP and PROLOG - difficult to follow, whether the reader is someone other than the author, or the author returning to the code after a period of absence.

1.2.5. Testing

Software testing is an important stage in software development, typically occupying 30-50% of development time. It is worth remembering that testing cannot show the absence of errors, only the presence of errors that need to be fixed. We can therefore never be sure that our system is error free; we can only obtain a reasonable confidence that it is working satisfactorily. It is helpful to draw a distinction between testing designed to verify the system from testing designed to validate it. There are many definitions for the terms verification and validation as applied to software systems but perhaps the most universally accepted are those proposed by Boehm [1981]:

- Verification; "Are we building the product right."
- Validation; "Are we building the right product."

Thus software verification is the process of testing that a piece of software meets its specifications and validation is the process of testing that a piece of software satisfies the requirements of the customer. Both are carried out throughout the development cycle although they can only definitively take place on completion of the product.

In a similar manner to that described in the above section on implementation, testing can be carried out either in a top-down or in a bottom-up fashion. Normally this will mirror the strategy used to develop the system. In addition a number of techniques for testing systems and constructing test data have been developed. These can be described using the taxonomy given in Figure 1.2. The figure shows that testing techniques can be divided into "black box" techniques, and "white box" techniques, also called "glass box" or "structured" techniques.

Black box testing occurs when test data is chosen using the requirements document, or detailed specification, and pays no regard to the internal working of the program. White box testing occurs when test data is chosen by reference to the structure of the program to demonstrate that the internal workings are satisfactory.

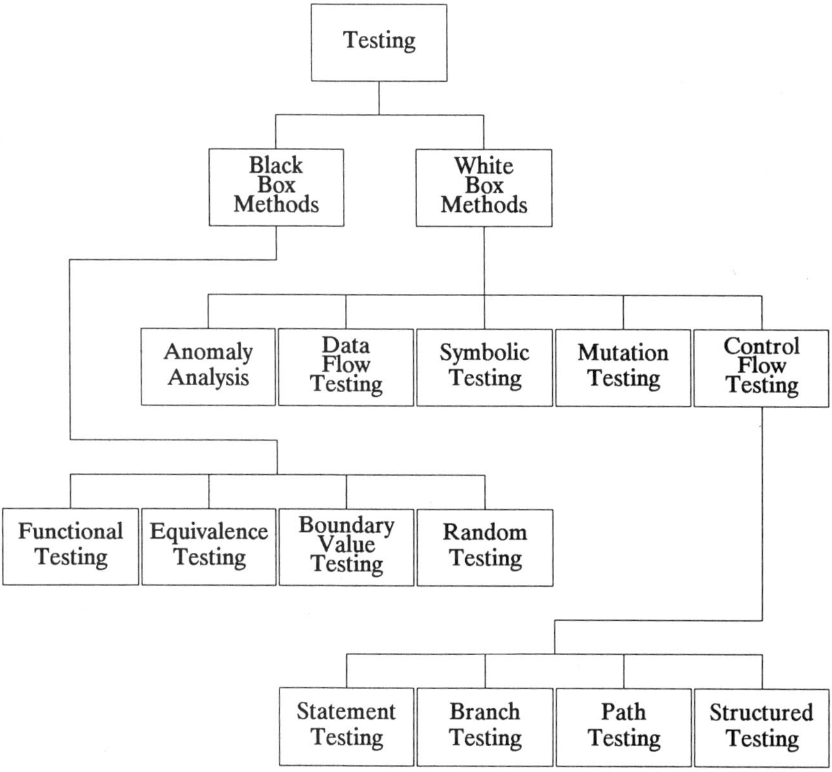

Figure 1.2: Testing taxonomy.

Black Box Testing Techniques

Black Box Techniques can be divided into:

1. Functional Testing. This is intended to demonstrate the working of each function in the requirements document for some typical requirement. For example an airline reservation system would test enquiring about availability, making a reservation, confirming a reservation, etc.
2. Random Testing. This method uses random values to remove any possibility of bias. A variant is to use "real" past data, where it exists.
3. Equivalence Testing. This is another method of designing test data. It divides the input domain into classes of data from which test cases can be constructed. This means examining the data which will be input to determine classes of data which should have the same (equivalent) effects. Thus:

- In the case of a range: three classes, values in the range, values below the range and values above the range.
- In the case of a specific value: three classes, that value, values below, and values above.
- In the case of a set: two classes, members and non-members.
- In the case of a Boolean: two classes, true and false.

We can construct test cases to exercise these classes exhaustively: when there is a failure it should be easy to determine which class of data is handled wrongly.

4. Boundary Value Testing. This is sometimes called "Extremal Value Testing". It is based on the insight that errors tend to occur at the limits of a data domain, rather than the centre. This method therefore uses these limit values to construct test cases as follows:

- In the case of a range: the lowest value, the highest value, and values either side of these values.
- In the case of a specific value: that value, a value just below and a value just above.
- In the case of an iteration: 0, 1 and the maximum number of iterations.
- In the case of an array: the first and last elements.

Boundary cases for both input *and* output can be examined using this technique.

White Box Testing Techniques

White box testing techniques include:

1. Anomaly Analysis. This involves examining the program, without running it, to look for suspicious constructs such as unused labels or variables.
2. Data Flow Driven Testing. Here test data is constructed to force the execution of different interactions between variable definitions and references in a program.
3. Symbolic Testing. With this technique selected paths are symbolically evaluated. Variables are initially assigned symbolic values. Then, when an assignment is executed the current symbolic values are used for the Right Hand Side and the resulting symbolic expression becomes the new value for the Left Hand Side.
4. Mutation Testing. Here a large number of small changes (mutations) are made to the program, one at a time. Test data which distinguishes the mutated version from the original must then be

found.

5. Control Flow Driven Testing. This uses test cases constructed to exercise control flow features of the program. There are a number of varieties:

   - Statement Testing - every statement is executed at least once.
   - Branch Testing - every branch (decision outcome) is executed at least once.
   - Path Testing - every complete program path is executed at least once. Often this is not practical as there will be too many (perhaps an infinite number of) paths (because of iterations).
   - Structured Testing - an approximation to path testing in which all paths which perform less than or equal to K iterations of loops are executed at least once. K is usually taken as 2. Variations are necessary when an iteration has a special feature which requires particular values of K to be tested.

To assist in some of the above techniques, automated testing tools have been developed. These tools can be either *static* or *dynamic*. Static tools analyse programs without running them. Some produce output intended to be useful in itself - such as anomaly analysis tools - while others produce information needed to employ other techniques, such as a list of branches or a list of Linear Code Sequences And Jumps (LCSAJs) which are a sequence of statements executed sequentially but preceded and terminated by a program jump (transfer of control). LCSAJs can be considered as the smallest units of program paths, and can then be used in control flow testing. Dynamic tools analyse programs by actually running them with test data - e.g. to trace execution, or record which paths and branches have been executed when carrying out control flow testing.

As yet little effort has been devoted to the exploration of the applicability of these techniques to KBSs, and hence the testing of KBSs is still something of a haphazard affair. Testing tends to be "black box" and involves the construction of test cases by the expert which are then run through the system to determine whether they produce results with which the experts will agree. This is often considered to be part of the stage of eliciting and refining knowledge from the expert, rather than as a distinct testing phase.

1.2.6. Maintenance

Conventionally the term maintenance refers to the process of keeping in working order and good repair some object such as a building or vehicle. In computer terms this translates to the process of modifying a program and its associated documentation after it has been delivered and is in use. The metaphor is not entirely accurate as in conventional terms maintenance does not include the addition of (say) an entire new wing to a building, whereas in computer terms it is taken to include the addition of further program features and routines.

The concept of software maintenance, as a separate phase, worthy of individual attention, also emerged as a direct result of the software crisis and it is now recognised that maintenance accounts for a considerable amount of the time and cost of the life-cycle of a software system. Although it is difficult to judge the costs of maintenance it is generally suggested that for traditional software systems maintenance costs exceed the development costs by a factor of between two and four [Boehm 1981, Kai 1988]. There is no reason to assume that this should be any different for KBSs - provided they have a reasonable operational life. Given this statistic it is surprising how little research energy is devoted to software maintenance, a branch of software engineering which is still perceived as distinctly unglamorous.

Maintenance in conventional systems has been categorised [Swanson 1976] under the following headings:

- Perfective Maintenance.
- Adaptive Maintenance.
- Corrective Maintenance.

Each of these is discussed in further detail in the next three subsections. In the following section some consideration is given to software maintainability.

Corrective Maintenance

Corrective maintenance is concerned with the correction of errors which are discovered after delivery. These errors may be considered to result from either:

- Programmer coding errors.
- Faulty software specification and design.
- Misunderstood user requirements.

Programmer coding errors are the simplest to fix. These may be either purely syntactic errors or errors in the "logic" of the program. A large number of such errors may be detected and removed prior to delivery of the software by using appropriate testing techniques. Syntactic errors may be detected using syntax checkers. These usually form an integral part of modern compilers. Syntax errors are thus generally discovered at compilation time. Implementation errors may be reduced by adopting suitable verification techniques, such as those mentioned above, to verify that the software meets its specifications. Alternatively the possibility of coding and implementation errors may be reduced by conducting program walk throughs.

Errors in the software specification and design are not so easily fixed as they are much more fundamental and often result in errors being incorporated within several individual program modules. For example a proposed algorithm may be wrong. Such errors can be reduced by adopting suitable software development techniques. The specification may be written in a formal specification language such as VDM or OBJ in which case the specification can be automatically tested. Alternatively a structured design technique such as JSP may be adopted. In addition the possibility of errors resulting from faulty software specification and design may be reduced by conducting specification and design reviews.

Misunderstood user requirements are the most serious form of error in the corrective maintenance category as these errors are implanted at the beginning of the software development life-cycle and hence will be passed all the way down the development cycle. One of the main motivations for software engineering is to minimise the risk of errors at this stage. It is argued that they can be greatly reduced by adopting rigid requirements analysis techniques such as those proposed in the SSADM or DSSD development methodologies. In addition requirements validation techniques such as requirements reviews can be adopted to improve the chances of detecting any errors as early in the cycle as possible.

Perfective Maintenance

Perfective maintenance encompasses changes required by the user which did not form part of the original user requirements but which are found to be desirable or necessary during the operation of the system. It is often the case that when a system has been delivered and has been in operation for some time the users identify additional necessary requirements or their requirements are broadened and further features become desirable. Typically these changes are concerned with system output and require alterations ranging from changes to the existing software to the addition of extra facilities. In the case of a traditional software system the ease with which changes may be incorporated into the system will depend not only on the structure of the program but also on the magnitude of the user's desired change.

Consider a traditional piece of software such as a company payroll system which passes instructions to the company's bank and generates wage slips. Adding another item of information to the wage slips will not require much maintenance energy if the information is already resident in the system's database or can be generated from information contained in the database. For example the users may wish to include each individual's tax code on the wage slips. Even if the additional item of information is not available in the database it may be added if the designer showed sufficient foresight as to anticipate such an eventuality by including empty fields into the data structure(s) accessed by the program. A more substantial amount of maintenance effort would be required if the data structure had to be rebuilt to incorporate the additional information as this restructuring may have repercussions through out the system. The degree of maintenance effort required to implement perfective maintenance to existing software is thus dependent on the degree of anticipation of user changes incorporated into the design.

The addition of extra facilities to a software system should not present much of a problem if a modular design philosophy has been adopted as this will serve to limit the effect that the addition of the extra code will have on the existing software. If we consider the payroll system described above an example of such a change might be the addition of a monthly report generating facility. This could be included by simply adding on a number of additional modules and where necessary interfacing with the existing code. The idea of structured programming is that minor changes in the specification should give rise only to minor changes in the code.

Adaptive Maintenance

Adaptive maintenance results from changes in the environment in which a system is expected to operate. Whereas perfective maintenance focuses principally on the output produced by a system, adaptive maintenance focuses on the input. As with perfective maintenance, the degree of maintenance effort required to implement adaptive maintenance is dependent on the degree of anticipation of changes in the environment exhibited by the design of the system.

If we again consider a payroll system it may be reasonably anticipated that the level of income tax and individuals employees' tax codes are going to change at regular intervals, normally annually and, in the UK, associated with the "Budget". This anticipation can easily be incorporated into the system by defining tax rates as global variables declared at the beginning of the program. Other changes in the environment may be more difficult to anticipate and harder to incorporate. For example in our payroll system the inclusion of a new type of tax may well require major restructuring of the software.

1.2.7. Software Maintainability

The degree of maintainability of a software product is a function of its understandability and consequently its adaptability. This in turn is dependent on the software development techniques adopted. Good software development techniques make software much easier to understand and hence maintain [Parikh 1986].

Software maintenance is often carried out by maintenance engineers who were not part of the original development team. Therefore the maintainability of a piece of software depends very much on its readability and understandability at all levels; analysis, development and operation. This in turn depends on the development and programming techniques used. In the case of traditional software, formal development methods should result in a well defined requirements definition and system specification produced according to some methodology so that they can be understood and maintained by all those familiar with the methodology used. Similarly well structured modular programs are much easier to read and understand than unstructured programs. This is because structured programming techniques lead to a clean and simple design. Also the principles of the design can be understood by anyone who understands the method used to structure the program. Further, modular programs are simpler to maintain because of the information hiding principles displayed by the small self-contained units which make up these programs [Wiener and Sincovec 1984]. Essentially the smaller the "unit of meaning" the easier the unit is to maintain, since such units can be considered independently of the rest of the program. Both modular design and information hiding form an important part of the Object Oriented Design methodology currently popular in the software industry [Booch 1986].

An important part of software maintenance is the infra-structure designed to support it. This is usually referred to as Software Configuration Management (SCM). SCM consists of a set of activities designed to manage change throughout the software life-cycle and particularly the change control process. This is the method intended to ensure that any changes to the system are made in a controlled manner, and so that the changes and the reasons for them are visible to those who need to work on the software subsequently.

There are a number of software tools available to assist in the SCM task. Examples include MAKE and SCCS (Source Code Control System). MAKE is designed to give software support for system building by ensuring consistency between source code and its corresponding object code [Feldman 1979]. SCCS is a software tool designed to help programming projects control changes to source code by providing facilities to keep track of system modifications and different system versions [Rochkind 1975].

Maintainability of KBSs

If maintenance has been a neglected phase in conventional systems it has been totally ignored in KBS. Partly this is a function of the relatively recent practical utilisation of KBS techniques, and hence the need for maintenance has not been great. One system which has undergone extensive maintenance - corrective, perfective and adaptive - is the DEC R1/XCON system [McDermott 1980, 1982]. This was a system built using production rules as the major means of knowledge representation and it was initially thought that the maintenance task would be relatively straightforward: all that was needed was to add additional rules, and allow the conflict resolution strategy of the system to sort things out. In practice, however, this has proved increasingly unsatisfactory, and the system eventually required an overhaul, amounting to a complete re-write [Soloway *et al.* 1987]. This suggests that the maintenance of KBSs is not the simple matter originally expected. It is the major aim of this book to explore maintenance issues and techniques with respect to KBSs.

1.3. CRITICISMS OF THE TRADITIONAL LIFE-CYCLE MODEL

Before leaving this brief survey of conventional software engineering, we ought briefly to consider some of the criticisms of the traditional "waterfall" model of the development life-cycle. Firstly it is argued that the division into a set of successive stages is entirely unrealistic: in practice the stages blur into one another, overlap, and require a good deal more iteration than the model allows. There is some truth in this, and it may be better to see the model as a fiction rather than a description of what goes on in software development. But if it is a fiction it is a useful one: even where the stage divisions are somewhat arbitrary they can, to a certain extent, be imposed on to the development process to provide essential review opportunities, and intermediate deliverables.

More serious are the following criticisms. One is that the traditional model relies on the possibility of producing a good, agreed specification of requirements. If this is not possible, either because the customer is uncertain as to what the requirements are, or because the customer cannot articulate or recognise the requirements, the whole development edifice will be constructed on insecure foundations. Moreover, in the traditional model there is a lengthy period of development in which the customer is not involved: this may alienate the customer from the system, and also prevents the customer from providing possibly valuable input and correcting misunderstandings during development. These criticisms have a good deal of validity, particularly where the application is breaking unfamiliar ground.

This has led to the proposal of an alternative model - the "prototyping" model (Figure 1.3). In the prototyping life-cycle the developer and customer define overall objectives, agree known requirements and identify areas needing further definition. Following this the developer produces a quick design, concentrating on aspects visible to the user. From this design a prototype is implemented, using existing program fragments and tools such as report generators to hasten the development process. This prototype then provides a working program which the customers can use to clarify and refine their requirements. When the customer's needs are satisfied the prototype can be discarded and a properly engineered system produced on the basis of the agreed

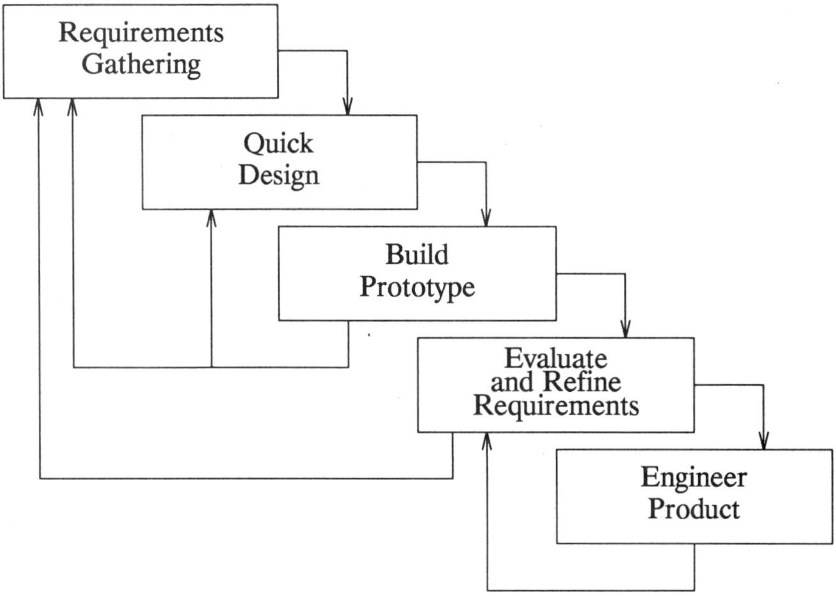

Figure 1.3: The prototyping software life cycle paradigm.

requirements discovered during the prototyping phase.

Prototyping can provide effective development, particularly in situation where there is much initial uncertainty, and helps increase customer confidence in, and identification with, the evolving system. There are, however, some drawbacks:

- There may be pressure to ignore or skimp the engineering stage and make do with the prototype.
- The need to get a program working quickly may lead to inappropriate design decisions which are then carried forward into the final product.

It is vital that the prototype be used only to help define requirements, and that a proper design is carried out when this is done.

KBSs often do begin from a situation of initial uncertainty and it is unsurprising that the prototyping (iterative) methodology was quickly taken up by developers of such systems; it is often now seen as the *only* way to develop such systems. The problem associated with prototype development, however, are critical to KBSs, because there is nothing corresponding to a proper method for well engineered development, and the final prototype is all too often seen as the finished system. Moreover the potential to get locked in to inferior design decisions is even greater in the case of KBSs. In this book we will not ignore prototyping, but we will suggest ways in which the lessons which are there to be learned from the more systematic development implied by the traditional model can be applied to KBSs.

1.4. SUMMARY

In this chapter we have given a broad overview of the discipline of software engineering as applicable to traditional software systems. It has been described with reference to the waterfall software life-cycle paradigm, the most generally adopted life-cycle for traditional systems, despite much criticism. Six distinct stages were identified:

1. System analysis.
2. Requirements analysis and definition.
3. Software specification and design.
4. Implementation.
5. Testing.
6. Maintenance.

These were discussed in some detail and the techniques and software tools available to support each stage identified. Where applicable parallels with KBS development were drawn. The aim has been to set the topic of software maintenance firmly within the overall discipline of software engineering.

In the following chapter we give an overview of KBSs and consider the development of such systems in the light of the software engineering principles that have been discussed here.

CHAPTER 2

Knowledge Based Systems

2.1. INTRODUCTION

In this chapter we give a brief overview of Knowledge Based Systems (KBSs) so as to provide some background to the rest of the work. The discussion concentrates particularly on the development of such systems as this has a considerable bearing on future maintenance. In a work of this kind an in depth description of KBSs as a whole cannot be provided, some familiarity with the subject is therefore assumed, readers requiring more information are referred to the many excellent text books that exist on the subject such as Rich and Knight [1991], Bench-Capon [1990] and Luger and Stubblefield [1989].

KBSs developed from expert systems. The latter can be defined as software systems that behave like an expert in some specific domain of application when solving problems in that domain. The essential characteristic of a KBS is that the knowledge representation and the means for manipulation of that knowledge are separated. Well known KBS applications include tasks such as medical diagnosis [Buchanan and Shortliffe 1984], chemical analysis [Lindsay *et al.* 1980], geological exploration [Hart *et al.* 1978] and computer configuration [McDermott 1982]. More recently KBS have been developed for real time process control [Inaba *et al.* 1991], nuclear power plant operation [Brown and Mayfield 1990] and marine navigation [Smeaton and Coenen 1990] to give a few examples. KBSs, according to their classical definition, also have to be capable of explaining their behaviour and their decisions to the user. An additional feature is often the ability to be able to deal with uncertainty and incompleteness of knowledge. This requires inexact or probablistic reasoning.

Traditionally a KBS is considered to consist of a Knowledge Base (KB) and an inference engine. The KB comprises the knowledge that is specific to the domain of application, including such things as simple facts about the domain, rules or frames that describe relations or phenomena in the domain, and possibly also methods, heuristics and ideas for solving problems in this domain. The inference engine then contains methods of manipulating the knowledge in the KB. The inference engine is usually written in procedural code which can thus be maintained using traditional methods and is therefore not considered to fall under the heading of KBS maintenance, which is essentially maintenance of the KB.

As with conventional software systems it is convenient to discuss the development of KBSs in terms of the life cycle paradigms that are applicable. These are described in section 2.2 below. However regardless of what life-cycle paradigm is adopted a number of particular KBS development phases can be identified:

1. Knowledge elicitation.
2. Knowledge analysis.
3. Domain conceptualisation.
4. Knowledge representation.
5. Implementation.
6. Testing.
7. Operation.
8. Maintenance.

Again these phases are not mutually exclusive, a great deal of overlap exists. In addition some phases, such as testing, pervade the entire development cycle. However, it is convenient for our purposes to consider each phase as being distinct from the previous and following phases so that each can be discussed in isolation. For the first seven identified phases this is carried out in sections 2.3 to 2.9. The maintenance phase is discussed in greater detail in chapter 4.

2.2. THE KBS LIFE-CYCLE

In the previous chapter the concept of a software life-cycle was introduced and the conventional waterfall model discussed. When considering candidates for possible KBS life-cycles the obvious starting point is to consider this and other existing conventional software life-cycles (see chapter 1). These life-cycles are principally concerned with systems, such as data processing systems, where the input data and end goals can be clearly defined. The problem is then simply a matter of how these goals can best be achieved. In most cases this is self evident and requires little more than appropriate specification and coding. However, in KBSs the end goals are typically not clearly defined, i.e. the goals are said to be "soft". Thus there is no clear concept of a KBS requirements specification. Further, whereas a conventional system can be said to be "correct" because it produces the correct output, this kind of evaluation of a KBS is not usually possible. This reflects the general difference between conventional systems and KBSs in that the latter are concerned with the encapsulation, representation and manipulation of knowledge, which is often abstract in nature, while the former are concerned with the processing of data which is clearly defined. The use of a purely traditional software life-cycle in the production of KBSs can therefore be considered to be inappropriate.

A number of alternative models to the traditional life-cycle have therefore been suggested in recognition of the special requirements associated with KBSs. The principal difference between these KBS life-cycles and the conventional life-cycle is that a specific knowledge engineering phase is included. This is the process of:

1. Acquiring knowledge (elicitation) about a particular problem domain from expert sources, either human or textual.
2. Analysing and conceptualising that knowledge.
3. Representing it in a suitable manner.

The knowledge engineering phase forms the most time consuming part of any KBS development and considerable research effort has been devoted to making this more efficient by the development of software support tools, techniques and methodologies. Some of these are reviewed in a later chapter.

KBS life-cycle paradigms can be broadly classified as either stage based (after traditional software life-cycles) or incremental (prototyping).

2.2.1. Stage Based KBS Life-Cycles

Stage based KBS life-cycles are analogous to the traditional life-cycle in that they consist of a number of development stages (Figure 2.1). Thus:

1. System analysis.
2. Knowledge engineering.
3. Implementation.
4. Testing.
5. Operation.

The essential differences between this and the traditional life-cycle is in the knowledge engineering phase during which knowledge elicitation, analysis, representation and specification takes place. The system is implemented and tested during the following two phases. Criticisms that have been levelled at KBS stage based life-cycle paradigms are that they are basically rehashes of the traditional waterfall life-cycle and thus incorporate the same disadvantages as those associated with this life-cycle. A further criticism directed at the stage base life-cycle is that it assumes that all necessary knowledge engineering can take place prior to the implementation, i.e. that a clear concept of requirements is derivable.

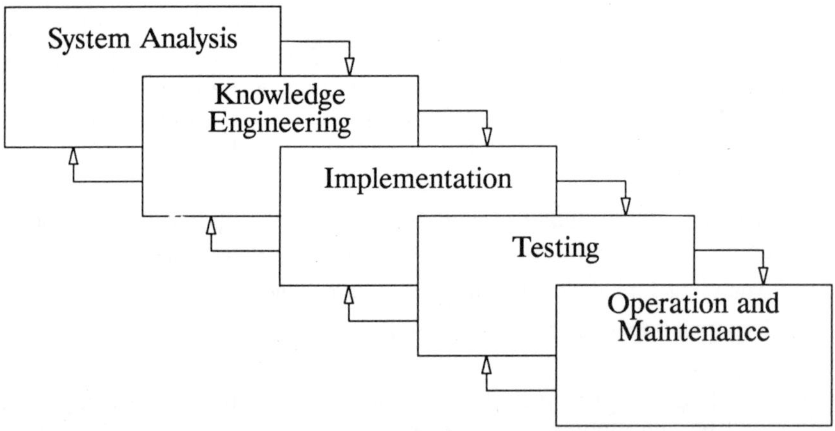

Figure 2.1: Stage based KBS life-cycle.

However, despite this well founded criticism, the stage based concept should not be abandoned as given suitable tools and techniques for use in the knowledge engineering phase. this type of life-cycle may still prove to be the most appropriate.

2.2.2. Incremental KBS Life-Cycles

The incremental, evolutionary or experimental life-cycle paradigm (Figure 2.2) is based on ideas concerned with rapid prototyping as implemented for the development of some traditional software systems (see 1.3). Prototyping was suggested as a remedy to "customer uncertainty" with regard to requirements for KBSs. In the incremental life-cycle a KBS is developed by first building a working system to address a subset of the problem domain, i.e a proto-type or pilot system. This system is then modified and expanded to encompass further subsets of the

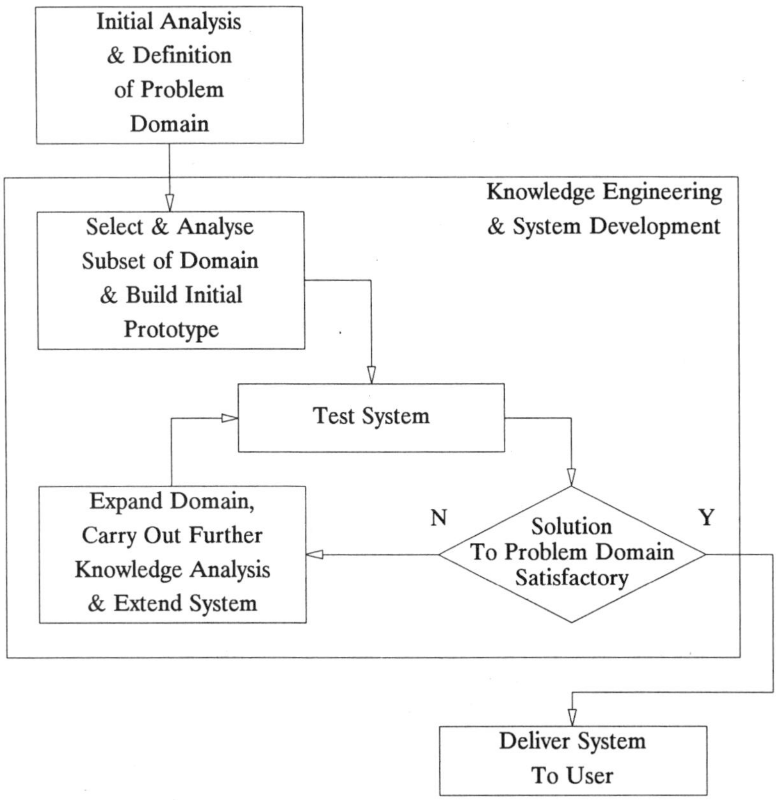

Figure 2.2: The incremental life-cycle.

domain in an iterative fashion and in consultation with the end users. This process continues until the entire domain is addressed and the system performs in a satisfactory manner. Adherents of this development method consider that given that KBSs are intended to emulate human expertise in some domain and that it is not clearly understood how humans carry out their tasks, proceeding in a detailed stage based manner as described in the previous section is not possible and therefore an experimental life-cycle is the only reasonable method in which to proceed. The incremental KBS life-cycle model has been used, with some success, in the development of several well known systems such as MYCIN [Buchanan and Shortliffe 1984].

Criticisms that have been levelled against it include:

1. It is essential that the end users are involved in the development.
2. The evolutionary increments are carried out in an unstructured manner without a specific plan and uncontrolled growth of the system often results.
3. Code is continually over written at each repetition. The continual change results in the structure of the software being corrupted, it eventually becomes incomprehensible, posing serious problems for future maintenance.
4. With a life-cycle model that includes frequent iterations it is difficult to identify management checkpoints to be used for planning and estimation.
5. Existing software management structures, which are mostly concerned with regular deliverables and where progress can be simply measured, do not easily map onto an incremental software process model.
6. Bad software engineering practices are encouraged resulting in inconsistency and redundancy problems with obvious adverse implications for the maintenance of the system at a later date as experienced in the development of XCON [McDermott 1982].

These disadvantages all have some force. However, it can be argued that the first is not a disadvantage but a desirable option in the development of KBSs. Further it can be argued that the absence of any clear concept of requirements at the outset means that KBSs can only be developed incrementally. The second of the above criticisms must thus be considered to be a "necessary evil" for systems where a precise requirements definition cannot be produced in advance. The third can be avoided by using modular methods, i.e. ensuring that the code is truly declarative so that sections can be removed and replaced without requiring additional patching. To meet the next two suggested disadvantages it is necessary for new management techniques to be inaugurated; this is still the subject of a considerable amount of research energy. Finally bad software engineering practices can be eradicated by adopting a rigid development methodology. This, however, requires a discipline that trades off against the ease of incremental development as originally envisaged; "just add a few more rules".

The incremental KBS life-cycle is the life-cycle described in Buchanan and Shortliffe [1984], and is of sufficiently wide acceptance as to be offered without alternative in Luger and Stubblefield's recent AI textbook [Luger and Stubblefield 1989]. It is well summed up in the latter:

> "Expert systems are built by progressive approximations, with the program's (sic) mistakes leading to corrections and additions to the KB. In a sense, the KB is "grown" rather than constructed. ... design proceeds through a process of trying and correcting candidate designs, rather than by such neatly hierarchical processes as top-down design." (p 300)

There have been a number of offshoots from the incremental model of the KBS life-cycle such as Boehm's spiral life-cycle [Boehm 1988] which, although aimed at traditional software systems, can be readily adapted to the development of KBSs [O'Keefe and Lee 1990] and is gaining popularity. Boehm's spiral life-cycle model incorporates many of the strengths of other models but has the major distinguishing feature that it creates a risk-driven approach to the software process rather than a primarily document, or code, driven process. It includes explicit stages for risk analysis and forces the system developer to express the criteria for entering and leaving each stage. Each level of software specification is followed by a verification step and the preparation of plans for the next cycle. Determination of entering and leaving criteria can help the developer set clear objectives for the system and allows the validator to evaluate the system without bias. The model proposed by O'Keefe and Lee exploits the strengths of both the incremental KBS life-cycle paradigm and Boehm's spiral model.

There have also been attempts to synthesise desirable elements from both the stage based and incremental KBS development life-cycle paradigms. For example the four-phase KBS life-cycle proposed by Agarwal and Tanniru [1990] which highlights the role of alternative development paradigms in the stage based life-cycle.

2.3. KNOWLEDGE ELICITATION

Knowledge elicitation, also sometimes referred to as knowledge acquisition, is the process of extracting, from expert sources, knowledge about a problem domain. Traditionally this has been carried out in an informal manner simply by interviewing recognised human experts in the problem domain or referring to written material. The process is often directed specifically at eliciting rules. Interviews are still the most popular knowledge elicitation technique. However, the result is often a large quantity of unstructured "raw" knowledge.

Attempts have therefore been made at formalising the interview process using structured, focused or systematic interviewing techniques and recording the results using interview protocols. These techniques are all well summarised in Diaper [1989]. Structured interviews are interviews designed to fit a prepared format, thus encouraging the production of consistent results: focussed interviews are intended to address a particular aspect of the problem domain; while systematic interviews involve the adoption of some system to ensure all relevant material is detected. Interview protocols are external records, possibly on audio or video tape, but more usually in the form of written transcripts, made during or shortly after an interview has taken place. Some software tools have also been proposed to enforce a structure on the interviewing technique.

A number of more formal elicitation techniques have been developed: a review is given in Grover [1983]. These include protocol analysis, goal decomposition, laddering, multi-dimensional elicitation and repertory grid elicitation. They are not necessarily designed to be used alone and each tends to favour a different kind of knowledge.

2.3.1. Protocol Analysis

Protocol analysis (also referred to as procedural simulation) refers to the automated or semi-automated analysis of "thinking-aloud" protocols. It involves the knowledge engineer observing the expert while he/she actually solves a problem. The result of the analysis can be considered to be a path through successive knowledge states representing the sequence of the problem solving events. Rules are then formulated in a *post hoc* manner. A criticism of protocol analysis is that the knowledge elicited tends to be primarily procedural. However, protocol analysis has been successfully adopted for a number of knowledge acquisition tools, for example KRITON (Diederich *et al.* 1987).

2.3.2. Goal Decomposition

In goal decomposition the problem space is represented as a hierarchy of goals with the solution to the problem at the top level. The knowledge engineer enters into the hierarchy at random and moves around it with prepared probes to explore it asking the expert to describe paths that can be used to achieve the goals.

2.3.3. Laddering

The laddering elicitation technique centres on the expert being asked to name important concepts of the problem domain in question. These concepts are then used as a basis for the interview to follow. Super types and instances of generic concepts are especially inquired about, allowing the derivation of a taxonomic structure.

2.3.4. Multi-Dimensional Elicitation

Multi-dimensional, or card sort, elicitation provides a qualitative multi-dimensional mapping of the elements in the problem domain. This is achieved by repeated sorts of a deck of cards, marked with the domain elements. On each sort, the expert is required to label the overall scale and the individual piles. Rules are then extracted through this classification of knowledge. Again the knowledge tends to be primarily procedural.

2.3.5. Repertory Grid Elicitation

Repertory grid elicitation techniques are used to determine the relationships between objects and to express the associations between concepts in a multi-dimensional construct space. In this respect they are similar to the card-sort elicitation technique described above. A number of elicitation tools have been developed based on the repertory grid technique. These include KSS0 (Knowledge Support System Zero), LaFrance's Knowledge Acquisition Grid and AQUINAS. KSS0 graphically represents the results of the repertory-grid after a hierarchical clustering analysis. The knowledge Acquisition Grid [LaFrance 1987] uses a two-dimensional space in which five forms of expert knowledge and six basic types of interview questions constitute the horizontal and vertical dimensions respectively. AQUINAS [Boose and Bradshaw 1987] is a KBS development environment where knowledge elicitation is based on the repertory-grid elicitation technique. AQUINAS is in fact a hybrid tool that can elicit distinctions, decompose problems, combine uncertain information, refine automatically and integrate expertise from different sources.

2.4. KNOWLEDGE ANALYSIS

Knowledge analysis may either take place once the knowledge elicitation phase has been completed or may form part of a highly iterative process together with the elicitation phase as in the MEKAS methodology [Nwana and Paton 1990]. During knowledge analysis the relevant knowledge is identified and extracted from the collected raw knowledge. The technique used depends very much on the knowledge elicitation method adopted. The more formal and structured the knowledge elicitation the more straightforward the analysis.

Traditionally this analysis has been carried out as follows:

1. Identify key words in the raw knowledge, typically entities.
2. Identify the attributes of these entities.

3. Identify the relationships between different entities and attributes within the domain.
4. Identify the operations that can be carried out on these entities to change their attributes and the relationships between them.

The principal criticism levelled at the traditional approach is that it produces an inconsistent and often superficial analysis. Alternative approaches that may be considered include ontological analysis, generic task modelling and deep modelling.

2.4.1. Ontological Analysis

An ontology is defined as "a collection of abstract objects, relationships and transformations that represent the physical and cognitive entities necessary to accomplish some task". Ontological analysis [Alexander *et al.* 1987] consists of the following steps:

1. Identification and analysis of objects in the domain and their inherent properties and relationships in a manner similar to entity relationship modelling.
2. Identification and analysis of the state space and the operations available that can change this space.
3. Identification and analysis of the knowledge structures that guide and use the operations defined in 2.

These stages are referred to as the static, dynamic and epistemic stages respectively. The aim of ontological analysis is to produce a formal specification of the knowledge elements needed to find a solution in a given problem domain by considering the entities, relationships and transformations necessary. As such it may be viewed simply as a formalisation of the traditional approach and hence be subject to similar criticisms, i.e it does not produce a consistent analysis.

2.4.2 Generic Task Modelling

Another proposed alternative is to use generic task modelling techniques as suggested by Chandrasekaran [Chandrasekaran 1985, Bylander and Chandrasekaran 1987] and Clancey [1985]. The notion behind generic task modelling, also sometimes referred to as the model driven knowledge acquisition technique, is to provide the knowledge engineer with sufficient information, in the form of interpretation models or generic templates, to know what type of knowledge to acquire and to direct future knowledge analysis. The underlying claim is that knowledge based reasoning tasks can often be decomposed into a number of generic tasks/models each with associated types of knowledge and family of control regimes. The disadvantages associated with generic task modelling are as follows:

1. The models tend to be pre-selective and have a very limited range of application. For example KNACK is a generic modelling technique aimed specifically at the development of electromechanical systems [Klinker *et al.* 1987].
2. There is no guarantee that the selected task is the correct task for the domain in question.
3. The number of available tasks can never be considered to be complete.
4. The selection of an appropriate model is often very complex.

Generic modelling, however, is a feature of several KBS development environments and methodologies. Examples include ROGET and MOLE, which were developed out of MYCIN [Buchanan and Shortliffe 1984] and KADS [Wielinga *et al.* 1992].

2.4.3. Deep Modelling

The philosophy behind deep modelling argues that superficial analysis results in the production of "fragile" KBSs and that, if we wish to build KBS which are more robust, what is required is a much deeper analysis to investigate the cause of decisions (causality modelling) and the mechanisms used to arrive at conclusions.

Deep Knowledge Based Systems (DKBS) emerged as a distinct topic in the mid 1980s. At that time the ALVEY programme was in operation, and was able to provide support for a first exploratory workshop in 1985. DKBS is still a current research project. A review of the progress of this research is given in Morgan [1990].

2.4.4. Textual Analysis Tools

A prominent sub-class of knowledge analysis tools are textual analysis tools. These are specifically aimed at the analysis of expert knowledge from textual sources such as manuals, codes of practice and legal texts. The textual analysis tools currently available allow the knowledge engineer to extract knowledge from textual sources and represent it in a meaningful form often using frame and rule language packages.

Usually the textual source must be partitioned into easily definable chunks. These chunks are then analysed by identifying particular entities and attributes in the text and the possible operations that can effect those entities and attributes. One example is the Cross-Referencing Editing Facility (CREF) which forms part of the KEATS methodology [Motta *et al.* 1988]. This allows the knowledge engineer to organise text by partitioning it into atomic entities called "segments" and grouping then into "collections". Relations between segments are then expressed using epistemological links. This then provides a basis for further data analysis. Another example is PED which forms part of the KADS methodology [Wielinga *et al.* 1986].

Often textual analysis tools incorporate hypertext facilities. Hypertext is a storage structure where information with attributes attached is stored in the nodes of a graph. Examples of tools that use hypertext type facilities include ACQUIST [Motta *et al.* 1989] and KANT [Storrs and Burton 1989]. These allow the user to carry out data analysis and domain conceptualisation though a process of abstracting and structuring the knowledge contained in raw texts.

Although designed specifically to analyse textual knowledge, textual analysis tools may also be used to analyse knowledge obtained verbally from human experts if the interviews are recorded in, or transcribed to, a computer readable form.

Textual knowledge analysis tools and techniques are often integrated with graphical tools to also allow the knowledge engineer to create a graphical representation of the domain. For example the KEATS methodology includes an intelligent Graphical Interface System (GIS) which allows the knowledge engineer to produce a free hand (but constrained) representation of the knowledge domain [Motta *et al.* 1988]. The ACQUIST textual analysis tool has a graphical support tool associated with it called MAPS [Motta *et al.* 1989].

2.5. DOMAIN CONCEPTUALISATION

In the domain conceptualisation stage the knowledge engineer attempts to impose a global structure onto the analysed knowledge to produce a model of the domain. To this end traditional flow diagrams, networks, tables or taxonomic hierarchies may be used. KADS supports the use of interpretation models to this end [Wielinga *et al.* 1992]. Alternatively an intermediate representation may be used.

During the domain conceptualisation task process "holes" often appear in the knowledge available necessitating a return to the knowledge elicitation stage. Indeed it is the ability to identify these holes and to use them to drive the elicitation process that characterises a successful methodology.

The use of formal methods to build the conceptual model of the domain will allow for the formal verification and validation of the domain and thus ease the domain conceptualisation task. A further advantage of formal conceptual models is that they can be automatically mapped onto a representation structure such as frames or rules. A disadvantage associated with formal domain conceptualisation methods is that they often impose limitations on the nature of conceptual model used to represent the domain.

Nwana and Paton [1990] suggest that conceptual models are built up using various techniques, i.e. metaphors and theories about the domain, each with particular advantages associated with them. They identify a number of characteristics of domain knowledge for which answers may be obtained. They therefore propose a methodology, MEKAS (Methodology for Knowledge Analysis) [Paton *et al.* 1991] that makes use of a set of conceptual models to represent the problem domain.

Recent developments to provide support for the knowledge engineer during the domain conceptualisation process include the intermediate or mediating representation approach. The idea is to use computer independent notations as a conceptual aid in the representation of knowledge gleaned verbally from human experts. Proponents of this method claim that premature coding of knowledge in KBSs is a hindrance to analysis and that by using a machine independent notation a more conceptual view of the domain can be gained. Further it is claimed that sub-sets of the knowledge may be encoded without affecting the analysis and that changes may be easily incorporated. Examples of such notations include Systematic Grammatic Networks (SGNs), conceptual schemas and the MAUDE Intermediate Representation (MIR). SGN are essentially a semi-formal notation which provide an empty structure into which a chosen domain of knowledge may be fitted [Johnson 1989]. A conceptual schema is an abstract description of some domain which is to be represented by a KBS. The best known example are Sowa's conceptual graphs [Sowa 1984]. Sowa describes these as forming "a knowledge representation language based on linguistics, psychology, and philosophy". In Sowa's graphs concept nodes represent entities, attributes, states and events, and relation nodes show how the concepts are interconnected. MIR is supported by a set of hypertext-like nodes that allow the user to link the source through to the final representation [Bench-Capon and Coenen 1991b]. The use of intermediate representations such as MIR has significant advantages for future maintenance and is discussed in detail in a later chapter. Critics of the intermediate representation approach consider that it results in a superficial analysis and that it adds an extra level of complexity to the development process which serves only as a link between verbalised knowledge and the implementation.

2.6. KNOWLEDGE REPRESENTATION

Once the expert knowledge has been analysed and the domain has been conceptualised the knowledge representation can be commenced. Several paradigms for representing knowledge have been suggested, the most popular are "if-then" production rules, propositional and predicate logic and structured objects (originally frames now more commonly objects in the object oriented programming sense).

Production rules are the most common due to their availability in the form of inexpensive shells. They contain premises or conditions in the "if" clauses and conclusions in the "then" clauses. They can have various interpretations (even within the same system) [Bratko 1986]:

- *if* precondition P *then* conclusion C.
- *if* situation S *then* action A.
- *if* conditions C1 and C2 hold *then* condition C does not hold.

Production rules are considered, by their advocates, to be a natural form of expressing knowledge. They are often used to define logical relations between concepts within a problem domain. Perhaps the best known example of an expert system that uses production rules is the MYCIN medical consultation system [Buchanan and Shortliffe 1984].

Propositional logic allows the construction of rules from propositions, or atomic formulas, and the logical connectives $\wedge$, $\vee$, $\neg$, $\Rightarrow$ and $\Leftrightarrow$ ("and", "or", "not", "implies" and "equality"). One advantage of expressing knowledge in this way is that the rules can be used to infer new knowledge. Thus given `A` and `A` $\Rightarrow$ `B` we can infer `B` (modus ponens). A disadvantage of propositional logic is the non-uniform structure of the rules constructed, which gives rise to problems when we wish to process the knowledge automatically. One solution is to convert the rules to a clausal form which is more uniform. A further disadvantage is that propositional logic cannot be used to express specific knowledge about individuals or general knowledge about classes of individuals. Predicate logic allows us to do this using the logical quantifiers $\forall$ and $\exists$ ("for all" and "there exists") in addition to the apparatus available in propositional logic. This allows us to reason about a particular domain as a relational structure.

The notion of frames, also sometimes referred to as classes, prototypes or structured-object descriptions, was first developed primarily for pattern recognition sub-systems, and especially for natural language understanding systems. The term itself was first introduced by Minsky for vision systems [Minsky 1975]. The theory behind frames has a lot of similarity with set theory although not all frame systems are defined in this way. Essentially frames are data structures which represent entity, or object or class, types. Like a semantic network, a frame consists of a collection of named slots, or facts or attributes, each of which can be filled by values or by pointers to other frames. Frames may be related in any number of ways. The most common is in a hierarchy of parent, sibling and child nodes so that inferences can take place between the nodes. Inferencing generally takes place through a matching process where by facts in (say) a database are matched to available slots or values are inherited from super classes. In the event of a successful match a slot is filled. When all the slots of a frame are filled, the frame is said to be instantiated. The frame then represents a particular entity of the type represented by the unfilled frame. In most frame applications only a limited number of slot values will be known. Candidate frames must therefore be selected and values found for the unfilled slots if possible. In effect the system will attempt to find a frame which best matches the known properties of the entities. How closely a frame matches a known set of slot values is indicated by a computed "match value".

Frame based, or object-oriented, representations are often considered to be more capable of dealing with complex situations than "if-then" production rules and predicate logic because they are more closely aligned to the way humans reason about problems, i.e. in clusters.

A criticism of frame based systems (and in many cases semantic networks) is that they are misleading, "they are able to represent only a fraction of what it might appear they can" [Brachman 1985]. For example frames cannot express even simple *composite descriptions* such as the "elephant whose colour is grey". Further frame based representations are more complex than production rule and predicate logic representations and hence are not as widely used. Their popularity is, however, growing with the introduction of more frame based KBS development tool kits such as NEXPERT OBJECT [Aiken and Sheng 1990].

There are also a number of programming languages available that exploit the concept of structured objects. Perhaps the best known is Smalltalk [Byrne 1991 and Goldberg and Robson 1983], an object oriented language which exploits extensive fact partitioning. Others include KRL [Bobrow and Winograd 1977] and KRYPTON [Brachman *et al.* 1983].

2.7. IMPLEMENTATION

The implementation stage can be considered to be analogous to the coding stage in the traditional software life cycle. There are a number of "expert systems" languages available in which the knowledge representation can be implemented. The best known examples are probably LISP [Steele 1990, Wilensky 1984] and PROLOG [Bratko 1986 and Clocksin and Mellish 1984].

LISP (LISt Processing language) was invented by John McCarthy in the late 1950s and is widely used, especially in the USA. It is intended as a functional language and has many dialects including Common LISP, Franz LISP and Inter LISP. It is also supported by powerful programming environments such as AI work stations.

The theoretical basis for PROLOG (PROgramming in LOGic) is formal logic, especially first order Predicate Calculus and the Horn Clause subset. The concept of PROLOG emerged in the late 1970s. Early developers included Robert Kowalski and Maarten van Emden at Edinburgh and Alan Colmerauer at Merseilles. DEC10 or Edinburgh PROLOG is now the *de facto* standard.

Alternatively a proposed KBS can be implemented using a shell language. These can be described as domain independent KBS frameworks consisting of only an inference engine and some explanation facilities; they incorporate no domain specific knowledge. To use a shell to build a KBS a shell with a suitable framework for the intended application must first be selected. The domain specific knowledge is then supplied by the user. Early examples include the research shells EMYCIN [van Melle *et al.* 1984] and KAS produced as part of the MYCIN project [Buchanan and Shortliffe 1984] and Prospector [Hart *et al.* 1978] projects respectively. Currently there are a wide range of commercial shells available. The principal advantage of using a shell is a significant reduction in the development time required to build KBSs. The disadvantage associated with the use of shells is that they are not Turing complete, i.e. not everything required to implement an expert system can always be written in the shell language. Thus, even with careful selection of a suitable shell, a number of design decisions will be imposed on the user. For example the knowledge may have to be represented using production rules of a specific form. This disadvantage serves to reduce the number of applications which any particular shell is suited for without the knowledge engineer frequently having to fall back on the underlying language in which the shell is implemented, normally PROLOG, LISP or C. These underlying languages support constructs such as objects, classes of objects (object schemas), generalisation hierarchies among the classes of objects, attributes (slots) of objects, property inheritance, relation schemas, facts and rules.

A variety of expert system tools kits and shells have been developed over the last decade. Three well known examples are briefly described below. Other shells that should be mentioned here include NASA Johnson Space Center's CLIPS, Intelligent Environment's CRYSTAL, Carnegie Croup's KNOWLEDGE CRAFT, IntelliCorp's KAPPA, Lockheed Missiles and Space Company's Lockheed Expert System (LES) and Neuron Data's NEXPERT OBJECT. A fairly comprehensive list of available expert system shells together with their key features is given in Mockler and Dologite [1992].

2.7.1. Inference Corporation's Automated Reasoning Tool (ART)

ART supports rules, frames, integrated backward and forward chaining, viewpoints for reasoning about hypothetical worlds, object-oriented programming capabilities and "multimethods". Multimethods are ART object-oriented programming procedures which allow the user to execute a procedure to send a message to a generalised group of closely linked objects instead of only to a single object.

2.7.2. IntelliCorp's Knowledge Engineering Environment (KEE)

KEE supports both rules and frames for knowledge representation, backward and forward chaining, object-oriented programming, an "active-values" mechanism, and "worlds". The active-value mechanism provides a way to attach procedures to frame slots so that when these slots are accessed or changed, specific procedures are executed. Worlds allows the user to hypothesise various situations and reason about them in parallel, thus enabling the generation and evaluation of alternatives.

2.7.3. General Research Corporation's The Intelligent Machine Model (TIMM)

TIMM [General Research Corporation 1985] generates its rules from examples, i.e, the knowledge representation is case based. TIMM is of particular interest here because it also incorporates some rule checking facilities to check for consistency and completeness. In TIMM inconsistency is defined as the situation where (a) a rule has the same antecedent as another rule but a different consequent, or (b) the antecedent of any rule overlaps the antecedent of another rule but with a different consequent, or (c) a rule with more than one consequent. The last two are a result of the method whereby TIMM generates its rules. The concepts of consistency and completeness are discussed in more detail later in chapter 8.

2.8. TESTING

Testing of KBSs involves the verification and validation of the content and operation of the KB and forms an important part of the KBS life-cycle. It is during this stage that many errors can be detected and the need for future corrective maintenance reduced. The possibility of future corrective maintenance, of course, cannot be eradicated completely. Many authors [Bachant and McDermott 1984] argue that it is essential to introduce a system into routine use so that inadequacies in the knowledge can be uncovered. It should also be appreciated that testing will also not alleviate the need for future perfective and adaptive maintenance.

There is a considerable amount of overlap between the types of error and anomaly that the developers of KBSs are attempting to eradicate and the type of errors and anomalies that we wish to avoid after a maintenance session has taken place. In fact the latter process can be referred to as KBS maintenance verification and validation. The essential difference between the checks that should be implemented during the testing verification and validation process and those that should be implemented as part of maintenance verification and validation is that the first is implemented on the entire KBS while the second impinges on only a part of it, the part that has been changed or is affected by the change.

Currently a considerable amount of work is being carried out in the development of KBS verification and validation techniques. The earliest examples include Suwa's rule checking program which was implemented on the ONCOCIN system [Suwa *et al.* 1982] and CHECK [Nguyen *et al.* 1985]. More recent examples include EVA [Chang *et al.* 1990] and COVER [Preece and Shinghal 1991a]. The work described by these projects has an important bearing on the checks that should be carried out after a maintenance session has taken place and is therefore discussed in some detail later in this work.

2.9. OPERATION

It is during the operation of a system that the need for maintenance, particularly corrective maintenance, comes to light; perfective and adaptive maintenance results from outside influences. This is discussed further in chapter 4.

The encoded knowledge in a KB is manipulated using a computer program referred to as the "inference engine". Generally the inference engine can be said to be either goal driven (forward chaining) or data driven (backward chaining). Backward chaining involves starting with one or more possible goals and attempting to show that they can be derived using the rules or frames in the KB and the input data. Forward chaining involves reasoning from the other direction, starting with the input data and then making inferences to establish everything that can be derived from that data. Forward chaining searches can thus rapidly expand since a virtually unlimited number of rules or frames may be examined.

2.10. DEFINITIONS

Prior to looking in much more detail at KBS maintenance it is necessary to establish some definitions. In the remainder of this work, with respect to KBSs, the following definitions are used:

Rule

This is an expression, comprised of propositions, consisting of a head and a tail or body, sometimes referred to as a consequent and an antecedent or a conclusion and a condition part, normally separated by an `if` in production rule forms or `iff` (read as if and only if). The head contains one or more propositions the truth or falsity of which is determined according to the truth or falsity of the propositions contained in the body and their connectives.

Clause

This is an expression in some normal form e.g. clausal, disjunctive or conjunctive normal form. We will usually express rules in clausal form, where the head is true if all the propositions in the body are true. A single rule will typically be equivalent to several clauses.

Proposition

A proposition consists either of a logical predicate with arguments, an Entity, Attribute, Value triple (EAV), an Attribute and Value (AV) or a string. They may be related by logical connectives. An entity is an object in a domain which may have certain properties. These properties are referred to as attributes which in turn have values. Possible values include true or false, numerics, literals or other entities.

Root Propositions and Attributes

A root proposition is a proposition which appears in the head of some clause, and does not appear in the tail of any clause. A root attribute is an attribute associated with one or more root propositions. The task which the KBS is designed to perform, involves establishing the root proposition.

Leaf Propositions and Attributes

A leaf proposition is a proposition which appears in the body of one or more clauses, and in the head of no clauses. A leaf attribute is an attribute associated with one or more leaf propositions. The significance of leaves is that values associated with them must be supplied to the system from some external source, not deduced. Values may be supplied either by explicit user input, or by retrieval from some external database.

Frames

Frames are data structures used in frame based systems that represent particular entity or object types. They are usually arranged in a hierarchy where sub-frames can inherit properties from super frames. When a set of facts is successfully matched to a frame the frame is said to be instantiated.

Slots

Slots are elements of a frame which represent particular attributes of the entity or object type described by the frame. Slots can be filled by values or pointers to other frames.

2.11. SUMMARY

In this chapter we have described the phases involved in the development of a KBS. Eight distinct phases were identified:

1. Knowledge elicitation.
2. Knowledge analysis.
3. Domain conceptualisation.
4. Knowledge representation.

5. Implementation.
6. Testing.
7. Operation.
8. Maintenance.

As in Chapter 1 the discussion commenced by considering the life-cycle paradigms that are applicable to KBS development. Two distinct categories were considered, stage based life-cycles and, the more popular, incremental life-cycles. The first seven development phases identified were then discussed in the following sections and some of the tools, methods and techniques available to assist in the implementation of each phase considered. The final phase, maintenance, is discussed in detail in chapter 4. However prior to this, in the following chapter, we give some consideration to what we mean by knowledge in the context of KBSs.

CHAPTER 3

Knowledge and Knowledge Representation

3.1. INTRODUCTION

Since we are interested in maintaining Knowledge Bases (KBs), it is well to be clear at the outset as to what knowledge bases are. Therefore in this chapter we will briefly review what kind of things are represented in a KB, and the ways in which they may be represented. Again, space will not permit us to go into a very detailed account of methods of knowledge representation: readers who want or need this are referred to specialist books which deal with these matters, such as Bench-Capon [1990]. As Knowledge Based Systems (KBSs) have developed a number of knowledge representation paradigms have emerged. For convenience we will divide them into two classes: *rule based* representations, which embrace production rule systems and logic based systems, and *structured object* representations, which include semantic networks, frame systems and object orientated representations. We will not advocate one over the other - indeed, we believe that a fusion of the two is most desirable - but in this chapter we will attempt to show the different slant on knowledge representation offered by these approaches.

3.2. WHAT KNOWLEDGE IS REPRESENTED IN A KBS?

A one word answer to the question of what is represented in a KB is "expertise". This is accurate, but not especially helpful. We need to decompose this term, and see what is involved in knowing about a domain. We will distinguish three broad topics: knowledge of the objects of a domain, knowledge of the tasks performed in the domain, and knowledge about how to deploy this knowledge - the meta-knowledge of the domain.

3.2.1. Knowledge of Objects

First, expertise will require that a person is familiar with the objects that go to make up the domain. Thus the car mechanic will know about gear-boxes, carburettors and fuel leads, and the medical expert will know about livers, hearts and arteries. We can summarise this knowledge as being in possession of an *ontology* of the domain.

But knowing of the existence of the various objects in the domain is not enough: the expert will also know what properties these objects typically have, and what properties they may sensibly have. Thus a fuel lead will have a diameter, but a gear box will not; a liver may exhibit cirrhosis, but a kidney cannot. Thus knowledge of an object will importantly include the *attributes* of the object. This notion of what it makes sense to say about an object can be expanded: attributes typically have some value, and the expert will have a variety of expectations about these values. Thus a gear box typically has five positions, but may have six if there is a fifth forward gear. The diameter of a fuel lead will normally lie in a certain range, and different values may be associated with different makes of engine. All of this comes together to provide a vocabulary for the domain - the objects it contains, the attributes of those objects and the values of those attributes for different objects - and constitutes part of what it is to have a feel for the domain, rejecting some statements as unlikely, and others as impossible.

As well as the attributes and properties of objects in the domain, the expert will know a good deal about the way the domain is organised and the role that the objects play in the domain. That is there will be knowledge of the *structure* of the domain and *function* of the objects in the domain. Structure will be concerned with certain key relations between objects: taxonomic hierarchies using the "is-a" relation, and part-whole hierarchies are two common examples. Thus a naturalist will know that a shad is a kind of herring and a herring is a kind of fish; a mechanic will know that a brake pad is part of the brake, and so on. Function will describe the purpose of objects in the domain, that the brake is needed to decelerate a car, or that the pancreas generates insulin which controls the level of blood glucose.

Additionally the expert will know a number of relationships between attributes, whether attributes of the same object or attributes of different objects. This knowledge may derive from definitions, so that the UK Social Security expert will know that a person is of pensionable age if his sex is male and his age greater than 65, or if her sex is female and her age greater than 60. Or they may represent universal generalisations: all tigers have stripes, although this is not part of the definition of a tiger. Sometimes they relate to sufficient conditions: it is enough to know that someone who has a safe pair of hands and sharp reflexes will be a good slip fielder. Finally, they may be no more than "rules of thumb". Such knowledge often appears to be of the same form as a universal generalisation, or a sufficient condition, but is different in that it is not always true. Sometimes this is signalled by the use of some qualification to the generalisation, such as "normally" or "usually". Rules of thumb are not always true because there are some exceptional cases to which they do not apply, but these exceptions are not stated explicitly, either because they are too rare to be of general concern, or because the mechanism which causes the exceptions to occur is insufficiently understood. In economics most principles are based on such rules of thumb: there we find statements like "the demand for goods varies inversely with its price, *other things being equal*". The addition of the last phrase recognises explicitly that the statement is not always true, but it is true most of the time, and it would be quite impossible to state the variety of factors which could make it false. For want of a better term we shall call all this knowledge *heuristic* knowledge, although heuristic is, of course, a rather weak term to apply to knowledge based on definitions or genuinely universal generalisations.

3.2.2. Knowledge of Tasks

An expert is not, of course, a simple repository of facts and theories about a domain. The expert will work in the domain, and will carry out a number of tasks. Thus the doctor must diagnose illnesses, the economist forecast performance, and the Social Security expert adjudicate claims for benefit, or advise people as to their rights. What distinguishes expert performance from inexpert performance is very often the way an expert sets about the task. "Knowing what to do" comprises knowledge of how to decompose the global task into a set of smaller sub-tasks, which can be carried out in a systematic order to ensure performance of the overall goal. The importance of appropriate decomposition cannot be overstated. In the well known AI example of the 15-puzzle, in which blocks are slid around inside a frame to achieve some desired arrangement, knowing that the way to proceed is to first get the first row right, then the second row, then the first column, then the second column, and finally shuffle the remaining tiles, will always provide a steady progression towards the solution. In contrast, without this strategy, the novice will flounder and very often repeatedly undo any progress that may have been made. Thus knowing how a task can be split into sub-tasks, and the order in which they should be undertaken is a key piece of expertise.

Complimentary to this strategic knowledge is tactical task knowledge. For many tasks there is no single best way of proceeding, but different methods are appropriate to different cases. Here the expert must have both a repertoire of methods so that the same method is not followed whether appropriate or not, and some means of identifying which of the methods is appropriate in a given case. To use a computer science example: there are a number of sorting algorithms, but their suitability depends on such factors as the number of items to be sorted and the state of the input data, since a method which works well on random data may not be so efficient on data which is already partially sorted. Here the expert will examine the detailed nature of the problem before deciding upon the method to use.

Finally, knowing how to perform a task will also involve knowing what information is required to perform the task, what information is available to perform the task, and how this information can be obtained. Sometimes the information can be found by querying the user, sometimes it can be inferred from other information in the database, sometimes it will be necessary to access a different computer system, and sometimes it may require the performance of further empirical tests or observations. The significance of the information and the costs of obtaining it may well have implications for which strategy is most appropriate.

3.2.3. Meta-Knowledge

The final component of expertise that we need to consider is the knowledge that an expert uses to determine how the rest of the knowledge will be exploited. For example, some of the knowledge about objects in the domain may be dependent on context; where rules of thumb are employed it may be helpful to have some indication of just how rare exceptions are; and which methods may be applicable only if certain preconditions are met. A further important form of meta-knowledge enables the expert to decide whether the problem presented to him is one with which he is not competent to deal.

Much of this - with the important exception of the confidence placed in rules of thumb - could be seen as meta-level *or* object level knowledge. Thus the context in which knowledge applies could be built in at the object level, and much concerning the suitability of task-solving strategies resembles the tactical task solving knowledge referred to above. We could therefore see the point at which the meta-/object level distinction is drawn as being somewhat artificial, and created in the encoding of expert knowledge by the design choices of the knowledge engineer.

Irrespective of these design choices, however, some meta-knowledge will be created by the encoding. This sort of meta-knowledge is not knowledge that the expert has concerning his knowledge of the domain, but knowledge which is required by the Knowledge Based System (KBS) a direct consequence of the encoding. This will include such knowledge as whether sub-classes in a taxonomy are exclusive, exhaustive or both; precedence in rules; and the meaning to be attached to whatever measure of confidence is used. This material is required by the KBS if it is to manipulate the knowledge in its KB correctly, but which cannot be expected to derive from the expert.

3.2.4. Volatility of Knowledge Base Contents

Since our specific concern is the maintenance of KBs, it is worth thinking here about how the knowledge in a KB is likely to change. Unfortunately there is no general answer: the ways in which different parts of the knowledge base are subject to change differ in different domains, and when domains are viewed from different perspectives. Thus, for example, in the medical domain, the basic components of the human body are likely to be static, and so from a diagnostic perspective things stay much the same. If, however, we turn to treatment, new drugs are developed, old drugs are superseded or found unsafe, fashions in treatment change, and more effective regimes are discovered. In the legal domain the situation is even worse in that many of the attributes that can be ascribed to people are dependent on legislation, and so when the legislation changes the rights and duties of citizens, so do the attributes they have and the values those attributes can take, and so even the vocabulary of the domain may not be stable. In the case of diagnosis of faults in machines new models are developed which require extension of the domain ontology. Depending too on how radical the new design is, this may lead to changes in task knowledge and even in meta-knowledge.

Also one should not overlook the fact that experts in every domain are continually extending and refining their knowledge. Sometimes it can be discovered that a universal generalisation is not so universal after all, and that it must be relegated to the status of a rule of thumb. Sometimes new relationships are discovered. Sometimes new task strategies are developed. These discoveries cannot be ignored if the KBS is to retain effectiveness and to continue to satisfy user requirements. Moreover, any model of the real world, whether the theory of an expert or a KB, must be an abstraction, and so necessarily exclude some detail. If and when some omitted detail becomes relevant, the model must be extended to accommodate this.

3.3. KNOWLEDGE REPRESENTATION

Having determined the kinds of knowledge that must be represented in a KBS, we now need to look at the strengths and weakness of knowledge representation paradigms. Although the expressiveness of rule based and structured object representations can be seen as equivalent in the abstract [Hayes 1979b], the style and focus of the different paradigms does have some real differences which mean that they are more suited to the representation of certain kinds of knowledge. This is what we shall discuss in this section.

3.3.1. Rule Based Representations

The primary focus of these representations, whether production rules or clauses of first order logic, is what we called "heuristic knowledge" above. Remember that we used the term broadly so as to encompass definitions and universal generalisations as well as rules of thumb. This should be unsurprising, as it is this knowledge which is most naturally expressed in the form of "if then" rules. These formalisms are also well adapted to the expression of task decompositions: production rules can be seen as expressing *actions* to be taken if certain conditions are satisfied, and the procedural semantics of logic programs allows a similar construction to be put on certain logic program goals. What is less well represented in these essentially *relation centred* representations is some of the more basic knowledge relating to objects in the domain.

Consider the following simple rule base relating to correct behaviour at traffic lights:

```
IF traffic-light red THEN driver-should stop.
IF traffic-light green THEN driver-should go.
```

The domain objects and their attributes are nowhere explicitly stated: they simply *emerge* from the rules. Thus we can infer that there are two states of traffic lights from these rules, but the knowledge that these states are exclusive is not recorded, nor that there is a further light, amber, nor that amber can appear in combination with red. Even if we extend the KB to include all the states that are in fact possible:

```
IF traffic-light amber THEN driver-should
                                    prepare-to-stop
IF traffic-light red/amber THEN driver-should
                                    prepare-to-go
```

we cannot tell from this that there are no other possibilities, nor still that the possibilities which are referenced in the rules are exclusive. This creates difficulties: first there is the practical difficulty that the conception of the objects of the domain represented in the KB can be verified only by an examination of the rule base as a whole, by an expert in the domain who has a full grasp of the ontology of the domain, and the deduction, also by that expert, of the conceptions implicit in the rules, which makes for problems when testing the rule base for consistency and completeness; second there is the more theoretical difficulty that rather fundamental domain knowledge is inevitably implicit rather than explicit. This further results in implicit meta-knowledge, such as the treatment of negation as failure in logic programs which requires the KB to be viewed as complete.

With regard to meta-knowledge there are two chief approaches taken in rule based representation - aside from the knowledge of the formalism implicit in the way in which the rules are triggered. One is to incorporate as much control knowledge as possible in the object level rules: this is the approach taken in many production rule systems such as MYCIN [Buchanan and Shortliffe 1984] and XCON [McDermott 1982], both of which make extensive explicit references to "contexts" to ensure the sensible application of rules. The other is to attempt to record such knowledge explicitly and to make use of this through a meta-interpreter, as exemplified by the MECHO system [Bundy *et al.* 1979]. The former approach has the advantage of the simpler system, but results in less straightforwardly understandable rules, the latter is a more complex system, but with explicit separation of control and object level knowledge. The kind of meta-knowledge which relates to the confidence to be placed in rules of thumb has also been represented in the rule based paradigm by providing a numerical means of measuring confidence and adapting the inference mechanism to propagate this measure through to conclusions drawn from such rules. MYCIN provides a classic example of this approach.

3.3.2. Structured Object or Frame Representations

Unlike rule based representations, structured object or frame representation are quite explicit as to the objects in the domain and their attributes. Sometimes too, although not always, it will be possible to state the nature of the values that can be taken by these attributes. Use of inheritance mechanisms - most notably based on the *is-a* relation - further allow objects to be grouped into hierarchies reflecting the structure of the domain. This focuses on objects, and the consequent bundling of information, which seems to accord with widespread intuitions as to knowledge representation, and accounts for much of the current popularity of this representation style.

Structured object representations are, however, less comfortable when it comes to representing the kind of heuristic knowledge which is the major strength of rule based representations. Some definitions can be captured through the use of specialisation into sub-classes and declaration of slot values, but this can cause a variety of problems if these techniques are not applied in a consistent manner, as well described in Brachman [1985]. Other kinds of heuristic knowledge can be represented as demons in frame systems or as methods in an object-orientated system, but such techniques often require the writing of code which may not be readily accessible to the domain expert. Similarly task knowledge tends either to be implicit in the system code which manipulates the representation, or forced to fit the representational scheme by defining tasks as objects in their own right.

Turning to meta-knowledge, structured object systems open up some very interesting possibilities. As well as classes of domain objects it is also possible to construct classes which refer to the objects found in the computer system. Thus, for example, there may be a class `Class` which describes classes and their attributes, and a class `Slot` which describes slots and their attributes. This means that the same representation can be used to record both knowledge of the domain, and knowledge about the way in which the domain knowledge has been encoded. Knowledge about the confidence to place in rules of thumb is not, however, so easily accommodated. Almost all structured object systems make use of default values, which mimic rules of thumb by allowing "typical" values to be inherited by class instances. Fillers either are or are not in slots, however, and so it hard to record the fact that the confidence reposed in these values differ.

3.3.3. Combined (Hybrid) Representations

Since both the representational paradigms have their strengths, some efforts have been made to combine the two. When structured objects are added to rule based systems this is seen as an attempt to provide structure to the KB; when rules are added to structured object systems the motive is to make heuristic knowledge more explicit and declarative. If the combination is made smoothly, these aims can be realised and the convenience of the representation enhanced.

In the MAUDE development environment [Coenen and Bench-Capon 1992a], referred to extensively in this book, a mixed paradigm is employed. In this system the structured objects are used exclusively to declare explicitly the vocabulary of the domain: no use is made of default values to represent what is typically the case. The representation of heuristic knowledge is all done with rules. In the MAUDE system the structured objects are also available to model meta-knowledge, although no provision is made to represent the degree of confidence in rules of thumb.

3.4. SUMMARY

We have seen that both the major paradigms express more naturally different areas of the expertise we wish to capture in a KBS. Which should be employed in a given case will depend on the nature of the domain being modelled, and on the predilections of the expert and knowledge engineer. We favour a mixed paradigm, and have used this in the MAUDE development environment. The essential difference between the paradigms is what is implicit in the representation: much relating to the ontology and structure of the domain in the case of rule based systems, and much relating to heuristic knowledge in the case of structured object systems. Also it should be noted that neither of the paradigms is at all good at representing the *function* of objects in the domain: this is at the heart of the criticism of KBSs which has led to work on "model based" or "deep knowledge" systems. Further it should be noted that at least some of the expertise will be implicit in the encoding and operation of the system. The implications for maintenance are both that explicit representation should be easier to maintain, and that the implicit expertise cannot be disregarded when maintaining the system.

CHAPTER 4

Maintenance of Knowledge Based Systems

4.1. INTRODUCTION

When expert systems first came to prominence, one of the major claims made for them was that, since they worked by manipulating a declarative representation of the knowledge pertinent to a problem, they lent themselves to easy verification by someone with that knowledge, easy extension, by the addition of extra knowledge, and easy maintenance, since obsolete knowledge could be straightforwardly replaced by current knowledge. Applying such a paradigm to the Knowledge Based System (KBS) sub-set of expert systems, it was envisaged that there would be one or more experts, whose knowledge would be elicited by a knowledge engineer capable of structuring and representing that knowledge in a form executable by the inference engine of the target system. MYCIN presents the classic example of this kind of approach. In practice things did not prove so straightforward.

In this chapter we introduce the concepts behind KBS maintenance. In chapter 1 we classified maintenance according to Swanson's classification [Swanson 1976]:

- Corrective maintenance.
- Perfective maintenance.
- Adaptive maintenance.

It is convenient to commence the discussion by considering this classification with respect to KBSs. This is carried out in sections 4.2 to 4.4 below. In section 4.5 we then discuss the importance of maintenance with respect to the wider adoption of KBS techniques.

Having established what maintenance is in the context of KBSs and with respect to traditional software systems we go on to consider the various facets of the KBS maintenance task. To this end we can identify a number of sub-tasks which can be organised into a methodology [Coenen 1992]:

1. Detection of the need for maintenance.
2. Determination of the nature of the change.
3. Global location of the section of the KBS that will be affected.
4. Determination of the nature of the required maintenance action.
5. Local identification of the elments in the KBS that will be directly affected.
6. Identification of the jeopardised sub-set of elements in the KBS that will be indirectly affected.
7. Implementation.
8. Testing.

A schematic for this process is given in Figure 4.1. From the figure it can be seen that as a result of local identification and testing further maintenance may be inaugurated before the system is returned to the end user. All the tasks identified are important to the successful implementation of KBS maintenance. All are considered in this chapter; some, however, warrant an entire chapter or chapters of their own and thus are only discussed in outline here and more fully later in this work. Where this is the case this is indicated in the text.

4.2. CORRECTIVE MAINTENANCE

In traditional software development corrective maintenance is considered to result from the discovery of system errors undetected prior to delivery of the system i.e. errors not detected during verification and validation. These are promulgated to the system maintainers through the medium of bug reports. In traditional systems verification is usually carried out with respect to a requirement specification document. However, in the previous chapter it was noted that the emphasis of KBS development is to produce a system that operates satisfactorily. There is thus no complete set of software requirements as is the case with traditional software systems, and therefore the concept of corrective maintenance due to misunderstood user requirements cannot exist. However, the user may still be dissatisfied with what the system does. We can thus define corrective maintenance for KBS as maintenance that is not perfective or adaptive. More precisely we can define

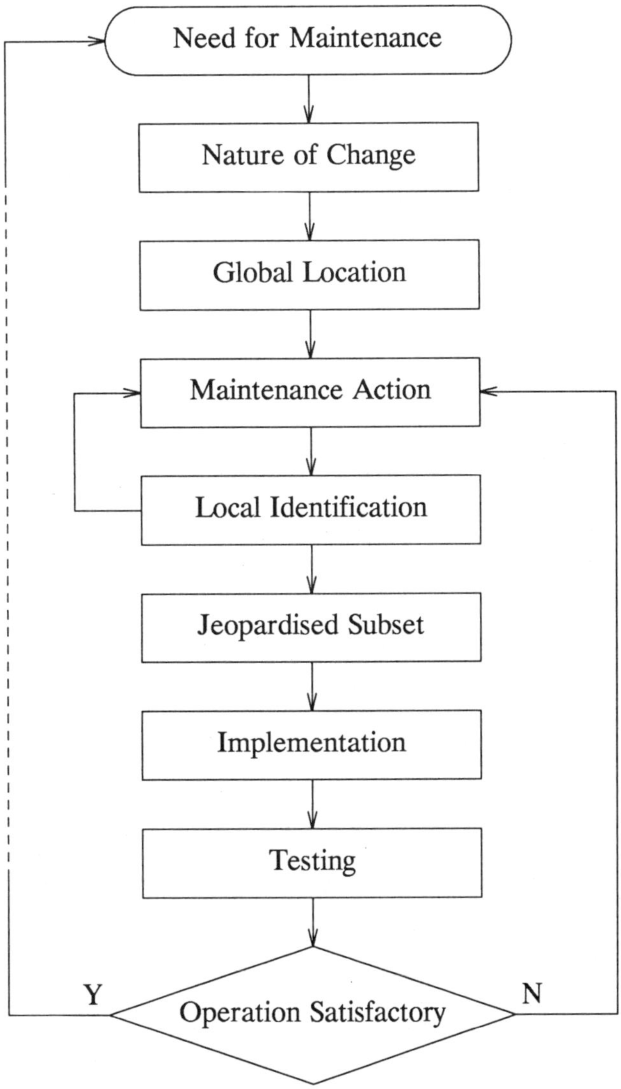

Figure 4.1: Schematic for a KBS maintenance methodology.

corrective maintenance for KBSs as maintenance required because a KBS is not behaving as it should. For example, given a particular set of facts a wrong conclusion may be drawn or a conclusion not arrived at. This may result from:

- Syntactic errors.
- Errors in identifying, formalising and encoding the knowledge obtained during knowledge analysis into the Knowledge Base (KB).

For traditional systems corrective maintenance is considered to represent between 17% and 21% of the total maintenance effort involved [Sommerville 1989, Pressman 1988]. Although there are no corresponding figures available for KBS there is no reason to assume that they would be very different. The amount of corrective maintenance for traditional software systems can be greatly reduced by adopting a rigid approach to the software engineering of the system accompanied by suitable testing methods and verification and validation techniques. Some of these benefits can be passed on to KBSs by adopting similar techniques.

4.3. PERFECTIVE MAINTENANCE

Perfective maintenance for traditional systems results from changes in user requirements. As a software system is used requests for new capabilities, modifications and general enhancements may be made. With respect to perfective maintenance the domain in which KBSs operate is usually very specific and thus perfective maintenance is restricted to the nature of the output or the amount of information displayed. Except where a process of incremental development has been chosen at the outset, it is rare for extra facilities to be appended to such systems. Perfective maintenance for traditional systems is quoted as representing between 65% and 50% of the total maintenance effort [Sommerville 1989, Pressman 1988], for KBSs this can be considered to be substantially less. Further, the amount of perfective maintenance can be reduced by adopting suitable system analysis techniques so that a fuller appreciation of the users requirements can be gained. This applies to both traditional software systems and KBSs.

4.4. ADAPTIVE MAINTENANCE

Adaptive maintenance results from changes in the environment in which a system is designed to operate. KBSs are particularly subject to this type of maintenance. This is because the "knowledge" displayed by these systems is often in a constant state of flux. The knowledge is usually obtained from expert sources through a knowledge engineering process. The nature of this expertise is continually subject to change as expert understanding increases and further knowledge elicitation is carried out.

For traditional systems adaptive maintenance is considered to account for between 18% to 25% of the total maintenance effort [Sommerville 1989, Pressman 1988]. For KBSs we can consider perfective maintenance to represent the largest part of the total maintenance effort.

Consider a particular KBS designed to provide British Coal's (BC's) Pensions and Insurance Division with decision support with respect to claims for industry related accidents [Bench-Capon and Coenen 1991a]. The need for adaptive maintenance here is considerable. Regarding the law itself, each year, BC estimate that there are between 10 and 20 court judgements in BC cases and another five relating to other employers, but with significance for BC. There are also up to 20 new relevant Statutory Instruments, and 10 Technical Instructions issued per year. In addition the policy of BC is modified from time to time, and some 10-15 such policy decisions are made in a typical year. Other changes arise out of changes in medical views, for example the acceptance that a particular substance can cause dermatitis; policy changes by other bodies, as when a particular firm of solicitors may start to issue writs if the claim is not settled in a certain period of time; and changes in the perception of methods of work or occupations. BC estimate that these will require another 30 changes per year. Thus the BC Pensions and Insurance KBS is subject to up to 110 changes per year, i.e. an average of approximately one change every three days. Some of these changes will be relatively minor, but none the less the cumulative effect of these changes indicates the rapidity with which a KBS dealing with this sort of application can go out of date if the appropriate adaptive maintenance does not take place.

4.5. IMPORTANCE OF MAINTENANCE

KBSs, over the last fifteen years, have undergone a period of steady development and are now approaching maturity. Facilities to develop large KBSs exist, for example development methodologies such as KADS [Wielinga *et al.* 1991], environments such as KEATS [Motta *et al.* 1990] and shells such as NEXPERT OBJECT [Aiken and Sheng 1990]. However, they have still not gained general acceptance; there are still a great many applications where the technology has not been applied. Why is this?

To answer this question we must return to the philosophy behind KBSs. By definition these systems are designed to behave like an expert in some specific domain of operation. As the expression "Knowledge Based System" indicates they are based on knowledge of a specific domain. However, all experts are continually learning therefore all knowledge is in a permanent state of flux. Thus for a KBS to be commercially viable it must be able to respond to the changes in the domain knowledge on which it is based, i.e. it needs to be maintained. However the maintenance of these systems has proven to be a difficult task. There are a number of reasons for this:

- Contrary to initial claims made when KBS were first introduced the nature of the representation techniques used do not lend themselves to traditional maintenance techniques.
- As illustrated in the BC example given above the frequency with which knowledge changes in many KBS domains is far in excess of that experienced for traditional software systems.
- There is almost a complete lack of suitable methodologies, techniques and software support for the KBS maintenance task.

The answer to the question of why KBSs have failed to gain more general acceptance can thus be firmly attributed to their lack of maintainability. This has been observed by a number of authors, examples include Bench-Capon and Coenen [1991a], Bratley *et al.* [1991a] and Bratley *et al.* [1991b].

4.6. DETECTING THE NEED FOR MAINTENANCE

Before any maintenance activity can be implemented the maintainers must first have become aware of a need for maintenance. The need for maintenance in KBSs is not always clear, particularly where adaptive maintenance is concerned. Generally the need for maintenance, regardless of the nature of that maintenance, can best be detected by the end users. The end users of course will not necessarily be domain experts, but they will be familiar with the environment in which the KBS is expected to operate, usually much more so than the maintainers of the system.

The need for corrective maintenance is usually promulgated by bug reports drawn up by the end users. Whenever a system appears not to behave as is it is intended to a bug report is filed. When a sufficient number of these reports have been gathered, or if a particularly serious bug is discovered, a maintenance session is inaugurated. This process is applicable to both traditional systems and KBSs.

Similarly the need for perfective maintenance is established in the form of requests by the end user. With respect to KBSs this is usually concerned with the nature and amount of output displayed. Often, while a system is in use, it becomes apparent that information which was originally not considered to be required is after all relevant or that the information displayed is in the wrong format. For example a UK Department of Social Security (DSS) system might display an applicant's age when in fact it is the date of birth that is required. Perfective maintenance to the structure of the KB may also be required as a result of expert suggestions and periodic scrutiny of the rule base. Again the process of requests for perfective maintenance is applicable to both traditional software and KBSs.

In the case of adaptive maintenance there is a danger that changes in the environment in which the system is operating may go unnoticed and hence the output of the system become erroneous. This is particularly significant for KBSs where the majority of maintenance consists of adaptive maintenance. The need for adaptive maintenance can only be recognised by monitoring the environment. How this is done depends very much on the domain in which a KBS is intended to operate. In some domains, changes in domain knowledge are well advertised. For example in legal domains, changes resulting from changes in the regulations on which the KBS is based are generally published in the form of Acts of Parliament and Statutory Instruments. However, external changes in the application of the law must also be monitored. The results of court cases pertaining to a particular sphere of interest are often collated and published. For example in the case of the DSS the principal reference work is Neligan, in the UK mining industry it is Kemp and Kemp. Alternatively in some domains, changes to the domain are promulgated in the form of company circulars etc. Typically these will involve changes in working practices, for example in a KBS designed to monitor a chemical processing plant the development of a new additive to be used for a particular process will necessitate a change in working practices. Similarly changes in the world in which a system is operating must also be monitored. Awareness of the need for maintenance may also come from notification by experts, from monitoring key information or may manifest itself through system malperformance. In most case the onus for detecting the need for adaptive maintenance is (again) on the end user.

Whatever the case the maintainers will be made aware of the need for maintenance by contact with the end user who will notify them of changes in their requirements through the medium of change requests and bug reports.

4.6.1 Who Should Carry Out Maintenance?

When the need for maintenance has been established by the end users this is passed on to whoever is to carry out the maintenance. Who these maintainers are will depend on company policy. A maintenance contract will often be taken out with either the original developers of the product or another software house. Alternatively maintenance may be carried out by an in-house maintenance team. The most desirable method is for the developers to carry out all maintenance. Even if the maintenance team is not made up of members of the original development team at least they will be familiar with the development techniques and methods used; further, internal sources of information will be available, for example members of the original development team may be contacted. Where maintenance is to be carried out by another software house it should be appreciated that the maintenance team involved are unlikely to be familiar with the product or the methodologies and techniques adopted in its development. If it is known in advance that maintenance is to be carried out by a third party it would be useful for them to be involved in the development process, if only as observers, so that some familiarity with the product can be gained. However, for sound business reasons, the development company is unlikely to be amenable to the involvement of what might be a rival software house in the development process.

Maintenance through maintenance contracts may not necessarily be the most cost effective method, especially where the end users have access to a substantial in-house IT department or where the product is developed in house. Again, where the product is developed externally, it would be useful if members of the IT department, who are going to maintain the system, were involved in the development process. In this case, because the maintainers represent the purchasers of the product, the developers may be much more amenable to this arrangement than the involvement of a third party.

4.7. DETERMINING THE NATURE OF THE CHANGE

To determine what maintenance action to take, having established that some maintenance is required, we need to consider the nature of the change in more detail. This can be viewed from a number of standpoints. In this work we consider two views, the applications view and the knowledge based view. The application view is a user view of the system and is concerned with changes to the domain in which a KBS is expected to operate. The knowledge based view is a developer's view and is concerned with how changes in the domain will affect the structure of the KB. It should be noted that from the end user's view there is little difference between a KBS and conventional software application: the user is of course not interested in implementation issues. In some domains there may be no difference between changes in the knowledge on which the KBS is based and its application; in others, such as legal domains, this distinction may be very much in evidence.

4.7.1. Applications View

From the standpoint of the application required changes to the KBS may be attributed to a number of sources depending on the nature of the domain:

1. Changes in the domain knowledge on which the KBS is based.
2. Changes in the application of the knowledge on which the KBS is based.
3. Changes in the environment in which the system is designed to operate.
4. Changes in system requirements.

Changes in Knowledge

A change in the domain knowledge on which a KBS is based may be considered to be either predictable or unpredicatable. Further the nature of the change may be considered to be either minor or radical. Different domains will be subject to different categories of change. If we take as an example KBSs operating in regulation based domains:

PREDICTABLE CHANGES. Some regulations are reviewed on a fixed time basis: for example annually or half yearly, in which case a change in the regulations may be predicted. These changes usually consist of minor up-ratings, for example changes in EEC fish quotas, DSS benefit rates, etc. Given suitable foresight the ability to respond to such predictable changes can be incorporated into a system without major restructuring of the KBS.

UNPREDICTABLE CHANGES. Unpredictable changes in regulations are usually in the form of amendments repealing, amending or adding certain sections. These are often "one off" changes promulgated through the medium of Statutory Instruments. For example the changes from Imperial to Metric Units that has affected many sets of regulations over the last two decades, or regulations to clarify or change the interpretation of existing regulations.

RADICAL CHANGES. Radical changes in regulations are generally unpredictable and are the most difficult to implement. If we consider a system designed to process DSS benefit claims then the recent change from Supplementary Benefit to Income Support may be described as a radical change.

A change in domain knowledge may result in either the introduction of a new concept or alter the relationship between existing concepts.

ESTABLISHING A CONCEPT. If we again consider a DSS system an example of a new concept could be the introduction of a new benefit, or of a new qualifying condition for an existing benefit.

Relationships between existing concepts may be altered by either adding a new relationship, deleting a relationship or modifying a relationship.

ESTABLISHING A RELATIONSHIP. If we consider a system designed to assess liability in road traffic accident claims we may have three legal concepts (A) negligence (B) statutory speed limits and (C) the onus on drivers to proceed with due care and attention. A new regulation may then be enacted that states that to show that a driver has been negligent it is necessary to show that the driver was exceeding the statutory speed limit and was proceeding without due care and attention. In other words a relationship has been created between these three concepts.

$$B \wedge C \Rightarrow A$$

REMOVING A RELATIONSHIP. A subsequent amendment may then remove the relationship between negligence and statutory speed limits in the case of emergency vehicles on the grounds that such vehicles should not be impeded by such restrictions when proceeding to the scene of an accident. Thus the relationship established between the above concepts has been removed in certain cases.

MODIFYING A RELATIONSHIP. Alternatively a subsequent amendment may alter the relationship between negligence, statutory speed limits and due care and attention so that to prove that a driver has been negligent it is only necessary to show that either the statutory speed limit has been exceeded or that the driver was not proceeding with due care and attention, but not both. Thus the relationship between the concepts A and B has been modified from an "and" relationship to an "or" relationship:

$$B \vee C \Rightarrow A$$

Changes in Application of Knowledge

The distinction between domain knowledge and the application of this knowledge is not always clear. It can be illustrated by considering a KBS operating in a medical domain. There may be two drugs which cure a particular disease one of which must be selected by the system. There may a heuristic which says select the cheapest, in which case changes in the price of the drugs would represent a change in domain knowledge. If, however, selection is in accordance with a government policy to "buy British" i.e. according to fashion, a change in this policy would represent a change in the application of the domain knowledge - that a group of drugs cure a particular disease. However, in this case where it remains true that two drugs cure a particular disease, changes in the country of manufacture would again represent a change in the domain knowledge.

Changes in the application of knowledge may be considered to be either external or internal:

EXTERNAL CHANGES. Again considering KBSs operating in legal domains the application of knowledge may change as a result of a decision by a superior tribunal.

INTERNAL CHANGES. The application of knowledge may change as a result of an administrative change initiated by the owner of the system.

A change in the application of knowledge may result in a condition either being established, modified or removed. In legal domains such conditions can be considered to be either sufficient or necessary. The distinction between a sufficient condition and a necessary condition can be summarised by considering the following two rules:

```
Rule 1:  Q ⇒ P
Rule 2: ¬Q ⇒ ¬P
```

In Rule 1 Q is a sufficient condition for P, in Rule 2 Q is a necessary condition for P. If we consider a coal mining application where an injury has occurred due to tripping:

ESTABLISHING A CONDITION. A judge may establish a legal condition that states that it is sufficient to show that a mine manager has been negligent (A) if a roadway was not free of obstructions

(B); and that it is necessary to show that the obstruction was in the roadway where the accident occurred (C).

$$\neg B \wedge C \Rightarrow A$$

MODIFYING A CONDITION. These conditions may then be modified by a later court case stating that it is sufficient to show that the mine manager has been negligent if a road way was not free of obstructions; and that it is necessary to show that the obstruction was in the roadway where the accident occurred and that the accident was caused by the obstruction (D). Thus the original conditions for A have been modified by the creation of an additional condition:

$$\neg B \wedge C \wedge D \Rightarrow A$$

REMOVING A CONDITION. A further court case may then remove all these conditions by stating that with modern mining techniques it is no longer sufficient to show that a mine manager has been negligent if obstructions are left in a roadway, and thus by implication that it is no longer necessary to show that the obstruction was left in the roadway where the accident occurred and that the accident was caused by the obstruction.

Internal changes can occur simply as a result of a decision by an organisation responsible for applying domain knowledge. This is important in legal domains as it can result in changes in the law without reference to judges or parliament. For example, it might be that whereas currently a birth certificate is the only acceptable evidence of age, the introduction of a national identity card scheme could allow the cards to be used for this purpose as well.

Changes in the Environment in which a KBS is to Operate.

Changes in the world or environment in which a KBS is designed to operate will result in the creation of new knowledge. This may manifest itself in a number of ways. We can identify four possibilities, although these may not necessarily be applicable to all domains.

ESTABLISHING A RELATIONSHIP. A new relationship between existing concepts may be established or discovered. For example that passive smoking causes lung cancer or that working in a noisy environment may cause loss of hearing.

REMOVING A RELATIONSHIP. An existing relationship may cease to exist. For example since the Middle Ages it has come to light that famines and natural disasters are not caused by witchcraft.

MODIFYING A RELATIONSHIP. An existing relationship may be modified, for example if we consider air pollution and car exhaust fumes the first is considered to be the product of the second. However this relationship has been modified in recent years in that the amount of pollution produced may be reduced by using unleaded petrol or the fitting of a catalytic converter.

ESTABLISHING A CONCEPT. A new concept may come into being. For example the Employment Protection Act introduced the concept of employees having property rights in their jobs, a concept that did not exist prior to the Act when employees could be hired and fired at will.

Changes in System Requirements

Changes affecting system requirements usually stem from the user. Not all changes in system requirements directly affect the KB itself. For example changes to the system interface, such as the display of additional information or a change in the manner in which information is displayed, or changes to the inference engine strategy or additional facilities, such as an explanation capability, may not affect the KB. However, the KB will be affected by changes in requirements which will necessitate a change in the breadth and depth of the KB or the manipulations performed on the existing KB. Typically such changes are the result of changes to the raw data with which the system is expected to operate. New information may become available, or the way in which it is presented may be changed, or alternatively certain information may no longer be readily available. Often this is the result of administrative changes within the environment in which the system is expected to operate.

Summary of Applications View

To summarise the above discussion, we have seen that the need to amend a KBS may arise from changes in (a) domain knowledge, (b) the way in which this knowledge is applied, (c) the environment in which it is applied or (d) system requirements. With respect to the first three causes for change, some changes may be regular and predictable (e.g. up-ratings), but in the majority of cases we cannot predict which areas will change, only that changes will occur. Changes are generally minor, affecting only a limited part of the KB, but there will be

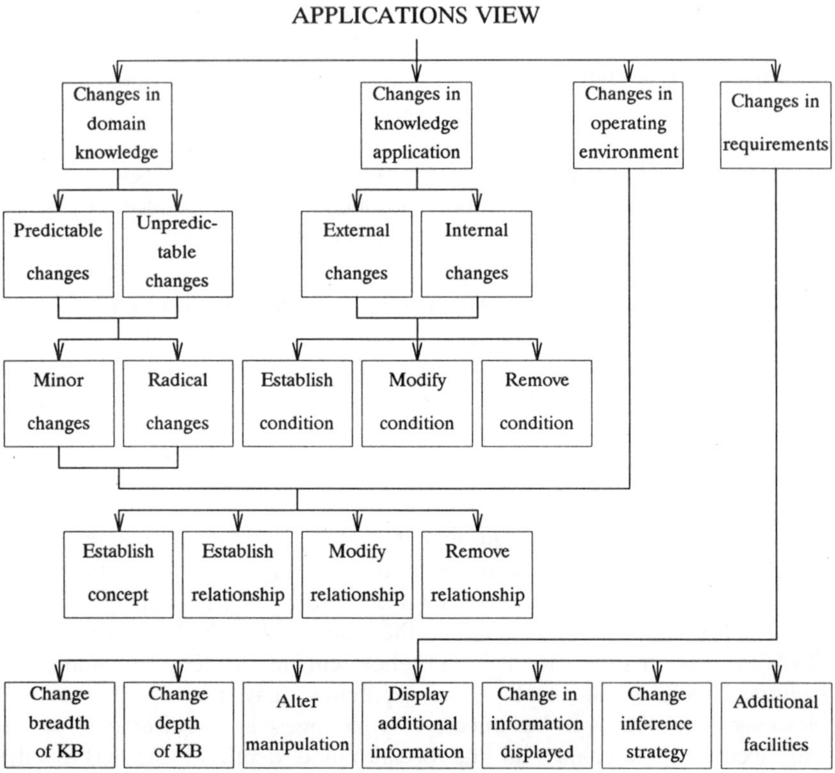

Figure 4.2: Applications view.

periodic radical changes, which will necessitate wholesale revision. Radical changes will always mean a major exercise.

The possible changes from an applications point of view are illustrated in Figure 4.2. Referring to this figure the possible knowledge changes identified can be summarised as follows:

- A new concept may be established (discovered).
- A new relationship between existing conditions may be established.
- An existing relationship may modified.
- An existing relationship may be removed.
- A new condition may be established.
- An existing condition may be modified.

- An existing condition may be removed.

With respect to changes arising from changes in system requirements, again referring to Figure 4.2, we can characterise the possible changes consequent on changes in system requirements as follows:

- The breadth of the KB must be increased or decreased.
- The depth of the KB must be increased or decreased.
- The manipulations performed on the existing KB added to.
- The interface is required to display additional information.
- The interface is required to display existing information differently.
- Changes in inference engine strategy.
- Additional facilities (e.g. explanations).

Some of these changes in system requirements will not affect the KB, others will. Broadly we can say that the first three will affect the KB, while the others will not.

4.7.2. Knowledge Based View

From the standpoint of the KB the need for maintenance can be because (a) the knowledge base is wrong in content or (b) the knowledge base is wrong in structure. We will introduce this distinction briefly in the following two sub-sections. The discussion is continued, in full detail, in chapter 8. A summary of the possible ways that a knowledge base may be wrong is given in Figure 4.3. The precise definitions of each item will be given in chapter 8. The importance of the distinction is that the two types of error arise from different sources, give rise to different types of maintenance action, require the involvement of different people, and require different kinds of tools for their treatment. Essentially, defects of structure can be identified, or at least suggested, by an examination of the knowledge base alone, without reference to the domain which it represents. This means that structural defects:

- Result from defective encoding of the domain.
- Require corrective maintenance.
- Can normally be remedied without reference to a domain expert.
- Can be identified by formal tools which examine the knowledge base statically.

In contrast, errors of content:

- Can only be discovered by the incorrect operation of the KBS.
- May arise either from inadequate elicitation or from changes in the external domain.
- Require a domain expert to fix.
- Need tools that will help in identifying the location of the defect, which will typically be dynamic, or relate to the sources or intermediate representation that was used in the encoding.

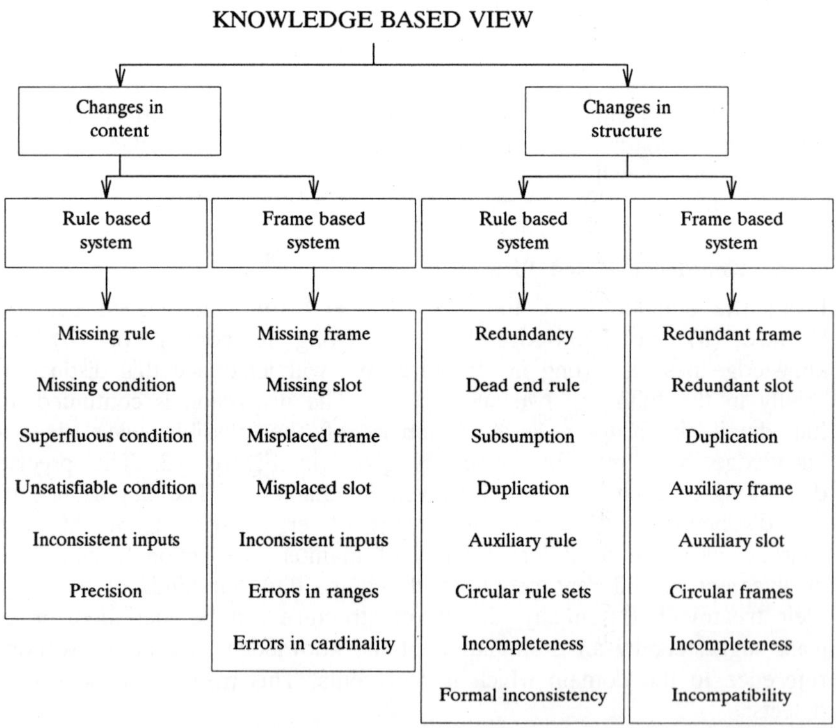

Figure 4.3: Knowledge based view.

Defects of Structure

There are a number of structural defects which a KB may exhibit. The precise nature of these potential defects will, of course, depend on the formalism used to encode the knowledge. Consider first the potential structural problems of a rule base. First there may be *redundant* rules, which play no part in establishing the system goals because they have lead to a conclusion not required to deduce the target goal. Second there may be *dead end rules,* which cannot establish the target proposition because they have unsatisfiable conditions. Thirdly we may have *subsumption,* whereby rules are duplicated by other rules, or their effect duplicated by one or more other rules. A fourth structural defect is referred to as *auxiliary rules,* where a rule could be eliminated by collapsing two rules together. Next we may have *circular rule* sets which will give rise to loops when executed by a backward chaining system. Then there is the possibility that the rule base may contain a formal *contradiction,* in that no model for the rule base can exist. Finally the rule base may be formally *incomplete,* in that there may be some combination of inputs for which no response can be given. All of these properties of a knowledge base can be detected by a static examination of the rule base considered in isolation from the domain. Each is considered in more detail in in chapter 8, and appropriate tools discussed in chapter 10.

As can be seen from Figure 4.3, most of these structural defects have parallels in frame systems, although because of the greater intrinsic structure of such systems, they are more often caught during development. A discussion can be found in section 8.3.

In should be noted, however, that although a defect can be identified as a defect of structure, investigation and correction may show that the problem is caused by a problem of content. Thus a dead end rule may occur because there is a *missing* rule, which should be in the knowledge base and which would enable the appropriate condition to be satisfied. Similarly the presence of an auxiliary rule may be explained by a desire to reflect the structure of the domain, or to provide for future extension of the knowledge base, and so be desirable. Never the less, consideration and identification of structural defects and anomalies is important, as it can be carried out in a relatively mechanical manner, and identifies features of the knowledge base which must be corrected or justified.

Defects of Content

Some of the the structural defects identified above require remedy by changing the content of the knowledge base, as when we correct a dead end rule by adding another rule. Other defects stem from a failure to capture knowledge adequately reflecting the domain; these include missing rules which, whilst not manifesting themselves in the structure of the KB, degrade its performance, missing conditions in rules, superfluous conditions in rules, conditions which cannot be satisfied because they require an attribute to assume an impossible value and so on. In frame systems there may be additional content problems, in that the cardinality of a slot may be incorrect, or the bounds put on the value of a slot may be incorrect. All of these defects are typically detected by a failure in the operation of the system, or when the fact that the knowledge on which the system was founded has changed in some way becomes known. Alternatively it may be possible to identify defects of content through the inspection of the knowledge base by a domain expert. Again a full discussion of these possibilities can be found in chapter 8.

Special mention should, however, be made of inconsistency. It may be that a knowledge base is not formally inconsistent, and yet excludes certain combinations of inputs. This may be wholly desirable in that such combinations cannot occur, and so their implicit inclusion is a valid part of the domain knowledge. However, if some of these combinations are in fact possible, then this is a serious defect, and one which will cause the users confusion if they attempt to supply one of these combinations. It is therefore highly desirable to check the knowledge base for this class of defect, and several tools to do this are discussed in section 10.9.

4.7.3. Classification of Changes

At this point we should recall Swanson's classification of maintenance tasks introduced in chapter 1 and discussed further at the beginning of this chapter. Corrections resulting from changes in the domain knowledge or its application, or changes in the world in which a system is expected to operate, may be considered to be adaptive maintenance. Changes in the system requirements may be considered to result in perfective maintenance. Finally, corrections to the KB because it is wrong in content or structure can be considered to be corrective maintenance. It can be argued that changes to the KB due to errors in its content is adaptive maintenance if it results from, for example, a flash of inspiration on the part of the developers. However, in this work we classify the maintenance resulting from required changes to a KBS as follows:

- Corrective Maintenance: KBS wrong in content or structure.
- Perfective Maintenance: changes in system requirements affecting the KB content.
- Adaptive Maintenance: changes in the domain, the application of domain knowledge or the environment in which the system is designed to operate, again requiring modification of the content of

the KB.

From the above it can be seen that special features of KBS maintenance derive in good measure from the greater need to accommodate adaptive maintenance. This bears out our earlier observations that adaptive maintenance is critically important for KBSs.

4.8. GLOBAL LOCATION

Having established the need for change and identified the nature of the change required the maintenance engineer will then wish to locate the section within the KB where the change is initially to be implemented. The starting point is to locate the area affected in the knowledge source. If the knowledge source is in the form of textual matter this can usually be accurately identified. If the source is more nebulous, for example a series of taped interviews with a domain expert this is much harder, especially, as is often the case, if related concepts are not all contained on the same tape but spread over a number of tapes. If the source knowledge resulted from unrecorded interviews with domain experts, i.e. the developers implemented the knowledge in rule or frame format directly, global identification will be even harder and may require recourse to the original domain experts. Thus in the first instance the ease with which the area affected can be identified depends very much on the format of the knowledge analysis. It is also worth noting that the use of an intermediate representation can be of value here.

Assuming that the area in the knowledge domain affected can be identified the next stage is to identify the particular elements of the KB that require attention. The ease with which this can be achieved will depend very much on the techniques used during development of the KBS. In the worst case it will involve the painstaking inspection of reams of code, an onerous and unenviable task.

From the above brief discussion it can be seen that the question of where to implement a required change in a KB depends very much on the nature of the development of the KBS as whole. Many development environments exist designed to facilitate knowledge acquisition, analysis, and representation. Some have been developed with a particular view to maintenance. Whatever the case the maintenance task will always be much simpler if a structured and formal approach to KBS development has been adopted. There are also a number of specific techniques that can be used to facilitate the location of the section of a KBS that will require attention as a result of changes to the source.

In the following chapter a number of KBS development

environments are described. The discussion on locating the section of a KBS that will be affected by a change and the tools and techniques available is then continued in chapter 7.

4.9. MAINTENANCE ACTIONS

Once the nature of the change and the area within the KB affected has been identified we can determine the type of maintenance action required. In most instances a maintenance session will involve the implementation of a number of maintenance actions. Usually a maintenance session is only commenced once a significant number of required changes have been gathered.

The possible changes to KBSs that may be required, as identified above, can result in a number of maintenance actions. With respect to a rule base system we can:

1. Add a rule.
2. Remove a rule.
3. Replace a rule.
4. Modify a rule.

Replacing a rule is defined as removing a rule from a given location and then adding another in the same location. Modifying a rule involves adding, removing, replacing or modifying one or more conditions in the head or tail of a rule.

With respect to frame based systems we may implement one or more of the following maintenance actions:

1. Add or remove a frame (class).
2. Add or remove a slot (attribute).
3. Add or remove a value.

Returning to the possible changes to a KBS that may be required, as discussed above, we can broadly consider that (a) the introduction of a new concept or a new relationship between existing conditions will require the introduction of new rule(s) or frame(s), (b) the removal of a relationship between existing concepts will involve the removal of a rule or frame and (c) the introduction of a condition or the removal of an existing condition or the modification of an existing relationship or condition will involve the modification or replacement of existing rules or frames. However, this is a very simplified view. In the following sub-sections each of these maintenance actions is considered in much more detail.

4.9.1. Introducing a New Rule

When new knowledge becomes available that has not previously been included in the KB new rules will need to be defined. If the change is small it may be sufficient simply to add an extra condition to an existing rule, i.e. the modification of a rule (see below). However new knowledge will normally result in the addition of a new branch to the rule hierarchy in which case the new rule (if only one is added) will represent a new leaf node. Adding a rule (the head of which is not currently available within the KB) as a leaf will require that the head proposition is tied into the rest of the rule hierarchy by ensuring that this proposition also appears in the rule or rules which are to call the new rule, this will necessitate the modification of existing rules. In addition consideration will have to be given to the mechanism that manipulate the "askable" propositions in the rule base if the conditions in the tail of the new rule are not currently referred to in the KB.

Alternatively a new rule may be introduced as a new root or in the middle of the rule hierarchy. Introducing a new rule in the middle of a rule base hierarchy is the most complex as it requires the "tying in" of both the head and tail propositions, i.e. attention must be paid to the rules that will call the new rule and the rules that will be called from the new rule. Introducing a new rule in the middle of a rule hierarchy will thus also require the modification of existing rules: these rules will at least need to be examined, the process is consequently more involved. Adding a new rule as a root is the simplest as it only requires the tying in of the tail propositions. This is a trivial operation in most cases, as such a high level rule will typically be expressed in terms of pre-existing conditions. Further it should be noted that the introduction of a new rule as a root is a rare event since it changes or extends the function of the KBS.

4.9.2. Removing an Existing Rule

As a result of a section of the source knowledge no longer being applicable rules may need to be modified or replaced (see below). In some cases this will mean the removal of an entire rule or group of rules from the rule base. We can consider the removal of a rule according to where it is located in the rule hierarchy. The removal of a root rule is effectively the same as altering the task that the rule base is expected to carry out as a new set of roots will be created. Removal of a root rule can therefore be considered to be an extreme form of rule base maintenance and in practice unlikely to occur. Removal of a rule in the middle of the rule base hierarchy will necessitate the knitting back together of the rule base. This will require the modification of the rules in which (a) the head proposition of the removed rule appears in the tail (assuming that the removed rule is the only one for this head), i.e. the rules that would have been used to call the rule which is to be removed, and (b) the rules in which the body propositions of the removed rule appear as the head, i.e. the rules that would have been called by the rule to be removed. In many cases matching these propositions will be a non-trivial operation. Removing a leaf rule will also require attention to the rules in which the head proposition of the removed rule appears in the tail. In addition removing a leaf rule will require attention to the the mechanism for manipulating askable propositions as new leaf propositions may be created.

4.9.3. Modifying or Replacing an Existing Rule

In most cases rule base maintenance will consist of modifying or replacing existing rules as a result of new conditions or relationships being created, removed or modified. Again the modification of a rule can be considered according to where it is located in the rule hierarchy, root, middle or leaf, or according to whether we are modifying the tail or the head propositions of the rule (or both). More concisely, however, the modification of a rule can be viewed as the process of removing a rule and introducing another, i.e. replacing it. The processes involved have already been described above.

4.9.4. Introducing and Removing Frames

Adding a new frame requires careful consideration as to where in the frame hierarchy it should be added. This can best be determined by the slots that need to be associated with the frame. If an existing frame contains a sub-set of the desired slots then it is a potential super-frame for the new frame. Clearly the frame with the largest such sub-set (i.e. the lowest such frame in the hierarchy) is the logical super-frame to choose. Next it must be determined which existing frames should be sub-frames of the new frame. The answer here is that existing frames with slots which are a superset of the new frame should be sub-frames of the new frame. This can only be done by inspection although assistance can be obtained using a frame hierarchy "browser" of some description.

Removing a frame is effectively like removing a set of slots.

However, existing sub-frames of the frame need to become sub-frames of its immediate super-frame. Problems will arise if any slots which are still valid are introduced in the frame to be removed or specialisation of values occurs, i.e. they are utilised by sub-frames of this frame. Clearly such slots must be re-introduced, either in the sub-frames or the immediate super-frames, as seems to be most appropriate.

4.9.5. Introducing and Removing Slots

One of the most basic maintenance actions that can be carried out to a frame based system is the introduction of a new slot or attribute or the removal of such a slot or attribute.

A slot can be added to a frame in two ways. Either it can be added directly to the frame, or it can be added to a super-frame, and so added to the frame in question indirectly by inheritance. Thus if a new slot is required, the first step should be to walk up the frame hierarchy to determine the appropriate point at which the slot should be introduced into the hierarchy. Note, however, that adding it to a super-frame will cause all the sub-frames of that frame to take on the slot, not only those on the path walked up. It will therefore be necessary to walk down all the paths to check that the new slot is inherited appropriately.

When removing an existing slot or attribute inheritance will necessitate that the slot also be removed from all the sub-frames below the point from which the slot is to be removed. We should therefore walk down the various paths to see whether we should reintroduce the slot at a lower level.

4.9.6. Introducing and Removing Values

Since some hybrid frame based systems which also incorporate a rule base, such as systems developed using MAUDE [Coenen and Bench-capon 1992b], allow for the specification of the possible values which can be used to fill a slot, we should also consider the addition of new values to a slot and the removal of existing values.

In practice a value will be added to a slot as a consequence of the introduction or modification of an existing attribute. The allocation of this additional value to an existing slot will not generally affect the operation of the existing class hierarchy. The exception to this is if rules exist that use the possible values of a slot to express negation. For example if we have a frame `paint` with a slot of the form:

```
Frame paint
slot(colour literal (red,green,blue,other))
```

and a rule:

```
(paint not PrimaryColour is true
if
not (colour is red)
and
not (colour is blue)
and
not (colour is green))
```

This will appear in the KB as:

```
(paint NotPrimaryColour is true
if
(colour is other))
```

Now the introduction of the value `purple` to the colour slot will invalidate the `NotPrimaryColour` rule as this will deduce that purple is a primary colour.

Because the inheritance mechanism of frame hierarchies will usually insist on strict specialisation, a value can only be added to a slot at the highest level at which that slot appears. If the rule which motivates the introduction of the new value refers to a frame which inherits the slot from a super-frame, either the value must be added to the super-frame, or some new slot must be created in the frame in question. If the value is added to the super-frame, of course, the rules for that frame in which the slot appears are jeopardised. Therefore, before a new value can be added, the user should examine the frame which introduces the slot to the frame hierarchy. This may not be the frame mentioned in the source change which motivated the introduction of the value, but the value may be added to this frame.

Removing a value from a slot jeopardises all rules which make use of that slot, and therefore these must also be either removed or modified (see above). Where the slot and value appear in the head of a rule this will usually result in the removal of that rule and any other rules hanging from it. Where the attribute and value are used in the tail of a rule the rule should be inspected so that the maintenance engineer can decide whether it is appropriate to remove the rule, remove the literal containing the removed value, or modify the rule in some other way. Note that the removal of a value will also cause that value to be removed from all sub-frames of the frame from which it is removed.

Although there seems to be a lot of extra work involved in hybrid systems to keep the frame and rule bases in step, this is in fact advantageous. Without the explicit record of the domain ontology represented by the frames in such a system it is all to easy to jeopardise rules unwittingly, with no way of identifying the potential problems.

4.10. LOCAL IDENTIFICATION

When the nature of the required maintenance has been established and the global area in the KB where it should be implemented identified the next step is to identify locally the elements of the KB that will require attention as a result of the proposed change. If we consider a frame based system where we wish to add a slot we will need to consider the method by which the slot may be set and also, assuming an inheritance mechanism, the sub-frames that may inherit the slot value.

Several techniques for local identification suggest themselves depending on the representation formalism used. The first possibility involves graphical representations of the KB as provided by rule maps or frame browsers. However, these tools require a certain amount of user interaction and depend on visual inspection for the identification of the appropriate elements. More desirable are mechanisms which automatically list the rules or frames that will be affected.

The tools and techniques available that can be used to support local identification are discussed further in Chapter 7 together with those appropriate for global identification.

4.11. THE JEOPARDISED SUB-SET

For testing purposes, in addition to the elements of the KB on which some maintenance action will be implemented, the maintenance engineer will also need to identify the elements that will be affected by the change but will not undergone any alteration themselves. Conceivably this could be the entire KB, however this would mean that the task that the KBS is intended to perform has been altered, a very unlikely event. In practice it is envisaged that only a limited number of elements of the KB will be involved. In a production rule, backward chaining, system, if a rule is added as a leaf then only the operation of that particular rule need be considered. In a forward chaining system the number of rules to be considered will be increased, but still limited.

The techniques to identify this "jeopardised" set of elements are similar to those required for local identification. Again full automation is the ideal to be aimed at: a list of jeopardised elements is the desired output.

4.12. IMPLEMENTATION

Having identified the nature of the required maintenance action(s) the next step is the implementation of the action(s). This usually involves a certain amount of programming in much the same manner as involved during the original development of the system. Most interpreters, development shells and environments include editing facilities. In some cases these are fairly sophisticated, incorporating a certain amount of syntactic and error checking capability.

The implementation of maintenance thus requires that the maintainers are familiar with the programming techniques used, e.g. PROLOG, LISP, or a shell or development environment language. If not a considerable learning period may be involved. Alternatively the KBS may be implemented using an intermediate representation. The principal advantage of the use of such a representation is that it can be easily understood by maintainers who were not part of the original development team and hence are not familiar with the development techniques used. The use of intermediate representations for KBS development is discussed in more detail in chapter 6.

4.13. TESTING

On completion of a maintenance session the maintenance engineer will wish to ensure two things: firstly that the maintenance action has been implemented correctly i.e. the KBS operates as required by the change. This is usually established by running suitable test cases. Traditionally "suitable" test cases have been defined as cases that contain some element of the changed rule or frame in the KB. However, suitable test cases are not necessarily the same as those that appear to be immediately relevant. The automatic generation of test cases is currently the subject of much research effort. Clearly for KBS maintenance purposes testing should be carried out with reference to the jeopardised sub-set of KBS elements as identified in section 4.11 above.

Secondly the maintenance engineer will wish to ensure that no errors or anomalies have been introduced that may affect the operation of the rest of the KBS. This can be carried out by using similar sets of tools as those proposed by many general KBS verification and validation tool kits. These have been well documented and are discussed in detail later in this work. Indeed there is a certain amount of overlap between the testing proposed here and KBS verification and validation in general. The significant difference is that the verification and validation carried out on completion of a KBS maintenance session impinges only on the sub-set of the elements in the KB identified whilst general KBS verification and validation focuses on the entire KB.

Where errors and anomalies are detected some further maintenance action may be required. The possible errors and anomalies that can exist are extensively described later in this work. It should be noted here, however, that the presence of an anomaly is not necessarily an error, it only indicates the possible presence of a error.

4.14. MAINTENANCE OF LARGE KNOWLEDGE BASED SYSTEMS: A CASE STUDY

There are very few reports concerning the long term maintenance of large KBSs. The two most notable are the reports concerning XCON given in Bachant and McDermott [1984] and Soloway *et al.* [1987]. XCON, originally referred to as R1, is a KBS used by Digital Equipment Corporation (DEC) to configure VAX-11 computer systems [McDermott 1980, 1982]. This domain is highly volatile since XCON is required to encompass new tasks as new products come on to the market. In this section we illustrate some of the maintenance issues discussed above with respect to R1/XCON.

XCON uses production rules. Some idea of the complexity of these rules can be obtained if we consider that in 1984 the number of elements in the conditional part of an XCON rule was on average 6.1; the minimum was 1 and the maximum 17. The action part of an XCON rule on average, in 1984, then has 2.9 elements; the minimum was 1 and the maximum 10.

The system has been used on a regular basis since its introduction in 1980. Since then it has grown steadily. In the first four years the number of rules grew from some 850 at the end of 1980 to some 3,350 at the end of 1983. By 1987 it had grown to 6,200 rules. Further some 50% of the rules had to be changed each year. XCON also has access to a database of product information which in 1984 contained 5,500 component descriptions and by 1987 some 20,000 descriptions.

As the number of rules and component details held by XCON increased, Digital's dependence on XCON also increased. It has thus become increasingly important that XCON's performance was also highly reliable.

The changes to which XCON is subject can be classified as follows:

- Minor refinements: adding knowledge to improve XCON's performance on an existing sub-task.
- Major refinments: adding knowledge required for XCON to perform a new sub-task.
- Functionality: providing the functionality needed to deal with new system types.
- Extension: extending the definition of the configuration task in significant ways, for example in 1983 XCON was extended to handle "multiple-CPU" orders.

Out of the 2,500 rules added to XCON in the first four years of its use, 10% are attributed to minor refinements, 40% to major refinements, 35% to provide extra functionality and 15% to extend the definition of the configuration task in significant ways.

Initially no formal development process was followed: rules were added in an *ad hoc* fashion and testing carried out according to the time available. As time passed the development process acquired substantially more structure and planned release dates were preceded by extensive testing of the system. However, as the knowledge base expanded it became increasingly more difficult to maintain. By 1987 the decision had been made to rewrite XCON in RIME. RIME [Hicks 1990] is a KBS development methodology/rule base language, produced by DEC, to facilitate maintenance, which produces OPS5 code (XCON was originally written in the OPS4 general purpose rule based language and later rewritten in OPS5). RIME is described further in a later chapter. However, the major advantages of XCON in RIME over XCON in OPS5 are considered to be:

- RIME is a high order language. OPS5 is an almost totally domain independent programming language whereas RIME has been developed specifically to reflect (a) the configuration task and (b) the maintenance of large rule bases.
- Homogeneity. The property that similar problems in a domain will have similar solutions which in turn makes for less idiosyncratic code.
- Predictability. The property that the decomposition in the code reflects the decomposition of the problem, hence the maintainer can predict the part of the code that needs changing.

4.15. SUMMARY

In this chapter we have discussed the concepts behind KBS maintenance in more detail. We have attempted to classify this maintenance by adopting Swanson's classification system for traditional software system maintenance, i.e. corrective, perfective and adaptive. After briefly considering the importance of KBS maintenance with respect to the general up take of these systems we go on to consider the components of a proposed KBS maintenance methodology. This commences with the initial detection and notification of the need for maintenance and goes on to address the identification of the more precise nature of the change. The latter is considered from two viewpoints, the applications viewpoint and the knowledge based viewpoint. Both are discussed in some detail and the identified changes classified according to the classification adapted from Swanson.

We next consider the global location of the section of the KB that will be affected by the required change. When this has been achieved we can determine the precise nature of the maintenance action(s) that will be required to implement the change. For rule base systems we may add, remove, replace or modify a rule. For frame based systems we may add or remove a frame, slot or value. When the nature of the required maintenance action has been established the next step is to identify locally the elements of the KB that will require attention. Further we need to identify all other elements of the KB, in addition to those on which some change is to be implemented, which will be affected (jeopardised) by the proposed change(s).

Finally we consider the implementation and testing of the necessary maintenance action(s). The chapter is concluded with a case study to illustrate the problems encountered when attempting to maintain a large KBS based on the experience of R1/XCON.

CHAPTER 5

KBS Development Methodologies and Environments

5.1. INTRODUCTION

We have seen, in chapter 1, that following a structured development methodology offers distinct advantages with respect to maintainability of conventional software systems. This is also true of the development of Knowledge Based Systems (KBSs): by following a step by step approach to development we can gain similar advantages. In this chapter several examples of such methodologies and environments, namely MEKAS, KADS, KEATS, MAUDE and RIME are described. Other KBS development environments which should be mentioned here include GEMINI [Montgomery 1988] and KRITON [Diederich *et al.* 1987, Diederich and Linster 1989]; there are many more. The GEMINI project was launched by the U.K. Central Communications and Telecommunications Agency (CCTA) early in 1988. It represented a national initiative to lay foundations for a publicly available expert systems development methodology to complement and integrate with SSADM [Cutts 1991] which had been adopted as the government standard for conventional systems. The final results of the GEMINI project have still to be published. KRITON is a development environment that can integrate several weak elicitation methods (e.g. protocol analysis, text analysis, interviews) to produce KBs that can be read and edited by domain experts. It does not produce executable code.

Before looking at the selected methodologies and environments in detail we should draw a distinction between KBS development shells, toolkits methodologies and environments, a distinction which is often blurred.

- Shells are principally aimed at the encoding of the knowledge that a KBS is required to use and have an implementation and representation strategy associated with them. They also often include various facilities for syntax checking etc. A brief discussion of KBS shells was given in section 2.7.

- Tool kits, as suggested by the term, are sets of interrelated tools designed to be used by KBS developers throughout the development cycle as they see fit, i.e. there is no real concept of an underlying methodology. Typically such tool kits will comprise elicitation, analysis, modelling and representation tools.
- A methodology, in turn, dictates a system of work to facilitate the development of KBS. As such a pure methodology may not have any software support associated with it, however, it has been observed [Motta *et al.* 1990] that the efficacy of a KBS development methodology is diminished if it is not supported by software tools. A KBS development methodology, in practice, can thus be said to be a system of work supported by a number of software tools.
- We can then say that a development environment consists of a software tool kit to facilitate the development of KBSs supported by an underlying methodology. They will of course also incorporate some concept of a shell to allow the implementation of knowledge. An environment thus encompasses a far wider range of activities than a simple shell, tool kit or methodology.

5.2. MEKAS (METHODOLOGY FOR KNOWLEDGE ANALYSIS)

The role of modelling in KBS development has been noted by many authors [Paton *et al.* 1991, Bench-Capon *et al.* 1991], some going as far as to consider that a KBS is itself a model of a domain, for example Bellman [1990]. Proponents claim that domain modelling has many advantages for knowledge acquisition and analysis. Critics, such as Linden, claim that system models are too specific to be of any practical use [Linden 1990]. Linden, however, goes on to suggest a meta-level model which can be tailored to fit any system.

The argument for domain models is as follows. Developers of KBSs face a number of practical problems when attempting to move this technology into routine use. One source of problems is that the analysis of the domain undertaken prior to the actual construction of the knowledge base is often unsatisfactory. Often it is carried out at too shallow a level and so fails to reflect the true structure of the domain; or it fails to recognise the boundaries of the embodied expertise, and the bias that may be introduced by concentrating on a particular task within the domain.

The importance of getting the model right has also been observed by many authors, for example Paton *et al.* [1991] and Svenson *et al.* [1991]. Svenson describes a system, ExpertiSZe, to be used by Dutch legislators in the process of preparing new legislation. The system consists of a number of modules: a consultation, a consistency and a simulation module, all based on a single rule model which must therefore be sound. The ExpertiSZe system carries out a number of tests on the model to ensure its correctness. These include tests on the parameters of the model, whether they are complete and whether any redundant parameters exist, and tests on the rule set for completeness, redundancy and subsumption and cyclic paths.

Paton *et al.* [1991] describe a methodology, MEKAS, which attempts to alleviate the shortcomings of the domain analysis techniques identified above by providing a method which will enable the knowledge engineer to begin with a thorough top level characterisation of the domain. By characterisation is meant a full description of the ontology, structure, functions and theories which underpin the domain, and which can provide a coherent framework within which to develop a knowledge base. Using such a framework will enable the knowledge base to be more readily identified with key aspects of the domain, aid verification and validation, and allow the incorporation of additional knowledge or revised knowledge, thus aiding maintenance and extension of the knowledge base. In MEKAS the approach to knowledge analysis, called SAAGS [Paton *et al.* 1991, Nwana and Paton 1990], consists of a four stage iterative modelling process (Figure 5.1). It receives a loose specification from a client as input and ultimately produces a comprehensive specification that provides the characterisation of the domain. The overall goal is to detail the structure and purpose of the domain within the context of its evolving theory. The principal stages are:

1. SPECIFICATION leading to the production of a characterisation of the domain. The top level features of the domain must be steadily accounted for in the successive iterations of this stage, which must also include relevant models and descriptive details such as the epistemic (domain) boundaries yielded by the analysis.
2. ANTICIPATION of the nature of the domain. The top-level features allow the knowledge engineer some anticipation of the breadth of the characteristics of the domain. Anticipation provides a way of critically testing the knowledge engineer's evolving understanding since these anticipations can be confirmed or disconfirmed in subsequent acquisition. The anticipation of top level characteristics will thus guide the domain-based knowledge acquisition process.

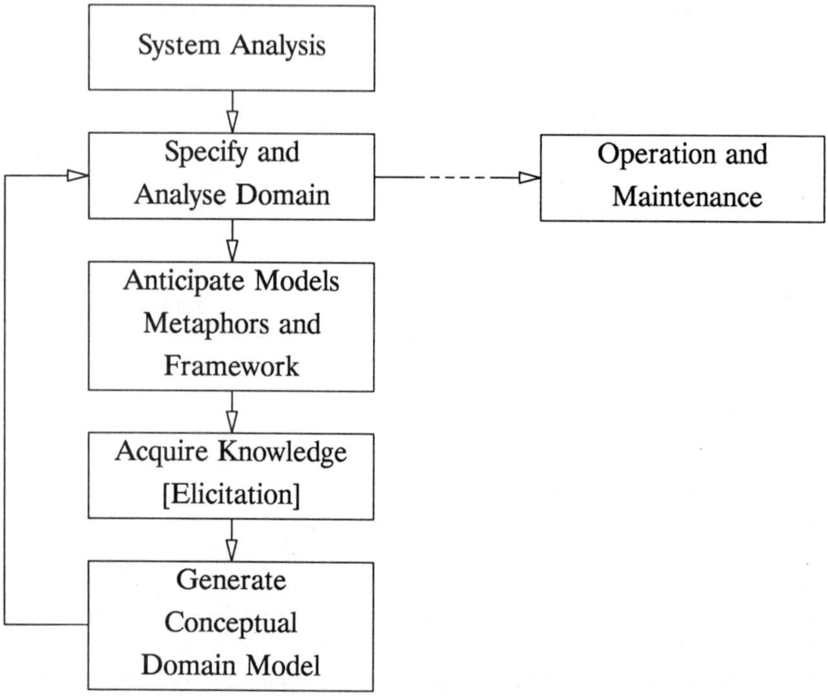

Figure 5.1: The SAAGS life-cycle.

3. ACQUISITION of knowledge. This includes: knowledge elicitation from experts and sourcing from other occurrences such as books and manuals etc. The outcomes from the anticipation stage are used to structure acquisition in a way which relates to the emerging nature of the domain.
4. GENERATION of models including the synthesis of outputs from the acquisition stage into a collection of models. These outputs drive the analysis forward and provide the explicit means for confirming, refuting or elaborating anticipations and thus prepare for an improvement of the specification.
5. The cycle now repeats with SPECIFICATION.

Domain modelling is also an essential part of many development methodologies and environments, for example KADS which is described in the following section.

5.3. KNOWLEDGE ANALYSIS AND DOCUMENTATION STRUCTURING (KADS) METHODOLOGY

The KADS methodology [Wielinga *et al.* 1986 and Wielinga *et al.* 1992] is supported by a stage based life-cycle, which incorporates generic task modelling techniques during the knowledge engineering phase, to build a set of models of the problem domain. A schematic of the KADS life-cycle is given in Figure 5.2. In KADS a modelling language is used to build up an increasingly more detailed representation of the system resulting in a knowledge hierarchy. A number of intermediate models are thus created, each model emphasising certain aspects of the system to be built.

The following knowledge engineering phase then comprises three basic stages:

1. Orientation.
2. Problem Identification.
3. Problem Analysis.

During the initial Orientation stage the entities in the domain are identified. This stage also incorporates a feasibility study and boundary definition. During the following Problem Identification stage initial knowledge elicitation and analysis commences and in particular the interface with the real world is studied and defined. Full knowledge elicitation and analysis then occurs during the third Problem Analysis stage. On completion of the knowledge engineering phase the design phase is commenced. KADS includes two separate tools, PED (Protocol EDitor) and CE (Concept Editor). PED incorporates hypertext facilities for fragmenting texts, creating links between fragments and grouping them together. This tool is a fairly typical example of the sort of textual analysis tool found in many KBS development environments, for example CREF as used by the KEATS development environment and KANT in the MAUDE environment (see below). These facilitate the extraction of knowledge from sources and its representation in a meaningful form which can be readily manipulated by the knowledge engineer. They are often supported by frame and rule language packages. Usually the text is partitioned into easily definable chunks. These chunks can then be analysed by identifying particular entities and attributes in the text and the possible operations that can effect those entities and attributes. CE allows the user to create conceptual hierarchies.

Disadvantages associated with the KADS methodology are the same as those directed at generic task modelling methods in general

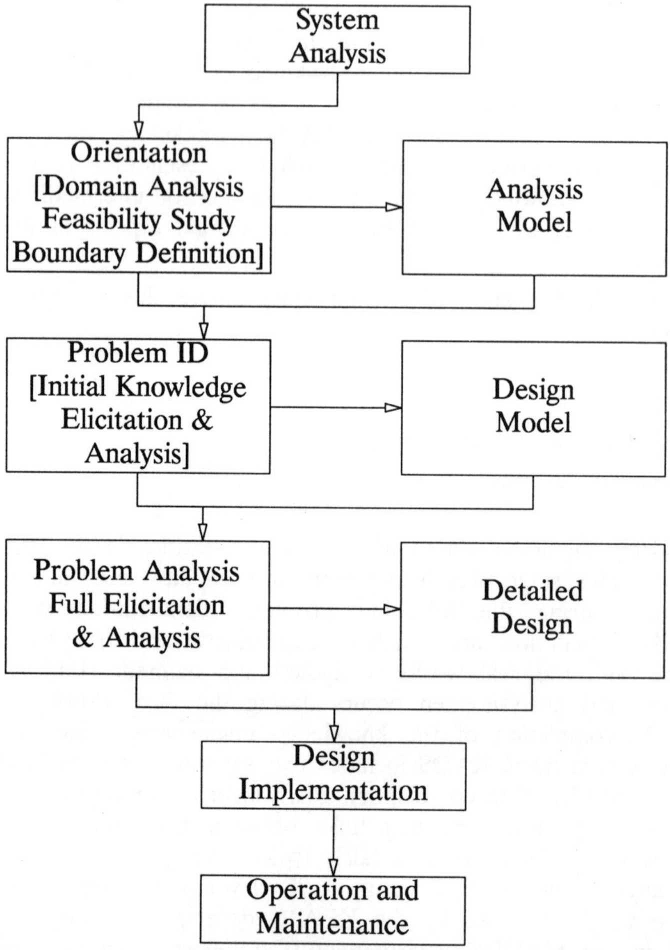

Figure 5.2: The KADS life-cycle.

(see section 2.4.2). The KADS environment is still, however, undergoing further development and in time proponents expect that a complete KBS development environment and methodology will emerge. This is the aim of the current KADS-II project. KADS-II is an ESPRIT funded project, based on the work of KADS-I (briefly described here), aimed at extending the current methodology to cover the full KBS development cycle.

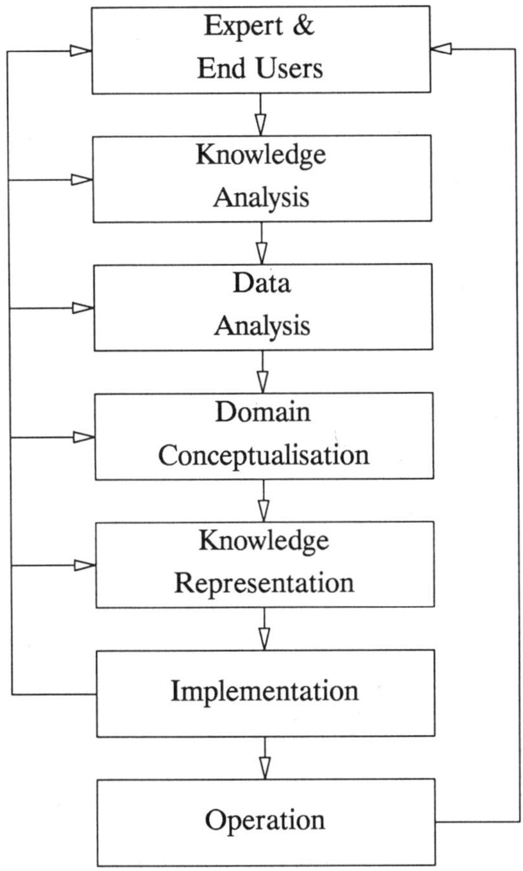

Figure 5.3: The KEATS life-cycle (after Motta et al. [1989]).

5.4. KNOWLEDGE ENGINEERS ASSISTANT (KEATS)

KEATS [Motta *et al.* 1988, Motta *et al.* 1989] is a KBS development methodology/environment designed to allow the user to map domain knowledge into frame structures which can then be interacted with using a rule interpreter. A block diagram of the KEATS life-cycle is given in Figure 5.3. It consists of a number of steps, starting with analysis of the domain represented in the form of documented knowledge obtained from experts. Knowledge engineering is viewed as a process of information transformation, in which knowledge is acquired and ultimately transformed to a formal representation, resident inside a machine. Motta refers to this process of transformation as model refinement.

Knowledge analysis is carried out using a textual knowledge analysis tool called CREF (Cross-Referencing Editing Facility). This allows the knowledge engineer to organise text by partitioning it into atomic entities called "segments" and grouping them into "collections". Relations between segments are expressed using epistemological links. This then provides a basis for further data analysis.

The knowledge thus obtained is encoded to form a knowledge base, using a language tool called the Knowledge Description Language (KDL). This results in a frame based representation to describe the properties of entities and classes. Inheritance is the basic mechanism for sharing and deducing properties of objects. KEATS uses a rule interpreter called the Context Oriented Production System (COPS), which interacts with the KB. The environment is fronted by an intelligent Graphical Interface Tool (GIS) which allows the user to produce a freehand, but constrained, representation of the knowledge domain.

The KEATS environment is also still the subject of further development. One of the more recent inclusions in the system is the ACQUIST textual analysis tool [Rajan *et al.* 1988]. This is an analysis tool that incorporates some hypertext facilities similar to PED. It allows the user to carry out data analysis and domain conceptualisation through a process of abstracting and structuring the knowledge contained in raw texts. It also has a graphical interface tool to support it called MAPS.

5.5. MAKE AUTHORING AND DEVELOPMENT ENVIRONMENT (MAUDE)

MAUDE [Coenen and Bench-Capon 1992b, Bench-Capon and Coenen 1991b] is a KBS development environment which incorporates features of isomorphism and an intermediate representation. Both are described in more detail in the following chapter. Unlike KEATS the MAUDE environment is specifically motivated by the need to produce maintainable systems. The developer starts with a number of source documents that have been suitably prepared. Knowledge analysis takes place using an analysis tool called KANT (Knowledge engineers ANalysis Tool) [Storrs and Burton 1989]. This analysis results in an intermediate representation stored in a series of structures which is then translated into the target representation to form the knowledge base. It is intended that where ever possible maintenance is carried out on this intermediate representation. To facilitate this MAUDE incorporates a linking mechanism, connecting the target rules and objects to the source data, and a number of software support tools. MAUDE is ideally suited to the construction of KBSs in domains, such as legal domains, where the source knowledge consists of a significant amount of textual material, by assisting the knowledge engineer in the analysis of these source documents.

A more detailed description of MAUDE, including a case study, is given at the end of this chapter.

5.6. THE RIME METHODOLOGY

The RIME methodology [Hicks 1990], like the MAUDE environment, is specifically designed to minimise maintenance in that it prescribes a methodology for the reduction of maintenance. The significance of RIME in the context of this work is that it was used to re-implement R1/XCON [Bachant and McDermott 1984] when maintenance problems began to threaten its profitability. R1/XCON was first put into production in 1980 and was, initially, highly successful. However, by 1988 the system had grown by 10,000 rules [Solway *et al.* 1987]. The resulting maintenance problems were such that eventually a complete rewrite was required (see section 4.15).

RIME consists of three components, a development plan, control characteristics and rule base characteristics. The development plan is similar to the traditional software development cycle and consists of the following stages:

- Defining and redefining the system.
- Extending and refining the system.
- Delivering the system.
- Evaluating the system.

Defining and redefining the system includes determining how to exploit expert system technology, determining if traditional software is appropriate for tasks, and designing the system to a wide variety of requirements. Extending and refining the system is concerned with KB management, on going knowledge acquisition, integration of multiple systems and system interface management. Delivering the system involves placing the system in production and includes release management and distribution, production installation and user support. Evaluating the system includes measuring its accuracy, performance, maintainability and fitness for the business need.

Traditionally KBS maintenance involves patching code. As the system's life-cycle proceeds this process continues and patches are placed on patches. This is because the maintenance engineers often change from one maintenance session to the next with the result that the current engineer, unable to understand the implications of the previous engineer's patching, leaves them in and puts further patches over the top of them. If the system behaves "correctly" the patch is considered to be satisfactory, without regard to the loss of fidelity of the representation to the domain. The result is increasing inefficiency. To substantial systems such as R1/XCON with a large number of users it is important that they are computationally efficient. To overcome this problem RIME uses a control structure to decompose problems into one of three types: procedural, declarative, or decision related. Each is implemented in a slightly different manner but the overall strategy is to decompose the problem in a layer-per-rule manner. Each rule corresponds to one layer of the problem. This strategy quickly identifies an incorrect path. The decomposition also results in a modular rule set which can be easily understood by the maintenance engineer. The layer-per-rule strategy is also carried over to the rest of the rule base. A software tool called SEAR produces RIME code through the use of standardised templates reflecting the layer-per-rule decomposition. SEAR enforces system programming practices and makes code more homogeneous and less redundant, the aim being to insure a standard representation of similar situations. In addition indexes are provided to assist the maintenance engineer in locating the appropriate section of code.

It is claimed that KBSs developed in RIME gain advantages of both homogeneity and predictability and hence are easier to maintain because code can be quickly located and understood.

5.7. MAUDE: A CASE STUDY

The Make AUthoring and Development Environment (MAUDE) was introduced in section 5.5. In this penultimate section of this chapter on KBS development methodologies and environments we consider MAUDE in more detail, firstly by looking at the architecture of the system, and then by considering the development process in depth by considering an actual example taken from a KBS built for British Coal's (BC's) Insurance and Pensions Division.

5.7.1. Overview

As outlined in section 5.5, MAUDE, like RIME, is aimed specifically at building maintainable KBSs particularly in regulation based domains. It was developed as part of the MAKE (Maintenance Assistance for Knowledge Engineers) project [Bench-Capon and Coenen 1991a, 1991b,

Coenen and Bench-Capon 1992a] which was a collaborative project between Liverpool University, BC and International Computers Limited (ICL).

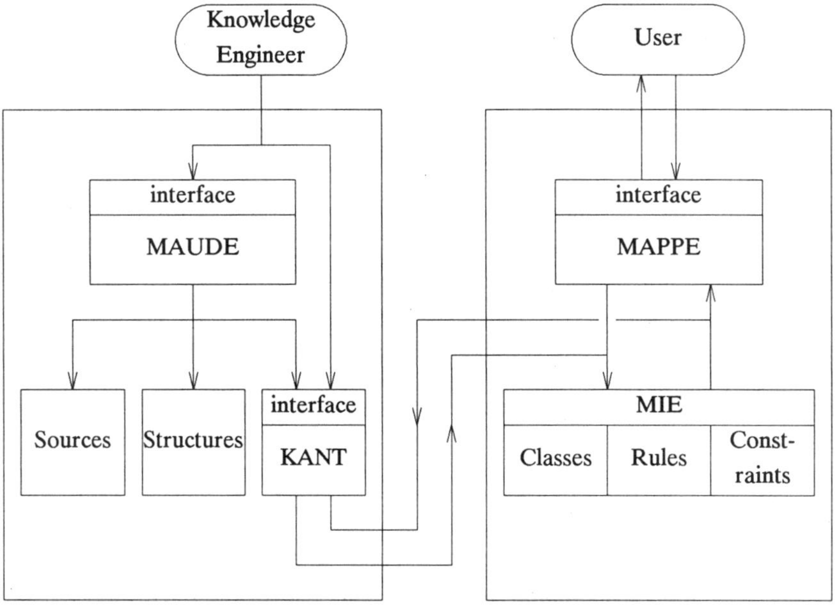

Figure 5.4: Schematic of the MAUDE KBS development environment.

The design of MAUDE revolves around three base windows, the KANT, MAUDE and MAPPE (Make APPlication Environment) Windows. A schematic is given in Figure 5.4. From the KANT base window sources can be selected and analysed. This is where the knowledge analysis of the application is carried out. The final result of the analysis is a set of rules, contained in a rule base, and a hierarchical object base, referred to as the class hierarchy, in an intermediate representation called the Make Intermediate Representation (MIR). This is essentially a simple language, with a formal, but flexible and easy to understand syntax, which is used to define objects and rules. In many respects it has similarities with a typed first order predicate logic with some extensions, for example to handle arithmetic. The nature of this intermediate representation and the advantages to be gained are fully described in Bench-Capon and Forder [1991]. The class hierarchy defines the vocabulary of object slots and values which can be used in constructing rules. It also describes the state of the application at any given time.

When established the MIR rule base and class hierarchy are compiled into the target representation used by the MAKE Inference Engine (MIE). Currently this consists of a clausal form called CMIR (Compiled MIR) but could equally well be any other target executable representation, for example that used in KAPPA or NEXPERT ONJECT. The MAUDE window is the user interface through which the MAKE maintenance tools are invoked. A full discussion of the tools available under the MAKE project is given in Bench-Capon and Coenen [1991b], additionally many of the tools are described in the appropriate sections of the following chapters of this work.

The MAPPE Base Window provides the end user view of the application. It is organised as a hierarchy of topics or question forms which the user is invited to fill in. The answers to questions are "asserted" into object slots as values, which in turn trigger rules in the rule base. The structure of this topic hierarchy is used to reflect the natural (task) decomposition of the problem.

Inferences are made, using the Make Inference Engine (MIE), by forward chaining with reference to the information available in the class hierarchy as supplied by the user. As the inferencing process continues further slots in the class hierarchy are instantiated. This process continues until all possible root propositions have been satisfied or no further inferencing can take place.

KANT is a hypertext like knowledge analysis tool originally built to assist in the development of a KBS to provide decision support for Department of Social Security (DSS) adjudication officers in the assessment of claims for benefits in local DSSs offices. This system was called the Local Office Demonstrator (LOD) System and was one of three applications built as part of the Alvey DHSS Large Demonstrator Project aimed at demonstrating the viability of KBS decision support in large, legislation based organisations [Storrs and Burton 1989]. KANT is designed to support the construction of KBS in domains, such as legal domains, where the source knowledge comprises a significant amount of textual material by assisting the knowledge engineer in the analysis of these source documents.

The advantages offered by the integration of hypertext facilities into the development of KBSs have also been advanced elsewhere. For example the TOROS-Hyper project [Delfs and Winkelmann 1991]. TOROS (Toolkit for Object and Rule Oriented System construction) is a hybrid development tool for object and rule oriented systems. The integration of TOROS with hypertext functionality means that facilities for the definition of, and navigation in, hyper-documents are added to the existing means for formal representation of knowledge.

KANT allows the user to search documents for key words and cut and paste relevant sections into a hierarchy of nodes referred to as KANT structures. In its simplest form each node can have some plain language text attached to it. In this case the structures are referred to as freestyle KANT structures. KANT thus readily supports the structuring of documents through the use of child and sibling relations, and through separable fields within a node. Child and sibling nodes are organised into a hierarchy consisting of a top level node, the root node, from which branch child nodes. Each child node can have siblings and further child nodes ending in a set of leaf nodes. Nodes can be folded into parent nodes or unfolded to reveal child nodes. In this respect the following notation is used:

+ A node which has been unfolded, i.e. its children are visible.

- A node that has been folded, i.e. its children are hidden.

O A leaf node, i.e. a node that has no children.

Individual nodes can also be linked to other nodes in other structures. To this end two more indicators are placed on either side of the +, - and O indicators already described. The left indicator will be one of:

* No links exist to the current node.

< Links exist to the current node.

The right indicators will be one of:

* No links exist from the current node.

> Links exist from the current node.

Other forms of KANT structure include MIR KANT structures and CMIR KANT structures. MIR structures are similar to freestyle KANT structures but are constructed according to a defined syntax. They are used to define the rules and object classes, and also the topics and questions to be used in the dialogue with the end user, using MIR. CMIR structures are the executable representation of MIR structures in that they can be interpreted by the MIE. Hence CMIR structures form the dynamic, instantiated, end user application.

The author is free to construct any number of KANT structures, with a variety of contents. However, the proposed methodology strongly suggests a number of specific structures.

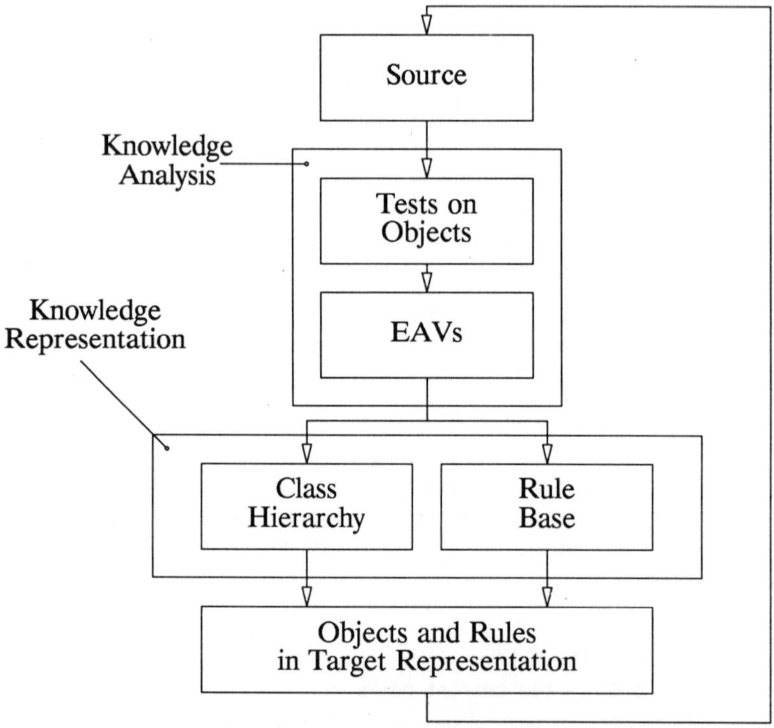

Figure 5.5: The MAUDE life-cycle.

5.7.2. The MAUDE KBS Development Methodology

KBS development using MAUDE consists of an iterative process in which repeated loops are performed, perhaps indefinitely, in that requirements will change over time and source material will be superseded. The MAUDE life-cycle is given in Figure 5.5. The proposed methodology suggests three strands of authoring material; this is illustrated with reference to the BC application in Figure 5.6. The dialogue strand results in the user interface and the object classes and rules strands in the class hierarchy and rule base respectively. As can be seen, a number of freestyle KANT structures are used in the analysis gradually building up to the definition of rules, object classes, topics and questions in MIR. It should be noted that during this analysis links are continually constructed so that any MIR definition can be traced back to the original source material and vice versa. The method actively encourages isomorphism between the source material and MIR definitions.

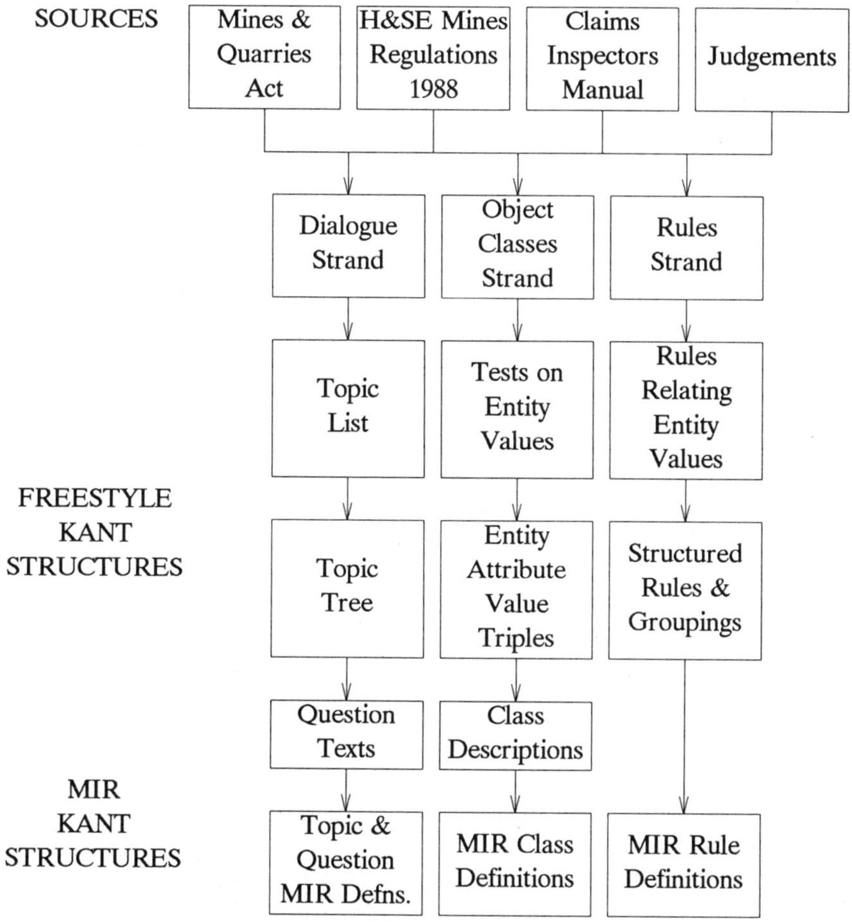

Figure 5.6: Strands of authoring material for a regulation based KBS for British Coal.

In more detail the KBS development methodology that supports MAUDE can be considered to consist of the following five basic stages:

1. Translate source documents into a form suitable for use in KANT (Kantification).
2. Pass through the source and identify attributes and their entities and the tests applied to them and store the identified tests on

objects in a freestyle KANT structure.

3. Identify Entity, Attribute, Value triples (EAVs) and store them in another freestyle KANT structure.
4. Use the tests on objects and EAV structures to build a suitable class hierarchy and accompanying rule base stored in MIR KANT structures.
5. Compile the MIR structures developed in 4 into the target CMIR representation.

A block diagram illustrating this process is given in Figure 5.7.

In the following sub-sections each stage in the development of the class hierarchy and rule base strands will be considered in further detail by considering a fragment of a KBS built for BC's Insurance and Pensions division using MAUDE. The BC system is designed to provide decision support for the processing of claims for work related injuries (Bench-Capon and Coenen 1991c). The fragment is concerned with the safety of buildings and structures on the surface of a mine.

5.7.3. Source Documents

The developer starts with a number of source documents that have been suitably prepared. This involves a process that has, inevitably, become known as "Kantification" where raw texts are taken and imported into KANT source format while preserving their original appearance. If we consider a fragment of legislation concerning the safety of surface buildings and structures taken from the the Mines and Quarries Act 1954; one of a number of source documents used in the development of the BC system:

Buildings, Structures, Means of Access, &c.

86. All buildings and structures on the surface of a mine shall be kept in safe condition.

87.-- (1) There shall be provided and maintained safe means of access to every place in or on a building or structure on the surface of a mine, being a place at which any person has at any time to work.

(2) Where a person is to work at any such place as aforesaid from which he will be liable to fall a distance of more than 10 feet, then, unless the place is one which affords secure foothold and, where necessary, secure handhold, means shall be provided by fencing or otherwise for ensuring his safety.

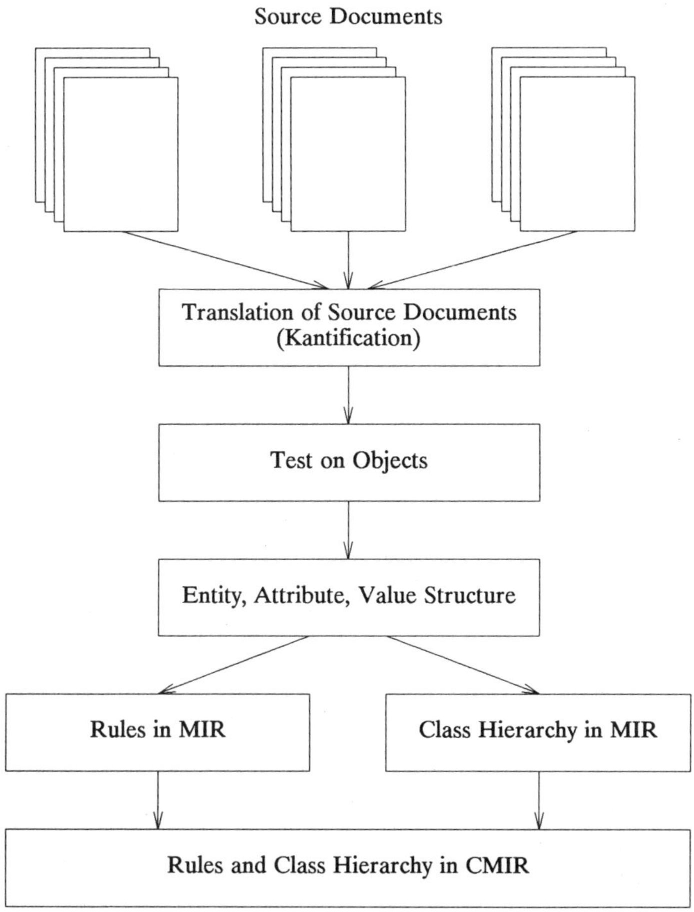

Figure 5.7: KBS development using MAUDE.

In its imported form this will consist of four blocks of text, the title and paragraphs 86, 87.1 and 87.2. These blocks or parts of them can then be copied into KANT Structure files where further analysis can take place.

5.7.4. Tests on Objects

After importation knowledge analysis is commenced by examining the relevant passages in the source material to gain a broad understanding of the domain. In some cases it is advantageous to collect

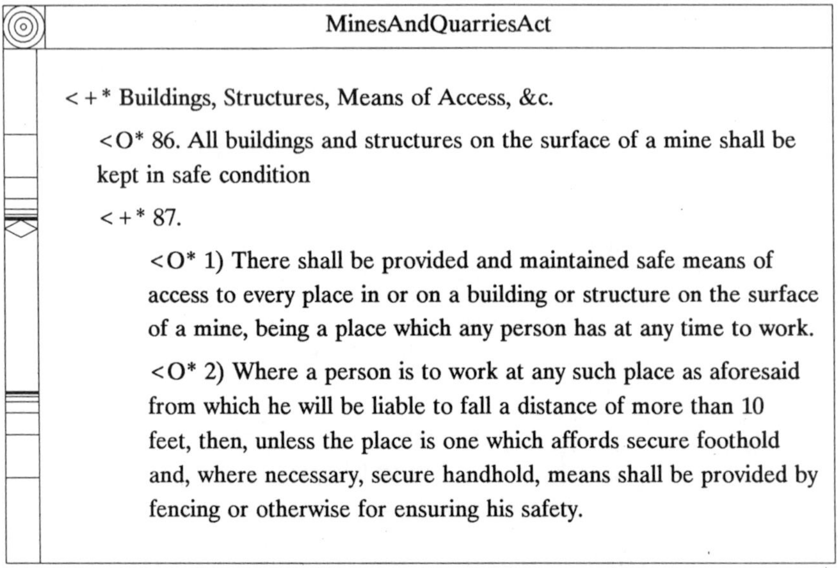

Figure 5.8: Freestyle KANT structures.

together the sub-set of regulations that are applicable to a particular part of the final application into a single KANT Structure file, using the copy and paste facilities provided with KANT. Figure 5.8 shows the above section of legal text copied into a freestyle KANT structure. Note the three indicators in front of each node indicating, in this case, that all nodes have been unfolded to their leaves and that links have been established from the nodes back to the source document. At any time the author may follow these links back to the source or, in time, forward to the rules and objects in the final application.

The methodology suggests that development commences by identifying tests on objects so as to discover the ontology and vocabulary of the domain from a problem orientated perspective. Objects can be identified by searching for nouns in the sections of source material of interest. Whether a test is relevant or not depends on what the task to be supported by the KBS is intended to establish and the grain size considered appropriate to the application.

If we consider the above imported regulations we can identify three principal entities: buildings and structures on the surface, places where persons work and high places where persons work, i.e. buildings, work places and high work places. It is important to appreciate that high work places are a type of work place and that work places are a type of building or structure. We can also identify a fourth implied entity. This is the mine manager who is responsible for ensuring that the regulations are complied with. The entity, mine manager, can be considered to be a type of manager which in turn is a type of person. We could identify further entities such as means of access, foothold and handhold. However, within the example fragment of legislation no tests are carried out on these entities and so they can be considered not to be relevant. There is also a question of grain size to be considered here. It may be adequate, for example, to consider the buildings and structures on the surface of a mine in the sample piece of legislation to be single conceptual objects. Alternatively if a test exists which applys to structures only, buildings and structures will have to be considered as two distinct objects. However, in the piece of legislation under consideration here no distinction is made between buildings and structures so they should effectively be considered to be the same thing. In practice the drafters of the act would have used the phrase specifically to preclude the possibility of a distinction being drawn between a building and a structure. This intention is most faithfully reflected by using a single object.

Having identified the relevant entities contained in the regulations we can consider the tests that may be performed on them. For example from section 86 of the Regulations we can identify a test to determine whether a building-structure is in a safe condition. Similarly from section 87.1 we can identify a test to determine whether a building-structure is a work place. At a higher level we can presume the existence of a test to determine whether a manager complies with the act or whether he/she is responsible for the building/structure in question. All relevant tests can be collated into a single freestyle KANT structure file and displayed in a KANT window as shown in Figure 5.9. Note that the * symbols on the left hand side of the `O` identifier before the `mine manager complies with act` and `mine manager responsible for building/structure`, indicates that there are no links back to the source. The * symbols on the right hand side of the `O` identifiers indicate that there are, as yet, no forward (downward) links to the rules and slots required.

5.7.5. Entity Attribute Values (EAV) Triples

The next stage in the analysis is to identify Entity Attribute Value (EAV) triples and store these in another freestyle KANT Structure file. We can identify the attributes associated with the entities and the values those attributes can have by inspection of the tests on objects and the source. Firstly, from the tests on objects file, we can extract an attribute for the entity mine manager that the manager complies with the Act and that this attribute can have the value true or false. More specifically, by referring back to the source, we can identify an attribute for the entity mine manager that the manager complies with section 86 of the Act. This thus gives rise to the EAV triple:

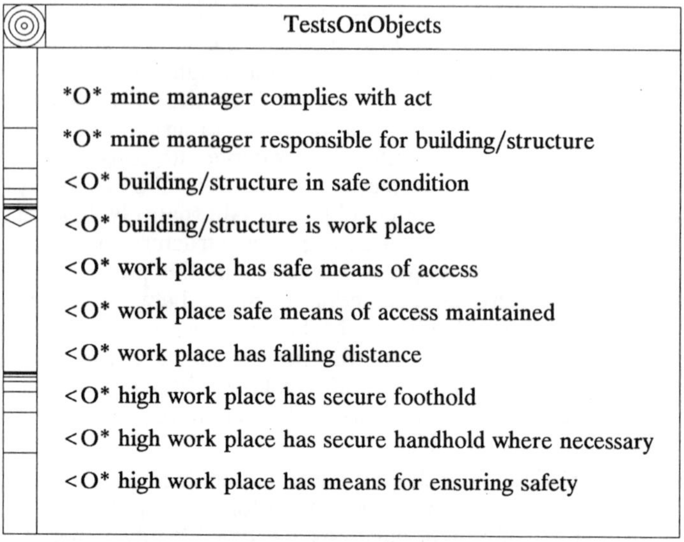

Figure 5.9: Tests on objects freestyle KANT structures.

```
mineManager - complies with section 86 - true, false
```

Again if we consider the entity building-structure we can identify further attributes and values. For example the attribute `in safe condition` which can have the value true or false, or `is work place` which can also have the values true or false. The EAV triples identified are stored in another KANT structure file of the form shown in Figure 5.10.

In constructing the EAV and tests on object structures care has to be taken to ensure that each structure or sub-structure bears a direct, one-to-one, correspondence with the source material i.e. isomorphism with the source is maintained. Further note that the tests on objects and EAV analysis stages are designed to minimise and contain the need for repeating the analysis as a result of problems located at later steps. Further it is recommended that the author uses source material terminology for Entity, Attribute and Value names wherever possible.

The tests on objects and EAV structures provide a sound basis from which to build a suitable class hierarchy and accompanying rule base stored in MIR structures.

EAVs

<O* manager - complies with section 86 - true, false

<O* manager - responsible for - building/structure

<O* building/structure - in safe condition - true, false

<O* building/structure - is work place - true, false

O work place - complies with section 87.1 - true, false

<O* work place - has safe means of access - true, false

<O* work place - safe means of access maintained - true, false

<O* work place - has falling distance - 0 to big

O high work place - complies with section 87.2 - true, false

<O* high work place - has secure foothold - true, false

<O* high work place - has secure handhold where necessary - true, false

<O* high work place - has means for ensuring safety - true, false

Figure 5.10: EAV freestyle KANT structures.

5.7.6. The Class-Hierarchy and Rule Base in MIR

From the tests on objects and EAV structures an object base or class hierarchy determining the vocabulary of the system, a rule base relating these triples and a hierarchy of forms representing the task are constructed in MIR. This is the intermediate representation on which all KB maintenance is to be carried out. The class hierarchy and rule base in MIR are stored in more formal MIR KANT structures. We will consider the construction of a class hierarchy and rule base with respect to the test on object and EAV structures created in the previous two sub-sections in this sub-section.

Considering the class hierarchy first, this is created by collecting the attributes and tests for each entity and then defining the attribute set for each entity. At the same time checks must be made for duplication and overlap. The entities are collected together in a class lattice, common attributes are placed at their highest common level. The result is a formal definition of entities, attributes and types in the MIR language. Each class has a unique class name and a number of slots describing attributes of that type of object, and the possible values that they may have. A feature of the class hierarchy is that sub-classes inherit attributes of super-classes so as to ensure that a sub-class is a strict specialisation of its super-class. In MAUDE inherited attributes cannot be cancelled as is the case with some other development environments, for example Intellicorp's Knowledge Engineering Environment (KEE). Slots in a class hierarchy are typically of the form:

```
"(" <attribute> "literal <true false> ")"

"(" <attribute> "instance" <className> ")"

"(" <attribute> "number" <numeric range> ")"
```

```
ClassHierarchy

*+*  Class definitions
   <O* MIRClass: mineManager
   ◇slot compliesWithS86 literal (true false)
   ◇slot responsibleFor instance buildingStructure
   <+* MIRClass: buildingStructure
   ◇slot compliesWithS87.1 literal (true false)
   ◇slot inSafeCondition literal (true false)
   ◇slot isWorkPlace literal (true false)
      <+* MIRClass: WorkPlace
      ◇slot hasSafeMeansOfAccess literal (true false)
      ◇slot safeMeansOfAccessMaintained literal (true false)
      ◇slot hasFallingDistance numeric ((0 big))
      ◇slot compliesWithS87.2 literal (true false)
         <O* MIRClass: HighWorkPlace
         ◇slot hasSecureFoothold literal (true false)
         ◇slot hasSecureHandhold literal (true false)
         ◇slot hasMeansForEnsuringSafety literal (true false)
```

Figure 5.11: Fragment of class hierarchy MIR KANT structure.

For the fragment of KB under consideration here the class hierarchy in MIR will be of the form given in Figure 5.11. The "◇" symbol simply indicates a field break. The value `big` is used in a numeric range to indicate no upper limit. Note that the class hierarchy is arranged so that sub-classes inherit attributes from super-classes. For example the sub-class `highWorkPlace` inherits the attribute `inSafeCondition` from the super-class `buildingStructure`.

With respect to the rule base we can pass through the sources, tests on objects and EAV structures again and identify rules. The resulting rule base will comprise a set of rules typically all branching out from a single top level node. For illustrative purposes in this work a simplified syntax for MIR rules is given below using a modified form of BNF (Backus-Naur Form). The symbol ::= means "consists of", | is used to separate alternatives and the angel brackets to enclose non-terminal symbols. A terminal symbol, enclosed in double quotes is simply one of the symbols that we use when writing a rule in MIR such as "and" or "or". A non-terminal symbol is then the name of one of the sub-structures of a MIR rule.

```
<rule> ::= "("<head> <neck> <tail> ")"

<head> ::= <proposition>

<neck> ::= "if" | "iff"

<tail> ::= "(" <disjunction> ")"

<disjunction> ::= <conjunction> |
          <conjunction> "or" <disjunction>
          <conjunction> "when" <conjunction>

<conjunction> ::= <proposition> |
          <proposition> "and" <conjunction>

<proposition> ::= <literalProposition>

<literalProposition> ::= "(" <attributeReference> "is"
                 literal ")"

<attributeReference> ::= <variable> <attribute>
```

Thus a rule has a head, neck and a tail. The tail consists of conjunctions and/or disjunctions. Literal propositions typically evaluate to true or false. Thus we can construct a rule to establish whether the mine manager complies with section 86 of the Act:

```
(manager compliesWithS86 is true
iff
(((buildingStructure inSafeCondition is true)
and
((buildingStructure isWorkPlace is false)
or
(buildingStructure compliesWithS87.1 is true)))
when
(manager responsible is buildingStructure)))
```

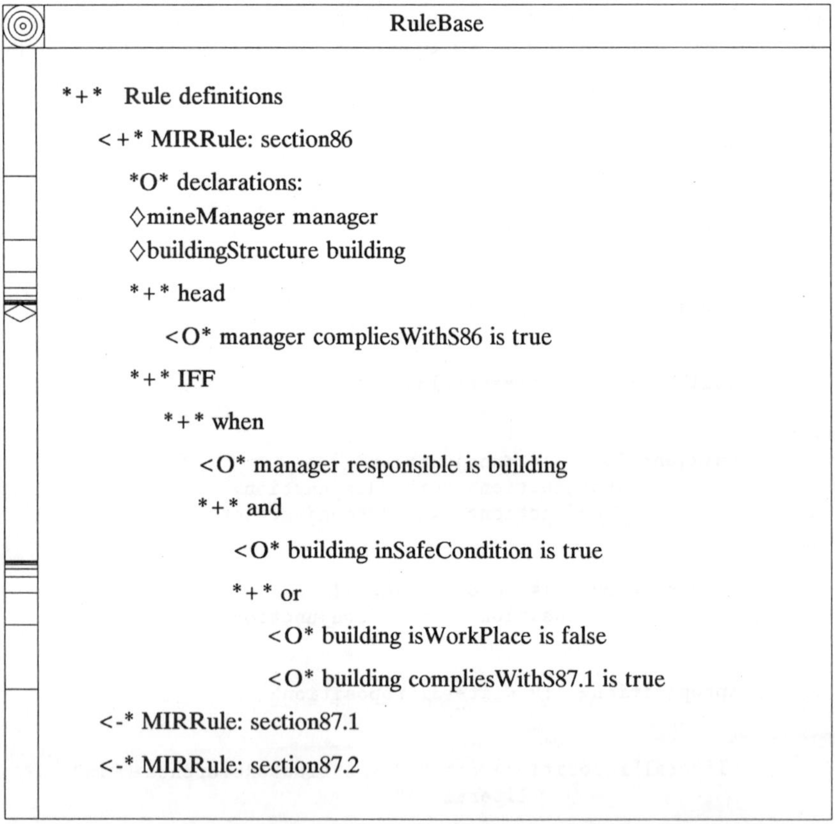

Figure 5.12: Fragment of rule base in MIR KANT structure.

Figure 5.12 shows the same rule as it will appear in a MIR KANT structure window. From the above and the figure it can be seen that the similarity with first order predicate logic is evident.

It is important to differentiate between rules and constraints at this stage. Rules are task dependent, and are thus arranged in a hierarchy headed by a top level rule representing the goal to be attained: further rules then branch of this top level rule down to a number of leaf rules. Predicates found in rules are therefore either (a) leaves, in which case their truth will be ascertained by direct reference to the class hierarchy or the user, (b) roots, where they are what the system is intended to establish, or (c) intermediate, where they need to be established from the rule base in order to establish some root. Constraints, however, are task independent. The rules represented in the example rule given above can be considered as constraints by replacing the "if" with the implies symbol from propositional logic i.e. $\Leftarrow$. Similarly "iff" (if and only if) can be replaced with the equivalence symbol i.e. $\Leftrightarrow$. The principal effect of this replacement is to licence additional inferences: whereas for rules only inferences concerning the head literal may be drawn, in constraints inferences may be drawn with regard to any of the component literals. Thus from `P if Q`, we can conclude only `P`, given `Q`, whereas from `P` $\Leftarrow$ `Q` we may conclude both `P`, given `Q`, and $\neg$`Q`, given $\neg$`P`. Similarly `P iff Q` licences only `P`, given `Q`, and $\neg$`P`, `given` $\neg$`Q`, whereas `P` $\Leftrightarrow$ `Q` licences `Q`, given `P` and $\neg$`Q`, given $\neg$`P` as well. The important issue here is that in a rule base redundancy and missing branches are significant, but depend on the notion of a purpose for the rule set in terms of what is to be given and what must be deduced. Different tasks may require different literals in a constraint to be treated as the head. Additionally, when considering inconsistencies in a task dependent rule base, it may be that an inconsistency is hidden by the restricted set of inferences that may be drawn, but exposed when the rules are considered as constraints.

5.7.7. Compilation Into CMIR

During the compilation stage the MIR class hierarchy and rule base are compiled into objects and rules in the executable target representation, CMIR. In the case of the rule base this will result in a set of clauses. In principle compilation of rules into CMIR involves translating the MIR rules into a clausal form. If we consider the rule constructed in the previous sub-section this will compile into the following (simplified) CMIR Clauses:

```
(manager compliesWithS86 is true
if
((buildingStructure inSafeCondition is true)
and
(buildingStructure isWorkPlace is false)
and
(manager responsible is buildingStructure)))
```

```
(manager compliesWithS86 is true
if
((buildingStructure inSafeCondition is true)
and
(buildingStructure compliesWithS87.1 is true)
and
(manager responsible is buildingStructure)))

(not manager compliesWithS86 is true
if
((not buildingStructure inSafeCondition is true)
and
(manager responsible is buildingStructure)))

(not manager compliesWithS86 is true
if
((not buildingStructure isWorkPlace is false)
and
(not buildingStructure compliesWithS87.1 is true)
and
(manager responsible is buildingStructure)))
```

5.7.8. Maintenance Features of MAUDE

The MAUDE development methodology encourages the production of maintainable systems in a number of ways. Firstly it enforces the use of an intermediate representation on which maintenance can be carried out and then passed on to the target executable representation. The user need have no knowledge of the target representation. It can be argued that the inclusion of such an intermediate stage simply adds an extra level of complexity to the life cycle. However, a language such as MIR is much easier to understand (Figures 5.11 and 5.12) and very much easier to relate to the original source expressions than more formal KBS languages such as PROLOG, LISP or CMIR. Further the clear separation of representation and programming of the results is desirable in itself in that it is the maintenance of the representation we should be addressing and not a program. Secondly it enforces a disciplined development approach similar to that provided by conventional software development methodologies, resulting in the production of systems that are objective and hence facilitates understanding by people other than the original author. Thirdly MAUDE encourages the development of systems that are easily adaptable by ensuring that the end result is isomorphic with the source material. That is to say that the structure of the class hierarchy, rule base and forms in the intermediate representation mirror the structure of the source material. The advantage of this is that if a particular section of the regulations is superseded or added to, only the relevant nodes in the tests on objects and EAV KANT structures and the appropriate sections in the MIR need be altered. To assist in the identification of these nodes and sections, linking facilities included in MAUDE allow the developer to link sections of the source material through to the target executable representation. These links are shown by the greater than and less than arrows (< and >) that can be located on either side of the identifiers found at the start of KANT and MIR KANT structures. Note that individual sections of the rule given in Figure 5.12 are linked back to previous stages in the development. Links also appear in the example of a freestyle KANT structure given in Figure 5.8. For a more in depth discussion of the benefits of isomorphism interested readers are referred to Bench-Capon and Coenen [1991c] and Bench-Capon and Forder [1991].

Other features of MAUDE, although not specifically addressing maintainability, but required by any usable methodology, are firstly that it is easily teachable. This has been well illustrated during the course of the development of the pilot for the BC application where two members of the threeman development team were totally unfamiliar with MAUDE and had not previously built a regulation based KBS, yet the pilot was completed within six man months. Secondly MAUDE also supports knowledge acquisition and representation through the tests on objects and EAV identification approach suggested by the methodology and through the use of KANT structures and MIR which serve to encapsulate the requisite knowledge.

5.8. SUMMARY

By following a structured development methodology the difficulties encountered when implementing future maintenance can be substantially reduced. The principal advantage is that of understandability. Provided that the maintenance engineers are familiar with the methodology and techniques used, the development process can be followed and the correct location, globally and locally, for the addition of (say) a rule and the associated jeopardised sub-set identified.

There are a great many KBS development methodologies and environments available. Five have been discussed here, namely the MEKAS and KADS methodologies for knowledge engineering, the KEATS development environment, and MAUDE and RIME which are both specifically designed to address maintenance requirements. The MAUDE environment is described in some detail by considering the development of a fragment of a KBS built for British Coal's Insurance and Pensions Division using the environment.

CHAPTER 6

Preventative Maintenance and Maintainability

6.1. INTRODUCTION

The most effective form of maintenance is to avoid it. As this is clearly not possible, given the unpredictability of the domains in which Knowledge Based Systems (KBSs) operate and the commercial constraints that necessitate their updating if they are to be considered a viable product, KBS should be built with an eye to future maintenance. We can identify two principal factors that will influence the maintainability of a KBS:

1. Understandability. If code can be easily understood it can be more easily maintained by maintenance engineers who were not necessarily members of the original development team.
2. Changeability. The ease with which the KBS can be extended and changes incorporated.

These two are related but understandability is the most important. The advantages, with respect to maintainability, of writing readable and hence understandable code are well appreciated for traditional software systems, this also applies to KBSs. Not all the features that make conventional code more understandable map simply onto KBSs, however. For example it is much harder to incorporate information hiding principles into Knowledge Bases (KBs), except where object oriented representation techniques are used. Further it should be noted that a KBS that can readily incorporate change through the use of some schema does not lend itself to maintainability if that schema cannot be understood.

The ease with which changes can be incorporated into a KBS is dependent on a number of additional factors, these include:

- The representation technique used. This should lend itself to the simple and efficient incorporation of change by displaying properties such as isomorphism and declarativeness. It should also, returning to our earlier theme, be understandable and decompose into independent units, so that the effect of change does not ramify through the whole system.
- The degree of anticipation displayed by the design. The KB should be structured with reference to the likelihood of change of individual items or groups of items of domain knowledge on which the KBS is based. This means, for example, that values susceptible to change shall be represented as parameters which can be picked up from a single source.
- Software support. Many software tools have been developed which, even if not specifically aimed at maintenance, can be used to greatly enhance the maintainability of KBS.

By building in maintainability into KBSs the amount of maintenance effort required at a later date can be reduced. When building in maintainability the following considerations should be included:

- The effect of a rule should be understandable in isolation.
- The KB should be structured in a similar manner to that displayed by the source material.
- The rule structure should be such as to be able to incorporate anticipated changes.
- The rule structure should display compositionality.
- The rule structure should display declarativeness.

In the rest of this chapter these ideas are expanded upon by focusing on the issues surrounding representations.

6.2. REPRESENTATION ISSUES

We noted in section 4.1 that when KBSs were first introduced it was claimed that, since they worked by manipulating a representation of the knowledge pertinent to a problem, they lent themselves to easy verification by someone with that knowledge, easy extension, by the addition of extra knowledge, and easy maintenance, since obsolete knowledge could be straightforwardly replaced by current knowledge. In practice, of course, things did not prove so straightforward. The process of verification was hindered by the fact that the expert was typically unable to understand the executable form of the rules. This meant that he was unable to say whether the from in which the rule appeared in the KB was, or was not, a faithful representation of his knowledge. This was quickly recognised in the MYCIN project, and facilities were supplied to use templates to "pretty print" the rules in a form approximating to English. This undoubtedly improved matters, although the expert was still expected to be able to cope with any intellectual contortions needed to express his knowledge in the production rule format, but the verification problem remained incompletely solved. This is because in such systems, the effect of the rules might well differ from their apparent meaning. As a simple example of this, consider synonyms. Suppose a KB contained two predicates `hasSpouse` and `isMarried`. The rules containing these predicates shown to the expert may well appear correct taken individually, and their inability to interact may go unoticed, since even if the "elegant variation" is picked up the expert will simply read them as synonyms, whereas the system will need to have this synonymity explicitly recorded. Aspects of control can make important differences too: a production rule system, which relies on specificity for its conflict resolution can work quite happily with rules such as `if context is configure cabinets then context is configure wiring`. This rule will not fire, given the conflict resolution strategy used, when there is some other rule appropriate to the existing context, and is used to change contexts. What it says, however, is simply nonsensical, unless one understands how the rule will be used in the overall working of the system.

Another, perhaps less obvious, and so less discussed, difficulty is that when the knowledge engineer encodes the knowledge that he has elicitated from the expert he will often bring together separately presented items into a single rule. The possibilities for this kind of thing can be illustrated by considering a UK Department of Social Security example involving category C Retirement Pension. The UK Social Security act states:

> "39(1) Subject to the provision of this Act:
>
> (a) a person who was over pensionable age on 5th July 1948 and satisfies such other conditions as may be prescribed shall be entitled to a category C retirement pension at the appropriate weekly rate."

To interpret this we need also to bear in mind the earlier section:

> "27(1) In this Act 'pensionable age' means-
>
> (a) in the case of a man, the age of 65 years; and

(b) in the case of a woman, the age of 60 years."

Now if we consider the kind of knowledge that an expert adjudicator might apply to decide claims for this benefit, we might see him allowing claims of men aged (at time of writing) 109 and over and women aged 104 and over. This would certainly pick out the correct group of people and would be the most convenient expression of the knowledge if the claim form gave the age of the claimant. It does, however, "compile in" both a certain amount of arithmetical expertise and knowledge of the current date, as well as the interaction between 27(1) and 39(1). If the claim form contained not the age of the claimant but the date of birth, however, this would not be the most convenient expression of the knowledge, since a calculation would be required to get the age from the date of birth, and the expert would be likely instead to operationalise the knowledge as "men born before 5th July 1883 and women born before 5th July 1888". This still conflates 27(1) and 39(1). The point here is that when experts operationalise their knowledge they will amalgamate knowledge from a variety of sources in the way which is of most use to them, but which may obscure some necessary (from a Software Engineering standpoint) structural information.

It is important not to obscure this information if we are to maintain the system effectively. If we used the operationalisation in terms of age we would not necessarily realise that the critical age had to be increased each year, since the benefit is not a simple old age pension payable on reaching a certain age. If we operationalised in terms of date of birth and there was a change to pension age, perhaps to equalise pension age between the sexes, the effect of this change to 27(1) would not be transmitted through to this conflated representation of 39(1), since we have not represented the connection between the sections. Thus the difficulties in maintaining a representation in which different pieces of legislation are brought together in a single rule seem evident.

Similar difficulties arise where the effect of a rule can only be understood in conjunction with other rules in the system. If we have a production system using specificity for conflict resolution and the first condition of every rule to denote the context to which it applies, we must ensure that any rules we add to the rule base conform to this strategy, otherwise it will be ineffective.

Thus we find in the encoding of a KB the potential for synonyms, distortions due to control, and conflation of knowledge from different sources, all of which militate against a straightforward interpretation of the KB by an expert, whether for the purpose of validation, extension or maintenance. Clearly careful consideration must be given to knowledge representation. To this end there are a number of considerations to address. These can be summarised as follows:

- Declarativeness.
- Compositionality.
- Isomorphism.
- Anticipation.
- Representation.

These considerations are discussed in the following sections.

6.3. DECLARATIVENESS

A KB displays declarativeness if each rule in the KB encapsulates a single item of "knowledge" and each group of rules or procedure deals with a single concept. The advantages of this are firstly that it will allow for changes in items of knowledge and concepts to be incorporated in such a manner that the effect on the rest of the KB is minimal, and secondly that it will enhance understandability. These advantage are also associated with the modular and information hiding principles displayed by conventional software development methods such as object oriented design.

Further the meaning of a fragment of the represented knowledge must be comprehendable in isolation. Contrast the following three PROLOG representations of the possession of navels, where we attempt to represent the knowledge that every person other than Adam and Eve has a navel.

```
R1a: has_Navel(adam,no).
R1b: has_Navel(eve,no).
R1c: has_Navel(X,yes):-person(X).

R2a: has_Navel(adam,no):-!.
R2b: has_Navel(eve,no):-!.
R2c: has_Navel(X,yes):-person(X).

R3b: has_Navel(adam,no).
R3c: has_Navel(eve,no).
R3a: has_Navel(X,yes):-person(X),X \== adam, X \== eve.
```

R1a and R1b express true facts, but R1c expresses the falsehood that everyone has a navel. It will often give the correct behaviour, but this will rely on two things. Firstly that R1c appears as the last clause of the procedure and a standard PROLOG execution strategy is being used, and secondly that backtracking will not occur. If backtracking does occur a second solution will ascribe navels to both Adam and Eve. In R2a and R2b the "cut" is used to avoid this latter problem (a solution imitated in various ways in production rule systems), although the order of the clauses remains necessary to give the correct behaviour. The cost is that we now have explicit representation of control in our clauses and we cannot really say that R2a and R2b express truths, or rely on the ability of our expert to understand them, since understanding now depends on some understanding of PROLOG as a programming language. R3a to R3c are correct in that they do represent true statements, both individually and collectively and in that there is no reliance on order or execution strategy.

Thus only R3 would satisfy the property of the individual clauses yielding their meaning without reference to the remainder of the KB or the inference strategy to be used. This simple example shows how declarativeness can be compromised even in the most straightforward of cases.

Maintenance can be greatly facilitated if statements in the representation are truly declarative. While almost all knowledge representation paradigms have declarativeness as an aspiration, in practice the use of, for example, conflict resolution strategies in production rule systems, means that it is not possible to detach a piece of a KB from its context and consider its correctness in isolation. If we want to ensure that localised changes to the source material result in correspondingly localised changes to the KB, we must be sure that there are no ramifications of changes resulting from a subtle alteration of the meaning of the statement deriving from its context in the KB. A full discussion of this problem is given in Bench-Capon and Forder [1991].

6.4. COMPOSITIONALITY

Compositionality is based on the idea that rules dealing with compound entities should be capable of being understood by understanding each individual simple entity making up a compound entity. This approach is analogous to top-down and bottom-up decomposition techniques used in traditional software development.

This can best be illustrated by considering an imperative language example. If we have a statement `a=6` this may be used in a number of different ways. For example:

```
if (a = 6) then ...
```

and

```
let (a = 6)
```

One represents a test and the other an assignment. The point being that the statement `a=6` cannot be understood in isolation, nor does it contribute uniformly to statements in which it appears. Languages, such as imperative languages, thus do not exhibit compositionality.

6.5. ISOMORPHISM

The philosophy behind isomorphism is that the KB should be structured in a similar manner to that displayed by the domain otherwise there is a danger of the KB being modelled on the structure of the analysis rather than the domain itself. To give a more specific case: if the KB is based on regulations the KB should be structured in such a manner as to reflect the structure of these regulations. Thus individual regulations, sections and sub-sections within the regulations should correspond to specific rules and groups of rules. Again the effect of this will be to enhance understandability and facilitate maintainability. Single changes in the regulations will correspond to identifiable rules or groups of rules, which do not derive from any other regulation, and therefore the scope of the jeopardised parts of the KB is limited and detectable: Regulations to rules can be one to many, but rules to regulations should be one to one.

Isomorphism can be achieved by a disciplined use of a representation rather than use of a distinctive representation, although certain extensions are required to languages such as PROLOG or any first order formalism. It should also be noted that by achieving a structural correspondence between the source and the code will enable the developer to record the provenance of all the items of knowledge in the representation, not a simple matter in the absence of such isomorphism.

The concept of isomorphism has been adopted in the methodology associated with the MAUDE KBS development environment described earlier. Isomorphism is discussed further in the following chapter. An interesting discussion of the subject is also given in Routen and Bench-Capon [1991].

6.6. ANTICIPATION

The degree of maintenance effort required to maintain a system is dependent, to a large extent, on the degree with which future changes are anticipated. This is particularly so in the case of adaptive maintenance. Knowing that the source material from which a KB has been designed is likely to change should lead to the development of a structure that can readily incorporate such changes. Alternatively the KB can be structured to avoid such changes. This can be achieved by a careful analysis of the source material. In the UK Department of Social Security example given in section 6.2, if this knowledge were encapsulated in a KB in the form of a statement "men over 109 and women over 104 are entitled to a category C pension" the KB would be incorrect within the year. The KB should therefore be structured in such a manner as to allow annual updating. Alternatively if the KB was structured so that date of birth was considered and not current age the need for this maintenance could be avoided.

In many domains it can only be anticipated that over a relatively short periods of time knowledge concerning the domain is going to change. Forecasting how it is going to change is much more difficult. If we consider a KBS which has as its domain some legal application we can anticipate that the knowledge displayed by the system is going to be affected by a number of possible changes in its operating environment. Statutes and regulations may be amended or repealed or new statutes and regulations introduced. Alternatively new precedents may be set in the courts resulting in different interpretations of existing statutes and regulations. Although such changes in the environment can be anticipated the nature of these changes cannot. The KB must therefore be designed so that new concepts and relationships can be introduced and existing ones altered or removed without requiring disproportionate restructuring of the rule base.

6.7. UNDERSTANDABILITY

KBS maintenance, as well as traditional software maintenance, can be summarised as the task of changing a body of code in some manner. Typically the maintenance engineer readily understands the nature of the change, he/she knows what needs to be done. The problem is in understanding the existing body of code and then knowing where and how to implement the change so as not to disturb the rest of the code. To facilitate understandability KBS developers should produce readable code. More specifically the KBS development should display the following features:

- Homogeneity.

- Predictability.
- Modularity.

The feature of homogeneity requires that similar situations should dictate similar solutions, making for more homogeneous and less idiosyncratic code. Homogeneous code uses a small number of stereotypic language constructs to achieve desired goals. The maintenance engineer should not be able to tell who wrote a particular section of code; each programmer in a development team should be using the same set of program "plans" to realise comparable goals.

Predictable code is defined by Soloway [Soloway *et al.* 1987] as having three properties:

1. The maintenance engineer should know where to look for answers to questions.
2. The engineer should not be surprised by what he/she finds.
3. Nothing untoward should be carried out, unknown to the maintainer, behind the scenes.

Thus in a production rule system if one rule serves more than one function, then (3) will be violated. Alternatively if rules intended to serve a related function are distributed over a rule base, the maintenance engineer may not realise that he/she needs to look in a non-obvious region for key rules and hence (1) will be violated.

As in traditional software engineering understandability of code can be enhanced if the interaction between system components is minimised, i.e. modularity. In KBSs this will involve such expediencies as rule clustering, partitioning and the writing of declarative and compositional code.

Understandability incorporating the above features can be introduced into a KBS by the use of good programming practices and by the use of formal development environments and methodologies. Good programming practices for KBSs are the same as those applicable to traditional software systems some of which were alluded to in chapter 1 of this work. A number of example of formal KBS development environments and methodologies were described in chapter 5.

6.8. PARTITIONING

The partitioning of KBs can have advantages for understandability, general maintainability, efficiency and suitability for parallel processing. A KB can be much easier to maintain if it is divided into chunks in such a manner that each chunk can be fully understood, and hence maintained, by one knowledge engineer.

One simple approach is to build a system made up of several KBs [Prerau *et al.* 1990]. PROSPECTOR [Hart *et al.* 1978] was developed in this manner. Alternatively, rules that contribute to a particular goal in a KB can be grouped together: R1/XCON [McDermott *et al.* 1982] can be considered to be subdivided in this manner. Since KBSs often use a large amount of computer resources research work has also been carried out to investigate the separation of the KB and memory so that each independent group can be processed on a parallel processor. There may however be a conflict between partitioning for efficiency and partitioning for maintenance. This increases the strength of the argument for intermediate representations where run time efficiency is not a consideration. The use of intermediate representations is discussed in the following section.

Jacob and Froscher [1990] discuss the partitioning of KBSs to facilitate maintenance. They suggest the partitioning of a KBS into a hierarchy of manageable groups by grouping rules that use or produce values for the same set of facts. A hierarchy must exist as there will also be some values that connect individual groups. Rules are flagged in the current group of interest that use facts generated by rules in another group, and facts in the current group of interest are flagged that are used by rules in other groups. This will then enable the knowledge engineer to be able to maintain a group of rules and at the same time issue warnings to other groups that will be affected.

6.9. INTERMEDIATE REPRESENTATIONS

Intermediate representations are used to represent domain knowledge, in a form that represents both the structure of the KB in the target representation and the source in a manner that can be easily understood by persons not familiar with the target representation. Their primary purpose is to provide an agreed basis for the knowledge engineer and his domain expert(s). It is therefore essential that the intermediate representation be couched in terms which will provide sufficient expressiveness to be acceptable to the expert, and sufficient formality that it will lack ambiguity and so be encodable in a chosen knowledge representation formalism without the need to resort further to the expert(s). Functionally, in the knowledge engineering process, intermediate representations serve to supplant the rough notes that any knowledge engineer would produce in the course of a knowledge elicitation, and to objectify these so as to allow communication between knowledge engineers, and perhaps also to provide a basis for a methodology which will help to teach people the knowledge engineering task.

From our perspective of concern with maintenance it can serve a further role in that changes, necessitated by the various requirements for maintenance, can be thought about first in terms of the intermediate representation, and changes to the executable KB derived from them. In this latter role it should be used much in the same way as the program structure diagrams of JSP are for COBOL programs, providing a view of the KB free from considerations dependent solely on aspects of implementation. This will mean that maintenance actions first are performed by adjusting the intermediate representation, and the consequent changes needed to be made in the KB derived from these.

Thus the intermediate representations are intended to serve as a medium of communication between a knowledge engineer and a domain expert; as an object which the expert can verify without reference to the behaviour of the system; as a means of enabling the knowledge engineer to organise his task of transferring expertise from expert to KB; and as a "model" of the domain knowledge which can be used as "a way in" to the KB for the purposes of extension and maintenance.

A number of formalisms have been proposed for intermediate representation: among the currently most popular are decision trees and the conceptual graphs of Sowa [1984].

The use of intermediate representations in the development of KBS has been advocated by many authors [Young 1987, Diederich *et al.* 1987, Watson *et al.* 1989, Johnson 1989]. One example of such a representation is the MAKE Intermediate Representation (MIR), introduced in the previous chapter. Further, a number of KBS verification and validation tools and techniques achieve a more general application by first translating the rules and/or frames in a target KBSs into a more universal representation so that verification and validation tools and techniques can be applied. These representations are akin to the intermediate development representations described here.

Finally it should be noted that critics of intermediate representations claim that they simply introduced another level of complexity in the development process.

The KBS development life-cycle proposed by those who wish to employ intermediate representations is something like that shown in Figure 6.1.

6.9.1. Features of an Intermediate Representation

We can identify a number of features that an intermediate representation must display if it is going to serve the purpose outlined above.

Firstly it is important that the expert be able to understand the representation independently of system execution, so that the system can

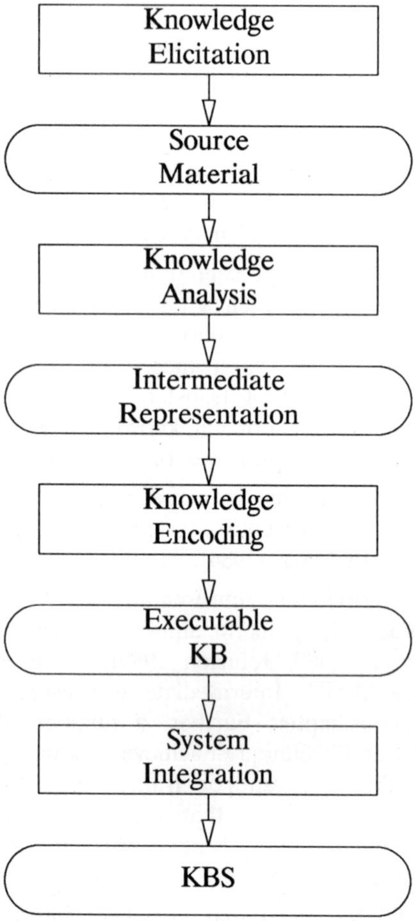

Figure 6.1: Stage based life-cycle incorporating an intermediate representation phase.

be validated rather than merely tested. This requires the following:

- Declarativeness. The meaning of a fragment of the intermediate representation must be comprehensible in isolation.
- Isomorphism. The intermediate representation should avoid conflating disparate items of knowledge into single structures. The requirement of isomorphism with sources can best be located in the intermediate rather than the executable representation, since it may well prove wise to conflate the knowledge sources in the executable representation to achieve certain behaviour or efficiency

goals. See, for an example Sherman's formalisation of the Income Tax law of Canada [Sherman 1987]. The intermediate representation will ensure that we are able to disentangle the conflations if required.

Secondly the intermediate representation should be "expert friendly" so that the expert may be able to grasp the formalism used to see whether the knowledge as represented really does reflect the knowledge as he/she would choose to express it. This is a problem area since a formalism is essential to avoid the ambiguities of natural language, but any formalism will need to be learned by the expert, and this may prove unacceptable. For example predicate calculus is unlikely to be acceptable to the majority of experts.

Another problem is concerned with synonyms or closely related concepts. This raises an important point: when developing KBS the major concern is that the rules in the KB are correct. The KB does not, however, consist solely of such dynamic knowledge: equally important is the static knowledge of the objects that make up the domain, the attributes that they have and the values that those attributes may have. This kind of dynamic/static division can be traced back to R1/XCON where the static knowledge of the components of the systems and their properties were stored in a simple database and the dynamic configuration knowledge in the form of production rules [McDermott 1980]. If no special mechanism for storing the static knowledge is used, the objects, their attributes and their values are emergent properties of the rules. An object exists by virtue of it being a potential instantiation for a variable in some rule, and the attributes and their values are known to exist by virtue of being mentioned in some rule(s). This lack of an explicit "domain model" means that there is no structured way in which potential objects, attributes and values can be retrieved from the KB. This can be a main source of conceptual duplication giving rise to the synonym problem alluded to above. Equally, actual features of the domain may be excluded from the KB because they do not appear in any of the rules; this may lead to faults in the KB, since this will mean that there can be some cases not covered by the KB. It also means that if the KB is extended or modified to include reference to such features they may be incorporated in a way not in accord with the existing KB.

A good illustration of this point can be found in the well known set of animal rules given in Winston [1984], in which we find the predicates "has dark spots" and "has black stripes". Clearly both of these refer to the markings of animals, but in the rules as they stand there is no connection between them. Similarly adding predicates to enable the identification of other animals "has white zig-zag stripes" and "has black spots" will accumulate information about the nature of markings without giving any indication of the possibility of systematic treatment of the concept of markings, and a mess is the likely outcome. For example how do black spots relate to dark spots? Our contention is that a more rational and extensible set of predicates could have been derived had some thought been given to the construction of a conceptual scheme showing the range of predicates and their relations.

One of the major advantages cited for frame based systems is their bundling aspect; that they break up the domain into related and relevant chunks of knowledge. If all the predicates applicable to a particular class of objects are grouped together through a frame mechanism, they will be easier to carry in the mind than if they are scattered through the rules of the KB in an unstructured way. This advantage can, however, be achieved in an intermediate representation through the construction of a conceptual scheme: there is no need to commit to passing this bundling through into the executable code. Indeed, there a different bundling may be appropriate since the emphasis will be on efficiency and behaviour rather than comprehensibility.

One additional thing the intermediate representation should allow, therefore, is the ability to express such a conceptual model of the static knowledge of the domain so that we can rationalise the predicates that we will use in the domain. This model will establish a language which will be used to construct the dynamics of the KB, and which can be used as a common language for knowledge engineer, expert and KBS. The intended role is similar to that of the T-Box in KRYPTON [Brachman *et al.* 1983]. Naturally the formalism used for this should conform to the same constraints as the rule formalism: fragments should retain their meaning in isolation from the rest of the KB, and there should be a structural correspondence between the domain model and the expert's conceptualisation of the objects of the domain.

6.9.2. The Executability of an Intermediate Representation

In the above discussion of the properties of an intermediate representation we have not considered whether the intermediate representation should be executable in any sense. Some would argue that it should be: proponents of logic programming would for example claim that such programs could serve as "executable specifications", an idea which is sufficiently close to our notion of an intermediate representation to be viewed as such. They argue further that such executable specifications might not be the best form in which to deploy the code in the final system: some transformation may be necessary for the purposes of efficiency, maintaining the distinction between intermediate and system representations.

The advantages of the executability of the intermediate representation are fairly evident: chiefly they result from the ability to get the best of both worlds in that not only can the KB be scrutinised, but it can also be tested against example cases so as to provide the kind of clarification that is achieved in the prototyping life-cycle.

It is not clear, however, that any formalism which is executable is sufficiently understandable by the kind of people to whom the intermediate representation is directed. If this is not the case the loss of the advantages conferred by having a representation which exhibits the properties described in the last section would outweigh the advantages of executability: we would, in effect, be forced to return to something closer to the prototyping life-cycle, in that the expert could understand the KB only by seeing its effect in use.

Before leaving this topic, we should perhaps consider a midway position: it may be that the representation is manipulable, although not executable. In this situation we would be able to carry out the kind of transformations mentioned with respect to logic programming, without necessarily being able to execute the representation directly.

6.10. SUMMARY

In this chapter we have discussed preventative maintenance on the grounds that the most effective form of maintenance is to attempt, to avoid it. The discussion focuses on the representation of KBSs, suggesting that by adopting a suitable representation we can gain advantages of understandability and changeability and hence ease the maintenance task. We claim that this can be achieved by using representations and implementation strategies that display features such as:

- Declarativeness.
- Compositionality.
- Isomorphism.
- Anticipation.
- Homogeneity.
- Predictability.
- Modularity.

Further we suggest that maintenance can best be implemented using an intermediate representation to provide a forum where the knowledge engineer and domain expert can meet. We also consider the advantages to be gained through the partitioning of KBs.

CHAPTER 7

Global and Local Identification

7.1. INTRODUCTION

In this chapter we consider the tools, techniques and design philosophies that can assist in the identification of:

1. The global area of a knowledge base (KB) on which some maintenance action should be implemented.
2. The local elements that will require attention.
3. The extended jeopardised element set to be taken into account when testing the system after a maintenance session has taken place.

7.2. GLOBAL IDENTIFICATION

The need for maintenance is usually promulgated to the maintainers of a Knowledge Based Systems (KBSs) by the end users of the system. Having established that a change is required, the next step is to identify the section of the KB where the change is to be implemented, i.e. establish from a global viewpoint the broad area of the KB where the change is to be effected. The simplicity with which this can be done will depend very much on the development techniques used to build the KBS and the type of maintenance required, corrective, perfective or adaptive.

If the KBS has been developed in an *ad hoc* manner than the only approach is a long and painful inspection of the code. If the KBS has been built in a more formal structured manner the task will be simplified. A number of formal development environments were described in chapter 5.

Where the required maintenance is adaptive or perfective there are a number of development philosophies/techniques that can be used to facilitate the detection of the area within a KBS which will require attention. These include isomorphism, linking and indexing. Isomorphism (introduced in section 6.5) is a design philosophy that requires that all rules/frames in a KBS should reflect the structure of the source data. Linking is a technique by which individual rules/frames, or parts thereof, can be traced back to the source and vice versa. Indexing involves the construction of a dictionary of rule base primitives which indicates where in the KB these primitives appear. By searching the dictionary appropriate key elements can be found and linked to the KB.

Where the type of maintenance required is corrective, i.e. the KBS is not operating as it should do, a number of software tools exist to help the maintenance engineer track down the rule(s) or frame(s) that are causing the incorrect result. These range from simple debuggers, through steppers to rule tracers. Alternatively the explanation facilities incorporated into most KBSs can be used to identify the problematic rule(s) or frame(s).

There is also a school of thought that existing rules or frames in a KBS should never be altered, therefore dispensing with the need for global and local identification. Thus if a rule base is not performing correctly this should only be addressed by adding new rules or frames to the hierarchy. This has been successfully implemented on the GARVEN-ES1 system [Compton *et al.* 1988, 1991].

7.3. ISOMORPHISM

The concept of isomorphism in the context of producing an understandable KB was discussed in the previous chapter. The intention of isomorphism in KBSs is that a KBS should reflect the sources from which it has been developed. The usefulness of isomorphism with respect to future maintenance will thus depend on the nature of the source. If the source already has a well defined structure then isomorphism will greatly aid maintenance. Good examples of such sources are legal documents such as acts of parliament which themselves are multi-layered logical structures [Routen 1989]. Alternatively if the source is very unstructured, for example an *ad hoc* collection of taped interviews with a number of domain experts, then isomorphism has little advantage to offer as rules/frames will be derived from many non-contiguous source fragments. In this case a process of analysis can identify the underlying structure of the domain. The KBS can then be made isomorphic to this structure [Paton and Nwana 1990, Paton *et al.* 1991].

Assuming a structured source, isomorphism supports maintenance both by aiding in the identification of jeopardised parts of the KB, given a particular change to the source material, and by the way it enables such jeopardised sections of the KB to be removed cleanly from the remainder of the KB and worked on in isolation. If in the case of a KBS operating in (say) a legal domain a section of source, for example a section in an act, is changed, an isomorphic representation will mean that only a well defined part of the KB will require attention, i.e. a single rule or frame or a small number of such rules or frames. Thus any maintenance need thus only be implemented on this rule/frame set and, if the representation is truly isomorphic, no other rules will be effected other than if the changed section of source relates to other parts of the source. In addition, by using suitable tools, verification and validation tests may be implemented on the identified rule set and thus the need to retest the entire KBS after maintenance has been implemented will be avoided. In addition, by achieving a structural correspondence, we will also be able to record the provenance of all items of knowledge in the intermediate representation. This is not a simple matter in the absence of such isomorphism, but which is vital if changes are to be followed through from source to KB.

An isomorphic KBS is thus easier to maintain in two ways: it is easier to identify the section of the KBS requiring change, and the effect of change is limited. Isomorphism also has advantages that pervade the whole life-cycle of the KBS. Not only is development facilitated and validation and debugging supported, but isomorphism also carries over into the execution of the system, enhancing the application from the users' perspective as well. These additional advantages are discussed briefly below.

Isomorphism has been adopted in the development of a number of KBSs, particularly legislative KBSs, for example the British Coal compensation claims system developed as part of the MAKE project [Bench-Capon and Coenen 1991b, Coenen and Bench-Capon 1992a] and the TESSEC expert system [Nieuwenhuis 1989].

7.3.1. Development

One reason for the slow adoption of KBSs in the practical world is that the task of constructing KBSs is seen as highly skilled, and therefore requires the development team to have rare personal qualities. One solution, widely adopted in conventional software systems, is to use a methodology which enables people to be taught to build the systems in a systematic way, thus reducing the need for individual inspiration. It has been found that by adopting the principle of isomorphism a very disciplined and teachable methodology, and one which permits the construction of the knowledge base to be spread over a multi-person team in an organised and sensible manner, results.

7.3.2. Validation

Isomorphism supports validation in two ways. First it results in a representation in which the components of the KB can be detached from the context of the KB and compared directly with a specific and identifiable fragment of source from which they are derived. This "by eye" validation is difficult, if not impossible, to achieve in representations which allow given rules to derive from several non-contiguous source fragments, or allow the representation of a given piece of source to be distributed across several rules.

Comparison of the KB with the source cannot, however, be sufficient to inspire complete confidence in the correctness of the KB: it is also necessary to run test cases through the system. Isomorphism helps here too, because the behaviour of the system is largely dictated by the structure of the original source. This means that when aberrant behaviour is detected it can be noticed more easily, because there is a deviation in structure from what is expected, as well as possibly a wrong answer being produced. Further the offending piece of the KB can then be detached, its parent source fragment associated with it, and corrections made without any need to worry that surrounding parts of the KB or source will be jeopardised by the changes.

7.3.3. System Execution

All of the above advantages are systems related, but isomorphism also impacts directly on the user. This is shown in two ways. Firstly the isomorphic representation allows use of a shared structure which makes the reasoning employed by the system very much more transparent to the user. Early expert systems were often criticised for a lack of topic coherence. Because the KB was structured in accordance with considerations pertaining to the KB rather than to the task or to the user, questions would often be asked of the user in an order which the user found difficult to relate to or explain. In contrast isomorphic KBs have a structure which corresponds to (say) familiar and accessible source documents, and therefore the motives for asking the questions can be explained by reference to this relatively well understood model, without need to consider an independent KB structure. This can be further exploited by the use of structured dialogues as used in the LOD system [Forder and Taylor 1991]. Instead of merely presenting the users with a form which requires them to answer questions without giving them a rationale for those questions or an idea of the consequences of their answers, the users can be presented with a dialogue which is tied to a particular section of the source, facilitating orientation, and which is structured in a way that corresponds with the source, allowing the users to employ their knowledge of those sources to select questions which are likely to have the most relevance and impact on the outcome.

A second advantage accrues when the user is faced with the need to come to a decision as to some vague or open textured concept. It is clearly impossible to anticipate every situation, and the resolution of open texture must therefore be left to the user. However, users, must resolve the question not in an arbitrary way, but taking into account the guidance provided for them, and with reference to previous decisions. Guidance and decisions are associated with particular fragments of the legislation, and because the rules reflect this structure, the specific guidance and decisions relevant to the point of the processing which has been arrived at can be selected and presented to the users. Were the rules not isomorphic with the source the associations could not be made. The need for harmonisation between rules, source and guidance is further discussed in Bench-Capon *et al.* [1992].

7.4. LINKING

Linking allows sections of knowledge in a source to be linked through to the final representation of the knowledge in the KB. The advantage for maintenance is that a change in the source can be quickly traced through to the rules or frames that need attention. At a local level linking can also be used to identify the related rules and frames that might be affected by a change to a particular rule or frame. This is achieved by tracing back from the rule or frame to be changed to any other section of the source that the rule or frame may also be derived from, and then, by tracing forward, identifying the other rules or frames also derived from those sources and so on. This linking process may be either implemented manually or using some automated tool.

When coupled with isomorphism linking becomes a powerful tool. Remember that the concept behind isomorphism is that individual chunks of source should, as far as possible, be represented by individual rules or frames. Using linking facilities a change in the source can be traced to the affected rules or frames; further the number of other rules and frames that will be affected will be limited. A number of KBS development environments support linking as well as isomorphic knowledge representation; a good example is the MAUDE environment [Bench-Capon and Coenen 1991b, Coenen and Bench-Capon 1992a]. This was described in depth in section 5.7.

A disadvantage of linking in most environments that use links is that the links must be established manually. A disciplined and formal development technique is therefore required. If the developers fail to include all necessary links the advantages for maintenance that can be gained will have been lost. Some consideration has been given to the automative inclusion of links but it is felt that this will often result in a plethora of irrelevant and spurious links which will only lead to confusion.

7.5. INDEXING

Another method of identifying the area of a KBS affected by a change, adopted in some development environments, is indexing. One example is the RIME KBS development methodology [Hicks 1990] which includes an indexing method to identify parts of the KB associated with particular identifiers.

Indexing involves the establishment of an index of (say) rule names or frame identifiers which are linked to the actual rules or frames in the KBS. This process is carried out throughout the development and on completion must of course be maintained in line with any maintenance that is carried out on the KBS. A change in knowledge can then be identified with a particular section of the KBS by inspection of the index in the same manner that a section of a text book concerning a particular subject can be found by inspection of the index. It should be noted that for this approach to operate successfully careful attention must be devoted to the selection of rule and frame names so that they are descriptive of the task they are intended to perform or the object they are intended to represent.

7.6. DEBUGGERS

In the case of corrective maintenance debugging tools can be used to discover the area of the KB that will require attention. A review of the debugging facilities available is thus given in this section.

The earliest form of debugging tools are the static tools such as those exemplified by the LISP break package [Wilensky 1984] and the PROLOG debug and trace facilities [Clocksin and Mellish 1984]. Such tools are found in most KBS development environments. For example the ORBS (Oregon Rule Base System) rapid programming environment [Fickas 1987] includes an INTERLISP break package which allows programmers to insert breaks into their rule bases. ORBS also provides tools such as a micro matcher which displays a low level account of the generation of a rule instantiation.

Static debugging tools, however, require a lot of interaction in that they require a substantial amount of user participation, have very low level commands and provide no indication of "how" and "why". A step up from these are automated debuggers. Automated debuggers incorporate some form of debugging strategy. Ducassé and Emde [1988] have identified four principal debugging strategies:

1. Checking Computational Equivalence. This is related to tutoring systems and consists of checking the computational equivalence of the program and of a correct implementation specified by a teacher.
2. Language Dependent Checking. For example type checking and consistency checking.
3. Recognition of Stereotyped Bugs. This is carried out either in the source of the program or in the execution trace.
4. Static or Dynamic Automated Filtering. This aims at reducing the amount of information the programmer still has to examine to localise a bug as opposed to the previous three strategies which aim at directly pointing to bugs. Possible dynamic strategies include Top-down Zooming, Retrospective Zooming and Divide-and-Query Algorithms.

The first three strategies are computationally expensive and further the first requires a correct implementation to already exist, and so can really only be applied to tutoring systems.

We should also consider meta-debuggers. These are programs which reside on top of basic debuggers. One example is Opium [Ducassé and Emde 1988]. Opium is a PROLOG meta-debugger that allows the maintenance engineer to develop debugging strategies.

Finally it is worth noting that given that KBSs are developed in a sequential manner, any bug, which is introduced at a particular stage, will be inherited by the following stages, where it may manifest itself. Therefore, debugging necessitates tracing back from the bug's manifestation, through the individual development stages, to its point of introduction. KEATS [Motta *et al.* 1990] supports this type of debugging by providing a coarse history for each model component throughout the model refinement process, allowing the user to inspect the development of a component from the source to the final operational implementation. The KEATS KBS development methodology is supported by a number of tools including TRI (Transparent Rule Interpreter) which supports the visualisation and debugging of rule base models. It represents the coarse-grained behaviour of a forward chaining rule interpreter.

7.6.1. Knowledge Base Refinement Systems

Knowledge base refinement systems, also known as knowledge rich debuggers, are principally aimed at speeding up the knowledge acquisition process. However, they can also be viewed as sophisticated debuggers. Examples include the TEIRESIAS system, KRUST and

SEEK and SEEK2. KB refinement systems assist the maintenance engineer (and the developer) to refine rules where the initial formulation of a rule is too general or too specific. They operate by allowing the manual or automatic running of test cases during which the user is asking whether a rule the system is about to apply should apply to the generated test case or not. If not the rule is too general and further refinement is required. If at the end of the inference a rule which should have been applied has not been applied, the rule is too specific and so requires some relaxation.

TEIRESIAS

The TEIRESIAS [Davis 1984] program marks the first attempt to automate KBS debugging, it is an interactive knowledge refinement and acquisition program which was built as part of the MYCIN series of experiments [Buchanan and Shortliffe 1984]. TEIRESIAS allows an expert to judge whether or not MYCIN's diagnosis is correct, to track down the bugs in the KB that led to incorrect conclusions and to alter, delete or add rules in order to fix the bug. During a consultation, a proof tree of rules is formed; facts form the leaves and the diagnosis the root. The tree shows which attributes were used to conclude other attributes. When a misdiagnosis occurs as the result of the addition of a new rule, TEIRESIAS uses the how explanation mechanism of the KBS to focus the expert's attention on rules lower down the proof tree which should not have appeared. This is achieved by comparing the tree with the attributes found in the if condition of the new rule. The program then proposes missing clauses if some attributes found in the if part of the model did not appear in the new rule.

KRUST

In KRUST [Craw and Sleeman 1990] the refinement of knowledge is automated. When KRUST is presented with a test case where the expert's conclusion differs with that produced by the KBS, it proposes and implements a set of possible refinements, based on the facts of the test case, to the KB so that the expert's conclusion is arrived at.

SEEK and SEEK2

Two systems for knowledge refinement, SEEK [Politakis 1985] and SEEK2 [Ginsberg and Weiss 1985] were developed at Rutgers University. SEEK is restricted to expert systems implemented in EXPERT which allows only inference rules expressed in tabular form, i.e. a restricted type of production rule formalism. To operate successfully SEEK requires two sources of knowledge:

1. The expert knowledge of the domain embodied in the KB

structures.

2. Case experience, in the form of a library of cases with known solutions.

Case analysis methods are then used to identify slight changes to the EXPERT-type rules which may correct any models which result in incorrect cases. SEEK suggests minimal changes under the assumption that the expert model is generally almost correct. Where an incorrect solution is arrived at, SEEK attempts to locate a partially satisfied rule for the expert's conclusion that is the closest to being satisfied and would override the model's incorrect answer. SEEK will then automatically advise the user on how best to refine the rule. The advice is generated on an empirical performance analysis of the rules. The types of advice are:

1. Increase or decrease a certainty factor.
2. Weaken the rule condition by removing components from the antecedent part.
3. Strengthen the rule condition by adding components to the antecedent part.

SEEK2 operates with more general KBS formats than the original SEEK, and if desired it may perform rule refinement automatically without reference to the user. It also incorporates a refinement meta-language, called RM, which describes both domain independent and domain specific meta-knowledge about the refinement process.

7.6.2. Steppers and Tracers

Tracers save the inference path used by the inference engine to draw particular conclusions for later inspection by a maintenance engineer. The trace can be displayed in one of to ways (a) as a text tree or (b) as a graphics tree. Several KBS development environments such as KEE and NEXPERT OBJECT provide rule execution traces.

Steppers allow the maintenance engineer to step through the inference process line by line so that (say) the point at which an incorrect instantiation is made can be located. Many include options to steer the inference process interactively.

Inference Tracers

Inference tracers, also sometimes referred to as rule tracers, provide the maintenance engineer with an audit trail of the inference process. This is essentially a record of all the rules that were activated to arrive at a conclusion. However no indication is given of which body variables had any impact on the conclusion and which did not.

Run Time Progress Graphers

Run time progress graphs depicting rule activations and instantiations as they are made, thus indicating the rules which were not fired as well as those that were.

7.7. EXPLANATION FACILITIES

By definition KBSs should be able to explain how they arrive at their conclusions. This explanation ability can greatly assist in the maintenance task. However, the explanatory capability of most expert systems is limited to what the system did, and so no deep justification is provided because the rationale behind the system's rules or methods is not represented.

Some authors [Neches *et al.* 1985] maintain that the explanation capability of KBS should be specifically developed to facilitate maintenance. This was illustrated by the XPLAIN system [Swartout 1983] which was based on two key principles: explicitly distinguishing different forms of domain knowledge present in the KB, and formal recording of the system development process. The claim was that this enhanced the capability of KBSs to generate explanations and justifications for their behaviour and hence made them more maintainable by making explicit the rationale behind the systems. This idea was developed further in the Explainable Expert Systems project [Neches *et. al.* 1985] which was concerned with developing a paradigm for building expert systems intended to provide for smoother evolution and enhanced explanation capabilities. The conclusion was that where explanation facilities are developed to facilitate maintenance they should allow ambiguities in the system to be tracked down and must make explicit the reason for rejecting and accepting propositions and how values may be arrived at.

Whatever the case, if a KBS is not behaving as it should, the cause of the problem, and hence the area of the KB which requires attention, can be identified using explanation facilities. Explanation facilities form an important part of all KBSs and are essentially intended to justify the findings of a KBS in a way that can be understood by the user, i.e. in the language of the domain. Micco [1988] lists a number of ways in which this information, for use by the maintenance engineer as well as the end user, can be arrived at:

Rule Tracing

This is the most common method adopted by many systems and has already been dealt with in the previous section. However, tracers tend to be cumbersome and do little to reveal the deep reasoning behind a system.

Canned Text

This works well for definition questions but is difficult to maintain. Moreover it may give misleading information because it is not derived from the system's actual execution.

Form Sentences

These draw on the facts known about a particular case and can be helpful to summarise the reasoning process.

Lists of Alternatives

These are lists of possibilities considered in ranked order. They provide a quick and convenient method of checking outcomes but do not explain how these results were arrived at.

Why/Why-Not Facilities

Some sort of deep reasoning capability which allows a system to list the reasons why a particular inference was made. Conversely, in response to the why-not question, the system can list the negative reasons why an inference was not made.

What-If Capabilities

It is also useful to provide a what-if capability which allows the maintenance engineer to explore and test the sensitivity of results by altering the input data.

7.8. KBS MAINTENANCE BY ADDITION TO THE KB

In the above sections we have concentrated on methods of locating, globally, the section of a KB where a change should be implemented. However, if we adopt a policy that we only refine the knowledge represented in the KB this process can be very much simplified. This concept has been suggested by Compton in a number of papers [Compton *et al.* 1991, Compton and Jansen 1988].

Compton observes that if a new rule is formulated as a result of a KBS producing an incorrect result this rule will be largely influenced by the context of the incorrect result as reported. This observation is based on Popper's falsification principle [Popper 1963] that we can never be certain that what we hypothesise is true, we can only disprove earlier hypotheses and replace them with an unproven refinement or new hypothesis. Thus any new rule can be considered not to be a global new rule but a rule to switch the interpretation from the incorrect to the correct conclusion. Compton thus suggests that all maintenance should be implemented by adding to the KBS without modifying or removing any existing rules. These new rules should then only be fired if the old rule which produced the incorrect interpretation is fired first. However, to allow the addition of rules in this manner a suitable representation must be adopted.

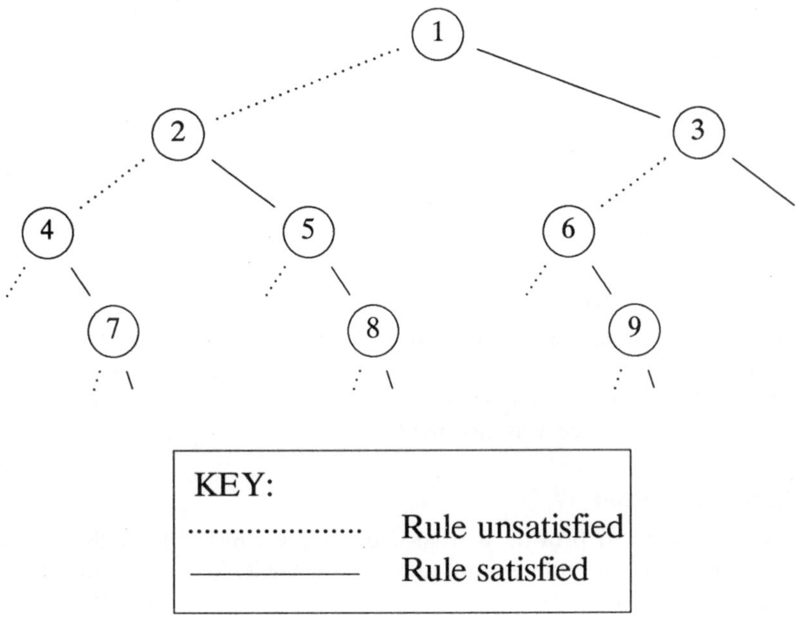

Figure 7.1: GARVEN-ES1 rule structure (after Compton et al. [1991]).

This principle has been implemented on the GARVEN-ES1 system, a KBS used to interpret thyroid hormone assay reports [Compton *et al.* 1988]. In the GARVEN-ES1 system the need for maintenance arises if an assay report, as judged by a team of domain experts, is not interpreted correctly. The rules in the system are represented in a tree structure (Figure 7.1) with a rule at each node. These nodes have two branches each, one of which is selected during the inference process according to whether the rule at the node is satisfied or not. Whenever a change in the system is required a rule is added in the form of a new node at the bottom of the tree. If the change is required because an interpretation is wrong the node will be attached to the satisfied branch of the last rule to be fired. If the change is required because no interpretation results the new rule will be added to the unsatisfied branch of the last rule to be fired.

This structure thus facilitates KBS maintenance by the addition of rules only. New rules are always added at the bottom of the rule hierarchy so that the task of identifying the area of the KB that requires attention is simplified. This also offers advantages in that the original rule base is never corrupted; it does not, however, guarantee that a new rule will not corrupt any existing rules. Thus after a maintenance session has been completed the KBS is checked using a data base of what Compton refers to as "cornerstone cases". These are cases which at some stage have instigated a change in the KB; each rule in the tree structure given in Figure 7.1 has one of these cornerstone cases associated with it. Every time the system's knowledge is changed the interpretations for all the cornerstone cases are checked to see that the additions to the system's knowledge have been genuinely incremental and have not corrupted the knowledge.

The GARVEN-ES1 approach to KBS maintenance does have limitations, however. It should be noted that, unlike XCON for example, the GARVEN-ES1 system has not been required to encompass new tasks, but has only been subject to minor corrections and additions to the system's knowledge.

7.9. LOCAL IDENTIFICATION

Having identified the section of the KBS that will require attention from a global standpoint, the maintenance engineer will then need to inspect the KB from a local perspective to identify the elements of the KB that will be affected by the implementation of the change as these may also require attention. There are a number of rule base viewing and representation techniques that can be used to achieve this end. These allow visual detection of the connections between elements in a KB. These viewing and representation techniques can be classified according to the following headings:

1. Petri Nets and Predicate-Transition Nets.
2. Decision Trees.
3. AND/OR Graphs.
4. Graphers.

There also some viewing/representation techniques that are usually used for verification and validation purposes which should also be mentioned here. These include evidence flow graph, decision table and incidence matrices techniques. The last two are described in detail in chapter 9. Evidence flow graphs allow a KB to be represented in such a manner as to aid the detection of unused inputs and sub-conclusions, unreachable conclusions and inputs between inputs and outputs [Becker *et al.* 1989].

A number of graphical tools, based on the above techniques, that allow the user to inspect a rule or frame hierarchy have been developed. To illustrate these tools, two, taken from the MAUDE development environment, namely the Datamap and the Class-Instance Browser, are discussed individually at the end of this chapter.

We should also consider the jeopardised frame/rule set here. This includes those additional KB elements that will be affected by a change although no specific maintenance action is to be implemented on them. This jeopardised frame/rule set can be identified using similar techniques to those described for local identification and is of particular significance when retesting the system after a maintenance session has taken place.

7.10. PETRI-NETS AND PREDICATE-TRANSITION NETS

Petri-net models are abstract, formal representations of information flow. They describe the input/output relationship between objects using a graphical representation. There are two types of node called places and transitions. Places are input and output objects (shown using circles) and transitions their functional relationship, i.e. the transformation of input places to output places (shown using a vertical bar or a square). The arcs between the nodes (shown by arrows) define the flow relation between the nodes. For example if we consider the following rule base:

```
Rule 1: A ∧ B ⇒ C
Rule 2:     D ⇒ E
Rule 3: C ∧ E ⇒ F
```

This can be represented by the Petri-net shown in Figure 7.2. Note that an arc should not connect two nodes of the same type. The transition/place relationship modelled can be succinctly summarised in the form of an incidence matrix (see Section 9.4). Sub-sets can then be established for the consequent of a particular rule of interest.

The dynamic behaviour of a Petri-net is controlled by the movement and propagation of tokens. The availability of tokens in input places can automatically trigger transitions that have these places as their inputs, and make their output places available (place tokens in

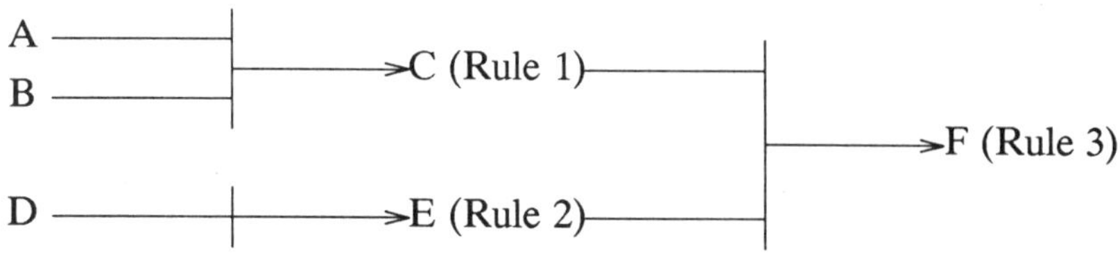

Figure 7.2: Example of rule base represented by a Petri-net.

them) for further propagation. Agarwal and Tanniru [1991] describe how a Petri-net model can be applied to KBSs, Pipard [1988] how they are used in the INDE rule checking system and Fidelak and Victor [1989] a method for verifying preduction systems using Petri-nets.

Predicate-transition nets [Genrich and Lautenbach 1981] are a special class of Petri-net in which a first order predicate is attached to each place.

In the KBS verification technique described by Fidelak the KB is automatically translated into a Petri-net and displayed. Each rule is translated into a transition by allocating a place to each condition and each action in the rule (the conditions and actions are assumed to be conjoined).

Returning to KBS maintenance, in the above example, if we wish to modify Rule 2 we can, by inspection of the Petri-net representing the rule base, easily identify the local elements of the KB that will require attention (we would have become aware of the need to alter Rule 2 through some global identification technique such as those described above, for example isomorphism or indexing).

7.11. DECISION TREES

Decision trees provide a graphical display of the rules used to reach an inference. Thus using the following example rule base:

```
Rule 1:  A ∧  B ⇒ ¬C
Rule 2:  D ∧ ¬E ⇒  A
Rule 3: ¬F ∧  G ⇒  B
Rule 4:  D ∧ ¬E ⇒ ¬F
```

a decision tree such as that shown in Figure 7.3 can be produced to indicate how ¬D is established given as inputs E, ¬F and H.

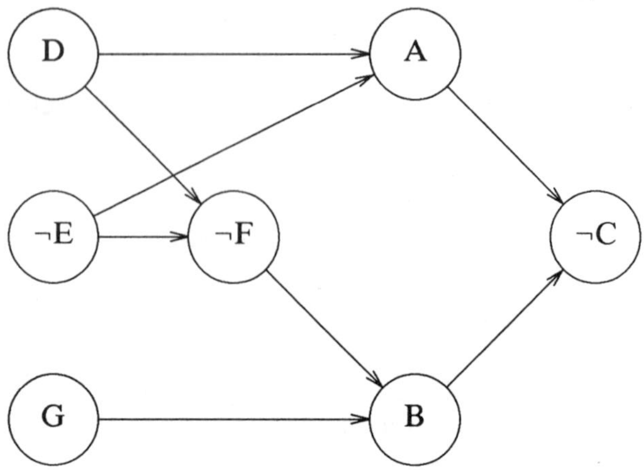

Figure 7.3: A Decision tree.

Now if we wish to modify Rule 2 by adding an extra conjuncted condition, `H`, to establish `A`, by inspection of the decision tree in Figure 7.3 we can quickly see that this should be added as a leaf proposition.

7.12. AND/OR GRAPHS

Decision trees, as discussed above, deal with conjunctions only. An "and-or" graph can be used to display a rule base so that conjunctions and disjunctions can be distinguished. If we consider the following rule base consisting of both conjunctions and disjunctions:

```
Rule 1: B ∧ C ⇒ A
Rule 2: D ∨ E ⇒ B
Rule 3: E ∧ F ⇒ C
Rule 4: G ∨ H ⇒ E
Rule 5: I ∧ J ⇒ H
```

This can be represented as an and-or graph as shown in Figure 7.4 where the arcs represent conjunctions.

If in this example, as a result of a change in domain knowledge, it is no longer necessary to establish `H` to show `E` we need to examine Rules 4 and 5. This can be established through some global identification technique. By inspecting the and-or graph in Figure 7.4 we

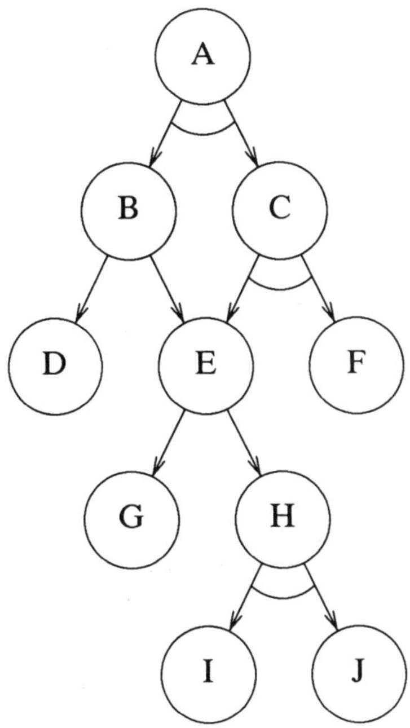

Figure 7.4: And-or graph.

can then see that the following maintenance actions are required:

1. Modify Rule 4 by removing the proposition `H` and adding the disjunction `I ∨ J`.
2. Delete Rule 5.

The disadvantage associated with and-or graphs (as well as decision trees) is that given a realistically sized rule base they often become unwieldy and impractical to use.

7.13. GRAPHERS

Graphers are software tools that produce directed graphs which express dependencies between literals. They are some times referred to as slot-rule dependency graphs or rule maps. One example is the Datamap [Coenen and Bench-Capon 1991] described below. Other examples include Yoon's Rulenet validation system which expresses dependencies of rule variables [Yoon 1989]. Again graphers display the elements that make up the rules/frames in a KB and can thus be used for local identification.

7.14. THE DATAMAP.

The Datamap [Coenen and Bench-Capon 1991] was developed as part of the Maintenance Assistance for Knowledge Engineers (MAKE) project [Coenen and Bench-Capon 1992a]. It produces a graphical view or tree structure of rules and slots to show the data path through a KB to the conclusions that can be drawn from the data. More specifically the Datamap is a directed (from left to right) bipartite graph which links attributes and rules. On the left hand side we will find the start attribute(s), with arcs to the rule identifiers in which the start attribute(s) act as the head. Arcs from these identifiers will connect to attributes in the body of the indicated rules. Further arcs will link to rule identifiers in which these attributes appear as the head (i.e. the attribute concerning which the rule indicated permits inference), and so on until the leaf attributes are reached.

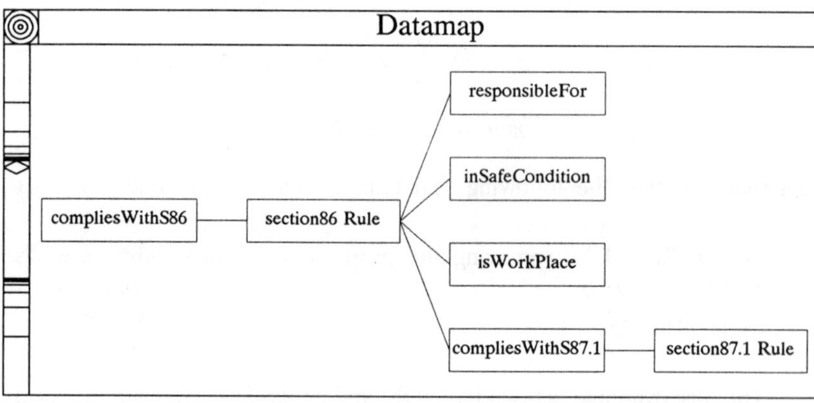

Figure 7.5: Datamap example 1 (root attribute option).

The Datamap may be drawn either from the root attribute(s) by default or any other start attribute as supplied by the user so that a lower portion of the tree can be investigated. The drawing is carried out from the desired attribute, first by identifying the rules in which the start attribute appears as the head, then the attributes in the body of the identified rules and so on. Figure 7.5 shows a Datamap drawn in default mode, it represents the rules developed in section 5.7 using MAUDE. Note that only a limited number of levels of rule-attribute pairs are drawn. This is because of the limited amount of screen space

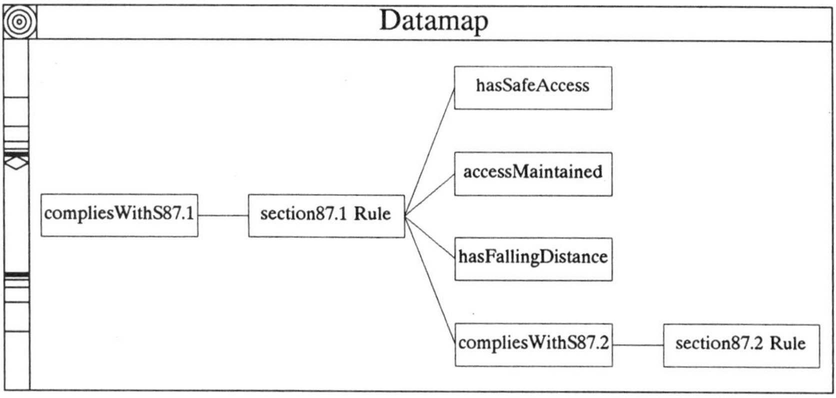

Figure 7.6: Datamap example 2 (start attribute option).

that it is envisaged will be available. The information displayed in these four levels, although restricted, is enough to allow the user to navigate through the KB. To obtain more information the user can scroll left (and back). Figure 7.6 shows a similar example, but where the maintenance engineer has selected the attribute `compliesWithS87.1` as the start attribute.

The thing shown most clearly by the Datamaps in Figures 7.5 and 7.6 is the relationship between attributes and rules. It shows in which rules attributes appear (through the arcs), and the role that they play in those rules. Thus having discovered a rule that requires attention the user can quickly identify the attributes associated with it and the other rules connected to it. The thing shown least clearly by the Datamaps in Figures 7.5 and 7.6 is which entities the attributes belong to. For example in Figure 7.5 the body attributes `inSafeCondition`, `isWorkPlace` and `compliesWithS87.1` refer to the entity `buildingStructure`. The attribute `compliesWithS86`, however, refers to the entity `mineManager`, the latter is in fact a relational attribute connecting the building to the manager; however, this is not apparent from the Datamap in the figure.

This ambiguity can be resolved by allowing the user to inspect the clause-proposition level of representation. In MAUDE this is the lowest level at which knowledge is recorded, it can be viewed and governs the "fine grain" behaviour of a system. An alternative Datamap can therefore be used to display this clause-proposition knowledge in a separate window by selecting an alternative view option. In this case the Datamap is drawn starting with the head proposition(s) derived from the selected start attribute. The clause identifiers in which this

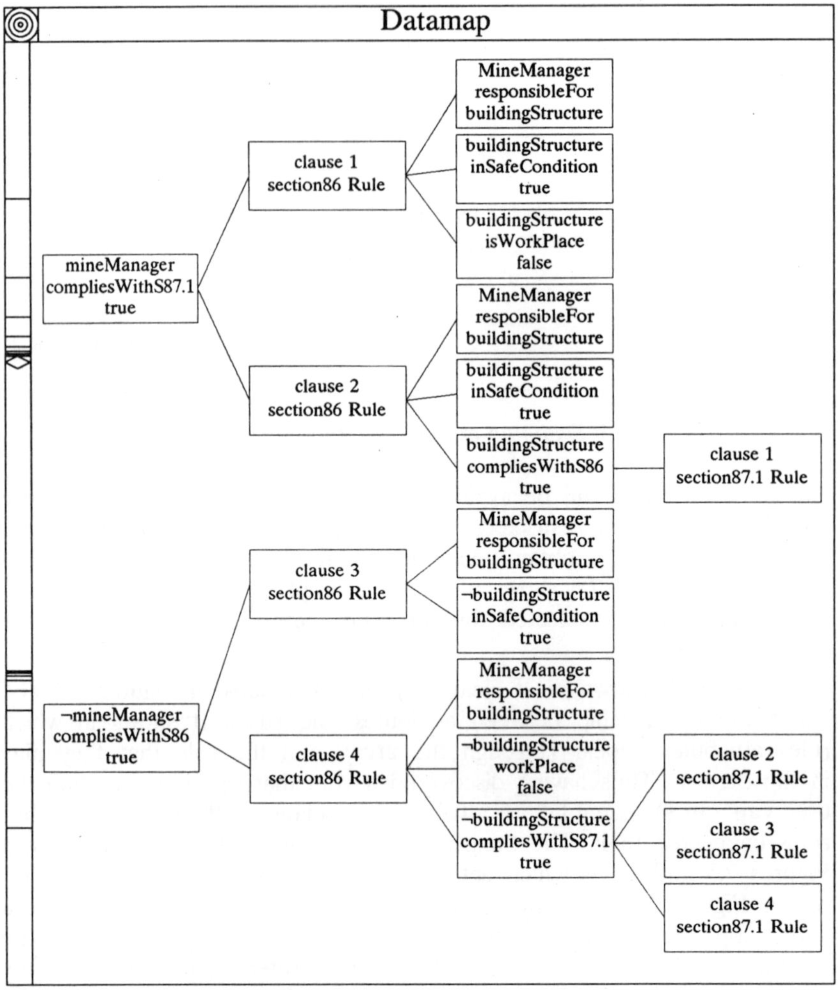

Figure 7.7: Datamap example 3 (clausal level).

proposition appears are then produced and displayed. This is followed by the tail propositions associated with these clauses, followed by the clauses in which these tail propositions appear as the head (if any). An example clause-proposition Datamap is given in Figure 7.7. Again because of the envisaged limited amount of space available only four levels of clause-proposition pairs are shown; however, the user is again free to scroll along the Datamap till the leaf propositions are reached. Due to the clausal form used in CMIR all propositional furcations in the graph represent conjunctions. Thus any two or more propositions branching out from a clause are conjoined, while any two or more clauses branching out from a proposition represent alternatives. In other words we can identify "and" and "or" connectors from the graph.

The clausal Datamap clearly shows the entities that each attribute refers to. Thus the fact that the `compliesWithS86` attribute refers to the entity `mineManager` is clearly identifiable. However, a disadvantage is a substantial increase in the amount of information displayed which can quickly lead to a very cluttered, and sometimes difficult to interpret, display, this is why it is recommended that the rule-attribute level should be used initially for global identification.

Thus, to summarise, the rule-attribute Datamap can be used to locate suspect rules (global identification). When found these rules can be examined to determine what other rules will be affected if the suspect rule is changed (local identification). It may be that the aberrant behaviour of the rule is the result of some unwanted, malformed or missing clause. This situation may be difficult to identify by inspection of the rule alone but can be discovered by inspection of the clauses into which the rule compiles. Finally the Datamap can be used to identify the jeopardised sub-set of KB elements.

7.14.1. Datamap Facilities

The Datamap, when coupled with the MAUDE development environment, provides access to a number of additional facilities. These include:

1. A head propositions option to produces a list of head propositions and their associated clause identifiers in a separate window. The option may be used to allow the maintenance engineer to inspect the head propositions associated with attributes and identify the clauses in which they are contained without referring to the alternative Datamap. The option may also be used to allow the engineer to inspect propositions associated with attributes to determine whether roots are complete.

2. A body propositions option to displays the body propositions in which a selected attribute appears and the clause identifiers associated with these propositions. The option will allow the user to inspect the propositions contained in the body of a selected rule, without referring to the alternative Datamap.

3. A root propositions option similar to the head propositions option

except that it returns "NONE" if the selected attribute can not be linked to a root proposition. This option could be used to determine whether an attribute, and hence the associated proposition, is a root attribute or root proposition. The option would also assist the maintenance engineer when determining whether the KB is adequate to establish the information that the application requires by inspecting the root propositions. The root propositions of the KB must be exhaustive with respect to the possible values of the root attributes required by the task, and must partition the possible values in the desired way. Lastly the root proposition(s) option allows the maintenance engineer to determine whether the KB establishes anything not required. It may be that an attribute we are not interested in appears as a root with respect to the KB, in which case we will waste inference in establishing it.

4. A leaf proposition(s) option similar to the body proposition(s) option described above except that the Datamap will return "NONE" if the selected attribute is not a leaf attribute. This option would allow the maintenance engineer to determine whether the information required by the KB to establish a desired propositions can be obtained. By examining the leaf propositions the engineer can see whether they are things that the system user can be expected to supply. If they are not, rules must be added to the KB to unfold them into ascertainable information. The option is also of use in determining whether all leaf propositions in the KB are required to establish a desired conclusion i.e. some leaf proposition may be unnecessary. This will involve finding all leaf propositions which appear only on paths leading to non-desired root attributes. Finally this option can be used to check for missing branches. The structure of the KB and class hierarchy (in the case of MAUDE) must be such that all values for leaf propositions can be obtained either by direct reference to the the class hierarchy or by explicit input by the user i.e. the completion of appropriate forms. If not, further rules may have to be added or maintenance carried out on the class hierarchy and/or forms available. In the MAKE application user input is defined through a task description. Linking this to the Datamap would enable the automative finding of missing branches.

5. A values option which, when selected, is used to display the values that an attribute may have by referring to the propositions in which the attribute of interest is contained. This option also assists in checking that there are no missing branches in the KB by allowing the engineer to match possible attribute values with the contents of the class hierarchy.

6. An entities option, similar to the values option except that it returns the entities associated with an individual attribute, again by reference to the propositions in which the attribute is contained.

7. When carrying out KB maintenance it will eventually be necessary for the engineer to inspect individual rules as they are represented in the intermediate representation. Thus a "display rule" option simply to display an entire rule will be useful. A possible use of this option would be to allow the maintenance engineer to check that individual rules represent the source data. Using an isomorphic approach to KBS development individual rules should represent individual blocks of source, which can be inspected at this point by links established in the analysis phase. This option will also allow the maintenance engineer to inspect the "and" and "or" connections in the body of a rule, which is something that is not identifiable by inspection of the Datamap itself.

8. A "display clause" option similar to the display rule option except that all the clauses that a rule compiles into are displayed. This may be required during a maintenance session again to allow the maintenance engineer to inspect the effect of the "and" and "or" connections in rules or simply to examine specific KB clauses.

9. Finally a "display sources" option to display the source blocks that a particular rule is linked to. It is suggested that the source blocks linked to a rule be displayed in a separate window. In some cases there may be a great number of these blocks, thus it may be necessary for the maintenance engineer to be able to scroll the source blocks so that they can all be viewed.

7.15. THE CLASS-INSTANCE BROWSER

The Class-Instance Browser was also developed during the course of the MAKE project as part of the suite of MAUDE maintenance tools [Bench-Capon and Coenen 1991b]. It is a static left to right directed graph which displays the hierarchy of classes in the class hierarchy and the instances of each class that have been created as part of executing a particular case. It allows the user to scroll systematically up and down the class hierarchy focusing on particular classes and instances. An example is given in Figure 7.8 which shows a fragment of the British Coal application developed in section 5.7. The figure shows the classes `mineManager`, `workPlace` and `highWorkPlace` and the instances `Fred`, `WindingHouse` and `PaintShop` which have been created. By clicking on a particular instance of a class all information available concerning that instance is displayed in a neighbouring window. Provision is also made to add instances or values of attributes associated with instances.

A number of other KBS development tool kits include a similar facility, for example KEE or LOOPS.

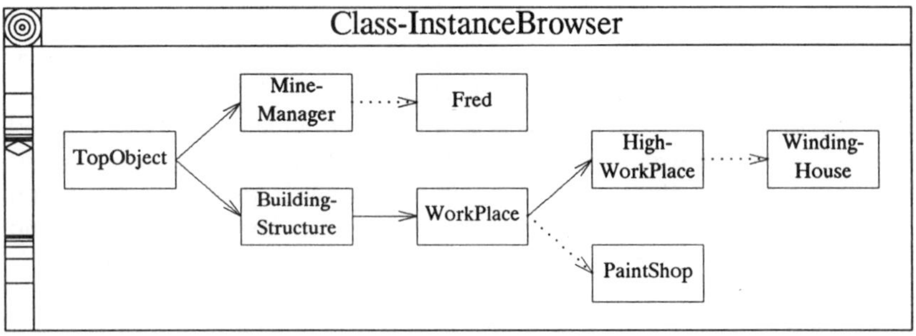

Figure 7.8: Class-instance browser.

7.16. HYBRID SYSTEMS

MAUDE is designed to produce hybrid systems where a class (frame) hierarchy defines the vocabulary for the rules in a rule base; maintenance of the hierarchy will affect the rules that use any slots that have undergone change. A tool to identify the rules which utilise the slots in question is therefore appropriate. This can be achieved simply by searching through the rule base and identifying all rules where the head or tail of a rule contains a changed slot. If we have a rule base of the form:

Rule 1: $\neg B(b) \vee C(a) \Rightarrow A(a)$
Rule 2: $D(a) \wedge E(b) \Rightarrow \neg B(b)$
Rule 3: $F(a) \vee G(a) \Rightarrow C(a)$

Where A to G are attributes in a class hierarchy which can have values (a), (b) or (c). We may wish to extend the range of possible values for (say) attribute B to include (d) in which case Rules 1 and 2 will be jeopardised. Rule 1 because B is contained in the tail (and we need to consider what we want when B(d)) and Rule 2 because B is contained in the head and so we need to consider whether we want $D(a) \wedge E(b)$ to imply B(d) or not. Simply recompiling Rule 1 will give the effective rule:

```
Rule 1.1: B(a c d) ∨ C(a) ⇒ A(a)
```

but since it was originally written in ignorance of the possibility B(d), it may be that:

```
¬(B(b) ∨ B(d)) ∨ C(a) ⇒ A(a)
```

is what is required. Similarly recompiling Rule 2 will give:

```
Rule 2.1: D(a) ∧ E(b) ⇒ B(a c d)
```

where as we may want only:

```
D(a) ∧ E(b) ⇒ B(a c)
```

Notice also that the answers may differ in the two cases: the recompiled version may be right for some rules and wrong for others.

We can also envisage a tool to identify slots which are jeopardised by the removal of a class because they are typed to that class.

7.17. SUMMARY

In this chapter we have considered the global and local identification of the elements of a KB on which some maintenance must be carried out. Global identification refers to the process of locating the broad area within a KB which requires attention. For example in a rule based system this may be a single rule or a group of rules; in a frame based system this may be a frame. Local identification refers to the process of finding the elements of a rule or frame which require attention, for example individual propositions or slots, and also the related elements in other rules or frames. We have also referred to the jeopardised set of elements in a rule or frame base, i.e. those KB elements that will be affected by a change. However, the jeopardised rule set will not necessarily be limited to the elements on which some maintenance has been implemented. The concept of a jeopardised rule set is important with respect to the testing of a system on completion of a maintenance session; this is discussed further in chapter 12.

We have identified a number of design philosophies and development techniques and tools that can be adopted for global identification.

These include isomorphism, linking, indexing, debugging tools and explanation facilities. For local identification there exist a number of graphical approaches to display a rule or frame base that will allow visual detection of the elements that will require attention. Examples that have been discussed include Petri-nets, decision trees and and-or graphs. We also consider a number of software tools that can be used for local identification, namely graphers such as the MAUDE Datamap tool and browsers such as the MAUDE Class-Instance browser.

CHAPTER 8

Errors and Anomalies

8.1. INTRODUCTION

One of the hazards associated with maintenance is that fixing one error in a system may have the additional effect of introducing new errors. Knowledge Based Systems (KBSs) are not immune from this danger. It is important therefore, after a maintenance session has taken place, to be able to review the new system so as to identify any errors that may have been introduced. We also make a distinction between *errors* and *anomalies*. Errors are clearly undesirable and will require further maintenance action to remove them; anomalies in contrast may not necessarily represent problems in themselves, but rather symptoms of genuine errors. Further, in some cases, the presence of certain anomalies may not be of significance, because although not strictly correct, they may not impair the functioning of the system.

In this chapter we consider, in detail, all the possible types of anomalies and errors that can occur in a KBS after a maintenance session has taken place. Many of the items considered have obvious parallels in the verification and validation of KBSs, since the defects that may result from maintenance can equally result from the initial construction of the knowledge base. Verification and validation of KBS has received considerably more attention that maintenance; thus, where applicable, we have drawn upon work carried out in this area. It should, however, be recognised that much of the published verification and validation work is concerned primarily with backward chaining production rule systems, and so is not always immediately relevant to KBSs based on other principles.

The major difference in between KBS maintenance and KBS verification and validation is that the first impinges on a system which is otherwise regarded as "correct". This opens up the possibility of limiting the parts of the Knowledge Base (KB) that need to be considered to those which may have been affected by the change, i.e. the jeopardised rule set.

Before commencing the discussion a short note on representations is needed. In this work we have concentrated on the three principal methods of knowledge representation used in KBSs: production rules, predicate logic and frame based representations. For the purpose of the discussion that follows there is no significant difference between production rule systems and predicate logic; we will refer to any system that uses these representations as a rule based system. Most of the work concerning the errors and anomalies that can occur in KBSs has been carried out on rule based representations. Parallels do exist with frame based representations (frame based representations can be translated into the predicate logic format). We will consider these parallels and also some potential errors peculiar to frame based systems. Thus the bulk of this chapter, the first part, applies to production rule and predicate logic systems, both forward and backward chaining; the second part relates this discussion to frame based systems. Finally we give some brief consideration to hybrid systems that use a mixture of frames and rules.

8.2. ERRORS AND ANOMALIES IN RULE BASED SYSTEMS

In this section we shall discuss in detail the errors and anomalies that may occur in a rule based system after a maintenance session has taken place.

In section 4.10 we identified four principal maintenance actions that can be implemented on a rule based system; we can add, remove, replace or modify a rule. We can identify a number of errors and anomalies that can result from the erroneous implementation of these maintenance actions:

- Redundancy.
- Dead end rules.
- Missing rules.
- Subsumption.
- Auxiliary rules.
- Circular rule sets.
- Incompleteness.
- Inconsistency.

A further set of errors can arise with respect to systems which include an indication of the level of confidence in rules and the inferences drawn from them, since the precision with which these confidence levels are calculated may be affected.

8.2.1. An Example Rule Base

In the following sections the anomalies and errors identified are defined and discussed in turn. To illustrate the discussion an example Knowledge Base (KB) is given. We have derived this example from a similar one given by Winston [1984] concerning the identification of animals in a zoo. This example was chosen because it is easy to understand and requires no specific domain knowledge. The KB is used to identify animals in a zoo which contains only tigers, lions, leopards (cheetahs - the rule base does not distinguish cheetahs and leopards), penguins and crocodiles. The KB is given below and by inspection of the comments associated with each rule we can see that it is littered with errors. For a fuller understanding these comments need to be read in conjunction with the sections which discuss the errors they identify.

Before continuing a number of points should be noted. Firstly the example rule base was produced without the benefit of using a development methodology or environment such as those described in chapter 5. This makes the rule base somewhat artificial, the consequence of which is that a number of the errors displayed would never have occurred if, for example, the KADS methodology, or similar, had been followed. Secondly, because of the many parallels between the errors and anomalies that can occur as a result of maintenance and those that should be identified during verification and validation of a KBS, some of the errors and anomalies displayed by the example rule base and discussed in the following sections have been included because they feature in much of the verification and validation literature. Finally some of the anomalies included, although considered to be errors by some authors, may not have any harmful effects in particular systems. For example some apparent anomalies, such as auxiliary rules, may be deliberately included in a KB out of a desire to maintain isomorphism with a knowledge source.

Our example rule base is as follows:

```
/* RULE 1: Absolute subsumption with RULE 6. */

animal type mammal
if
animal laysEggs no
and
animal gives milk

/* RULE 2: Compound subsumption with RULE 9, RULE 8 and RULE
10 (RULE 10 subsumes RULE 2, RULE 8 and RULE 9) and also
produces an indirect inconsistency between RULE 10 and
RULE 11 through RULE 8. */

animal type carnivore
if
animal eats meat

/* RULE 3: Ungulate is a redundant value for type; the rule
can thus be considered redundant; also complex subsumption
with RULE 4. */

animal type ungulate
if
animal feet hoofs
and
animal type mammal

/* RULE 4: Ungulate is a redundant value for type, the rule
can thus be considered redundant; also complex subsumption
with RULE 3. */

animal type ungulate
if
animal feet hoofs

/* RULE 5: An auxiliary rule to RULE 16. */

animal type reptile
if
animal skinCover scales
and
animal laysEggs yes

/* RULE 6: Absolute subsumption with RULE 1. */

animal type mammal
if
animal gives milk
and
animal laysEggs no
```

```
/* RULE 7: In circular rule set with rule 15, the rule also
implies that any animal that is not both a bird and a penguin
does fly (assuming that a negation as failure strategy is
used). */

animal flys no
if
animal type bird
and
animal isa penguin.

/* RULE 8: Compound subsumption with RULE 2, RULE 9 and
RULE 10. */

animal eats meat
if
animal feet claws
or
animal teeth pointed
and
animal eyes pointForward

/* RULE 9: Compound subsumption with RULE 2, RULE 8 and
RULE 10; also direct soft inconsistency with RULE 11 and
with RULE 12. */

animal isa tiger
if
animal type mammal
and
animal type carnivore

/* RULE 10: Compound subsumption with RULE 2, RULE 8 and
RULE 9 and also indirect soft inconsistency with RULE 11
through RULE 2 and RULE 8. */

animal isa tiger
if
animal type mammal
and
animal feet claws
and
animal teeth pointed
and
animal eyes pointForward
```

```
/* RULE 11: Direct inconsistency with RULE 10 and indirect
soft inconsistency with RULE 10 through RULE 2 and RULE 8. */

animal isa lion
if
animal type mammal
and
animal type carnivore

/* RULE 12: Direct soft inconsistency with RULE 9 .*/

animal isa lion
if
animal type mammal
and
animal type carnivore
and
animal skinCover tawny

/* RULE 13: Shares an irrelevant literal (animal isa cheetah)
with RULE 14. */

animal isa leopard
if
animal skinCover spots
and
animal type mammal
and
animal type carnivore
and
animal isa cheetah

/* RULE 14: Shares an irrelevant literal (animal isa cheetah)
with RULE 13. */

animal isa leopard
if
animal skinCover spots
and
animal type mammal
and
animal type carnivore
and
not animal isa cheetah
```

```
/* RULE 15: A Dead end rule (since animal type bird cannot be
established), and in addition forms a circular rule set with
RULE 7. */

animal isa penguin
if
animal type bird
and
animal flys no
and
animal eats fish

*/ RULE 16: RULE 5 is an auxiliary rule to this rule.  */

animal isa crocodile
if
animal type reptile
and
animal type carnivore
and
animal feet claws
```

8.2.2. Redundancy (Missing Links)

The concept of redundancy is often confused with that of subsumption. In this work a KB is considered to contain redundancy if a rule, or group of rules, plays no part in establishing the root proposition(s) of the KB. We make this distinction because we believe that a KBS is designed to solve one or more tasks, and that therefore anything in the supporting KB should make some contribution to the tasks it was designed for. Subsumption, to be discussed in a later section, in contrast concerns a rule which could have a use in solving the task were its function not usurped by some other rule. In the animals rule base the task that the KB is intended to perform is to establish the identity of animals. RULE 3 and RULE 4 are therefore redundant because they play no part establishing the identity of any animal: the conclusion that an animal is an ungulate is not used to identify any sort of animal. However, the head attribute - `type` - of these two rules *is* used by other rules: for example RULE 9 uses the types mammal and carnivore. Note also that type is not an exclusive attribute, so knowing that an animal is type ungulate cannot be said even to exclude any possibilities. In some representations this fact that a redundant rule may assign a useless value to a useful attribute can make them difficult to detect. It may also be important to record the fact that the attribute can take this value for the attribute, and this may be an argument for leaving such rules in the KB. A purer form of redundancy is the situation where the redundancy in question concerns an attribute rather than a value for an attribute: i.e. an attribute not referenced in the tail of any rule. This situation would have existed in the example had the heads of RULE 3 and RULE 4 been `animal ungulate true`. In such a case the whole attribute is irrelevant to the task, and there seems no good reason to retain such rules. We can therefore make a distinction between redundancy of attributes and redundancy of certain values of otherwise useful attributes. We will refer to the first as absolute redundancy and the second as partial redundancy.

Redundancy may result because of an error in the head of the redundant rule or because there is a missing rule which should be in the KB to link the apparently redundant rule to the other rules, in which case the redundancy undoubtedly represents an error and will adversely affect the operation of the system. Alternatively it may be that the redundant rule is simply there because it is an earlier version of an existing rule that has not been expunged, in which case the existence of the redundancy will not adversely affect the KB. Lastly it may be that the redundant rule is included in the KB in anticipation of future maintenance, i.e. the arrival of a giraffe, zebra or other ungulate in the zoo, in which case it should not be lost altogether.

In Chang's EVA system [Chang *et al.* 1990], which is designed to be implemented on backward chaining systems, redundant rules as defined here are referred to as containing unreachable literals. A consequent literal is considered to be unreachable if it cannot be matched by any antecedent literal of any rule.

Ginsberg [1987] considers a rule in a KB to be "redundant" if it contains one or more rules which can be removed without changing the set of conclusions asserted by the KB for any valid input. It should be noted that this definition also covers subsumption as defined in this work (see section 8.2.5).

There are many other attempts to define redundancy. Cragen and Steudel [1987] suggests that redundancy occurs where the same logical conditions satisfy more than one rule, but the actions are the same, i.e duplication. Agarwal and Tanniru [1991] and Nguyen *et al.* [1987] also equate redundancy with duplication, as do Stachowitz and Combs [1987]. Stachowitz and Combs also refer to subsumption as redundancy. We prefer to distinguish duplication from redundancy and consider such duplication to be a special form of subsumption, namely absolute subsumption. Subsumption is discussed in section 8.2.5 below.

Irrelevant Literals

If we have two rules, designed to infer some literal, `C`, which are duplicates except for the fact that a literal `A` appears in the body of Rule 1 and `¬A` in the body of Rule 2, or vice versa, the literal `A` is redundant because it does not play any part in establishing C, which can be inferred whether A is true or false. A is therefore considered to be an irrelevant literal, since the rules would be better combined with A omitted since the presence of such a literal will at best lead to inefficiency and at worst mean that a justified inference cannot be drawn until the value of A is determined.

Thus if we have two rules:

```
Rule 1:  A ∧ B ⇒ C
Rule 2: ¬A ∧ B ⇒ C
```

The literal A is irrelevant and the rule can (and should) be combined into the single rule: B ⇒ C. In our animals rule base RULE 13 and RULE 14 contain the literal `animal is a cheetah` with a positive occurrence in RULE 13 and a negative occurrence in RULE 14. This literal can therefore be considered to be irrelevant in the context of these two rules, and they would be better combined into a single rule in which the literal was omitted.

Nguyen *et al.* [1987] use the term "unnecessary if conditions" to describe this situation. They also identify a special case where two rules have the same conclusion but one rule contains a single condition that conflicts with an `if` condition in the other rule which has two or more conditions:

```
Rule 1: A ∧ B ⇒ C
Rule 2:     ¬A ⇒ C
```

The first condition in rule 1 is not needed, since if A is false, ¬A is satisfied, but both rules are still required, since the second is required when ¬B, and C remains unproven when both ¬B and ¬A. The two rules should be presented as follows:

```
Rule 1a:  B ⇒ C
Rule 2a: ¬A ⇒ C
```

This preserves the basic structure of the two rules but removes the ambiguity.

8.2.3. Dead End Rules (Missing Leaves)

In this work a dead end rule, a term originally used, with obvious application, in relation to systems that use backward chaining, is defined as a rule whose antecedent cannot be satisfied because it contains a literal which cannot match either a fact, i.e. it is not askable or obtainable from any other external source, or a literal in the consequent of any other rule. This definition is also adopted in the EVA system [Chang *et al.* 1990 and Stachowitz and Combs 1987]. A dead end rule indicates a deficiency in the rule base in that either:

1. An error exists in the tail of the dead end rule, since it cannot have been intended that an unsatisfiable condition be included in the rule.
2. A missing rule exists which is intended to satisfy the antecedent in the suspect rule.
3. Arrangements should have been made for the user or some other external source to satisfy the antecedent by establishing it as an askable fact.

In a forward chaining system the equivalent situation arises when there are inappropriate leaf literals; i.e. the current leaves do not represent askable propositions. In such cases we must write rules to allow them to be inferred, or specify the external source from which they may be obtained.

If we consider our animals rule base RULE 15 may be considered to be a dead end rule if we assume that the predicate `animal type bird` is neither a fact nor something which the user is intended to supply.

8.2.4. Missing Rules

Missing rules may exist whenever either a redundant or dead end rule is detected. In the first case a rule may be required to provide the link between the head of the redundant rule and the rest of the KB. In the second a rule may be required so that the facts in the consequent part of a dead end rule can be matched. Such missing rules can be detected by an examination of the KB, but a KB may also be considered to contain missing rules if it is incomplete, in the sense of failing to establish conclusions in all circumstances. This is a rather different problem - one of content rather than structure - and is discussed in section 8.2.8 below.

8.2.5. Subsumption

As observed earlier the terms subsumption and redundancy are often confused or considered to be synonymous. We have already discussed redundancy in section 8.2.2, in this section we consider subsumption. We can identify several types of subsumption, namely:

1. Absolute Subsumption.
2. Complex Subsumption.
3. Compound Subsumption.

These different types of subsumption are discussed in turn in the following sub-sections. Subsumption does not normally affect the operation of a rule base, since subsumed rules will not ordinarily affect the outcome, unless the system estimates the level of confidence in its conclusions. In systems which do attempt to estimate levels of confidence two rules with the same effect may erroneously strengthen a conclusion. Problems can also result in a system which does not use confidence levels when, as the consequence of the need to change the KB, one rule is altered whilst the other is left in place with the incorrect effect.

Absolute Subsumption

We define absolute subsumption as straightforward duplication; i.e. the KB contains two or more rules which have identical antecedents and consequents except, perhaps, for the order of the literals. For example the following two rules are duplicates:

```
Rule 1: A ∧ B ∧ C ⇒ D
Rule 2: B ∧ C ∧ A ⇒ D
```

This is illustrated in our example rule base by RULE 1 and RULE 6, where the conditions and the conclusions of the two rules are the same, with only the order of the conditions changed. Absolute subsumption may represent either an error in the content of the rule, for example if a mistake has been made when writing of the rule, or an error in the structure of the KB; for example the author of the duplicate rule may have been unaware of the existence of the original. In the former case the rule must be rewritten, in the latter case one of the copies needs to be removed.

Absolute subsumption is referred to by Suwa *et al.* [1984] as "redundancy" and by Agarwal and Tanniru [1991] as "absolute redundancy". Suwa's definition for "redundancy" is the situation where two rules succeed in the same situation and have the same result.

Absolute subsumption usually does not adversely effect a KBS other than making its operation slightly less efficient. Problems will arise, however, if some maintenance action is implemented on one of the duplicates and not on the other. Also, where a KB incorporates a scoring system, such as certainty factors, duplicate information may lead to erroneous increases in the weighting of inferred conclusions.

Complex Subsumption

Complex subsumption occurs when one rule is a more specialised case of another. Thus when two rules have duplicate consequents and the antecedent of one is a subset of the antecedent of the other, or when two rules have duplicate antecedents and the consequent of one is a subset of the consequent of the other, or a mixture of these states, we have complex subsumption. This definition is supported by that given by Suwa *et al.* [1984] who define subsumption as the situation where two rules exist that have the same result, but one contains additional restrictions on the situations in which it will succeed. In our example rule base we can see that RULE 4 subsumes RULE 3 because RULE 3 contains the extra condition "animal type mammal".

Alternatively if we consider the following two rules:

```
Rule 1: B ∨ C ⇒ A
Rule 2: B ∧ C ⇒ A
```

The second rule is subsumed by the previous rule, which will succeed if either of the conjuncts in Rule 2 are true.

Rules can, as we use the term, be arbitrary expressions. It is often helpful to re-write rules into a normal form such as clausal form. This is standard when the KB is written in Horn Clauses or production rules which do not permit disjunctive conditions. If we do this we can identify cases where individual clauses deriving from rules are subsumed although the rules as a whole may not be subsumed. A subsumed clause is either:

1. A clause which is generated from a rule which is wholly subsumed.
2. A clause which is generated from a rule which is not wholly subsumed but which need never play a role in establishing a root proposition because a more general clause supersedes it.

An example of the latter is as follows. We may have two rules:

```
Rule 1: (B ∨ C) ∧ (D ∨ E) ⇒ A
Rule 2:              C ∨ F ⇒ A
```

We can translate these rules into the following clauses:

```
Clause 1.1: B ∧ D ⇒ A
Clause 1.2: B ∧ E ⇒ A
Clause 1.3: C ∧ D ⇒ A
Clause 1.4: C ∧ E ⇒ A
Clause 2.1:     C ⇒ A
Clause 2.2:     F ⇒ A
```

Here Clause 2.1 Subsumes Clauses 1.3 and 1.4. Thus individual clauses may be subsumed without the rule from which they stem being subsumed, since Clauses 1.1 and 1.2 remain unsubsumed. None the less we would probably want to rewrite Rule 1 so as to exclude C, and eliminate clauses 1.3 and 1.4 from the KB, thus:

```
B ∧ (D ∨ E) ⇒ A
```

This kind of example shows that the identification of subsumed rules and clauses should best take place at the clausal level of representation, a subsumed rule being seen as one in which all its clauses are subsumed.

Complex subsumption is referred to by many authors as redundancy [Ginsberg 1987, Nguyen *et al.* 1987, Stachowitz and Combs 1987 and Chang *et al.* 1991]. Chang defines "redundancy" as follows:

> "Given two rules R1 and R2, if the LHS of R1 subsumes the LHS of R2, and if forward chaining is used, then whenever R2 can be fired, R1 also can be fired. Therefore, any actions in the RHS of R2 which also occur in the RHS of R1 will be redundant."

Thus if we have two rules:

```
Rule 1:       A ⇒ C
Rule 2: A ∧ B ⇒ C
```

Rule 2 will be "redundant" according to Chang and exhibit complex subsumption according to the definition used in this work. Had Rule 2 had two actions, say `C ∧ D`, then `C` alone would have been redundant, and a version of this rule would still have been required:

```
Rule 2a: A ∧ B ⇒ D
```

Again this situation is most clearly seen if the rules is analysed into clauses.

Complex subsumption can be considered to represent an error of content in the writing of the rule. In many cases the author would not have even been aware that a risk of complex subsumption existed.

The presence of complex subsumption will not necessarily always be an indication of an error. In KBSs which use certainty factors rules which are more specialised forms of other rule quite often feature so that the more restrictive rules add weight to conclusions made by less restrictive rules. In such cases the author needs to be very clear as to the effect of these extra rules on conclusions. Although complex subsumption will always affect efficiency, in a system where the first successful rule is the only one to succeed, a problem will only arise if one of two subsumed rules is modified or deleted and the other is left unchanged.

Compound Subsumption

Compound subsumption occurs as a result of chained inferences. Thus if we consider RULE 9, RULE 2, RULE 8 and RULE 10 in our animals example rule base, `animal isa tiger` in RULE 9 is true if `animal type mammal` and `animal type carnivore` are true. `animal type carnivore` is established by reference to RULE 2 and is true if `animal eats meat` is true which in turn is established by RULE 8. However, this chain of inferences is effectively summarised by RULE 10, where the conditions of RULE 9 have been unfolded into the conditions supplied by the other rules. We therefore say that RULE 10 is subsumed by RULE 9, RULE 2 and RULE 8. Alternatively if `animal isa carnivore` and `animal eats meat` were neither inferences required by some other rule nor information that the user could potentially supply we could say instead that RULE 10 subsumes RULE 9, RULE 2 and RULE 8, since there would be no benefit from having the three rules instead of one.

Similar examples are also given by Charles, for the MELODIA verification program, and Preece who both refer to this type of subsumption as "redundancy".

Charles in the MELODIA verification program [Charles 1991] considers a rule R to be redundant if the set of rules {KB - R} is equivalent to {KB}. According to this definition if we have a set of rules:

```
Rule 1:       A ⇒ E
Rule 2: A ∨ B ⇒ C
Rule 3: C ∧ A ⇒ E
```

Rule 3 is "redundant" because E can be deduced from A alone using Rule 1. However, in this work we would consider Rule 3 to be subsumed by Rule 1 (complex subsumption) or, if E played no other role in the system, that Rule 1 subsumes Rules 2 and 3 (compound subsumption). This is an important point - what is subsumed cannot be determined except by reference to the task towards which the KBS is directed.

Preece and Shinghal [1991a, 1991b] state that "redundancy" exists where for two or more expressions in a KB, given all possible fact bases, the result is the same. More formally Preece states that for a KB with n rules, I1 ... In, rule Ij is "redundant" if it is a logical consequence of rules I1 ... Ij-1, Ij+1 ... In. For example if we consider the following:

```
Rule 1: A ⇒ B
Rule 2: B ⇒ C
Rule 3: C ⇒ D
Rule 4: A ⇒ D
```

Here Preece would claim that Rule 4 is "redundant" because it can be inferred from Rules 1, 2 and 3. We would consider that Rule 4 is subsumed by Rules 1, 2 and 3 (compound subsumption) or if B and C were not required by any other rule, or capable of being supplied by the user, that Rules 1, 2 and 3 were subsumed by Rule 4 (also compound subsumption).

8.2.6. Auxiliary Rules

An auxiliary rule is a rule that has been included in a KB purely to reflect the structure of the domain (isomorphism), or to add structure and comprehension, or to facilitate future modification. However, undesired auxiliary rules may introduce inefficiencies into the KB, and so they should not be introduced without some such good reason. For example one very common use of auxiliary rules is to replace a disjunction by a single predicate which succeeds if either of the disjuncts is satisfied. This can eliminate disjunctions from rules, and hence make them easier to read. Moreover, we can perhaps stipulate further conditions where the disjunction may hold, although we cannot say which of the disjuncts is responsible for its truth.

If we consider RULE 16 and RULE 5 in our animal rule base, the predicate `animal type reptile` does not need to be established through a separate rule to show that `animal isa crocodile` is true because there are no other reptiles in our zoo, and so the head of RULE 5 could simply be replaced by `animal isa crocodile`. In this case, however, we may wish to retain the auxiliary rule so as to allow for the introduction of other reptiles to the zoo.

Agarwal and Tanniru [1991] give a similar but simpler example involving auxiliary rules:

```
Rule 1: A ⇒ B
Rule 2: B ⇒ C
```

Here Rule 2 is considered to be an auxiliary rule to Rule 1 as both rules can be collapsed into the single rule:

```
Rule 3: A ⇒ C
```

We could argue that a KB contains auxiliary rules if we can contrive a rule that subsumes two or more existing rules in the KB. For example in the above case Rule 3 subsumes Rules 1 and 2 (compound subsumption).

8.2.7. Circular Rule Sets

Circularity presents an urgent problem in backward chaining systems when a KBS contains a set of rules such that an non-terminating loop can occur when the rules are fired. Thus:

```
Rule 1: A ⇒ B
Rule 2: B ⇒ A
```

This is illustrated in our example rule base by RULE 7 and RULE 15. `animal flys false` is established by RULE 7, in which `animal isa penguin` is established by RULE 15 in which `animal flys false` is established by returning to RULE 7 and so on.

We can distinguish between direct cycles, where the rule calls itself, and indirect cycles, where several rules are involved. This distinction is also made by Stachowitz and Combs [1987]:

INDIRECT CYCLE.

```
Rule 1: A ⇒ B
Rule 2: B ⇒ A
```

DIRECT CYCLE.

```
Rule 1: A ∧ B ⇒ B
```

However, in the case of a direct cycle it is hard to envisage a situation where a developer would write such a rule.

In some forward chaining systems, for example systems developed using MAUDE, circular rule sets do not result in a non-terminating loop and are therefore not considered to represent an error, since occasions can be envisaged where either one of the rules would be effective. In some cases where inference is forward chaining there may be a distinct advantage in introducing this kind of circularity. For example in a forward chaining system we may have two rules that would, in a backward chaining system, call each other: one that produces a value for an attribute temperature in Fahrenheit and another that produces the value in Centigrade. This would be useful in a forward chaining system when the temperature might be asserted using either scale, since the appropriate rule would then fire to convert the temperature to the alternative scale.

8.2.8 Incompleteness

In this work a KB is considered to be incomplete if there exist possible legal sets of facts from which no useful conclusion can be inferred.

Preece and Shinghal [1991a, 1991b] refer to incompleteness as a "deficiency" in a KBS. They consider a KB to be deficient if there exists a permissible fact base from which no conclusions can be inferred. For example if we consider the following rule base (where the Arabic numerals represent values for the attributes `A` to `E`):

```
Rule 1:          A(1) ∧ B(1) ⇒ C(1)
Rule 2:          C(1) ∧ D(1) ⇒ E(1)
Rule 3:          C(1) ∧ D(2) ⇒ E(2)
Rule 4: A(1) ∧ B(2) ∧ D(1) ⇒ E(3)
```

and `A`, `B` and `D` are leaf attributes which can have the values of `(1)` and `(2)`. There are eight possible combinations in which the values for these leaf attributes can be combined, constituting eight legal sets of facts or *fact bases* as they are sometimes called:

```
{A(1) B(1) D(1)}
{A(1) B(1) D(2)}
{A(1) B(2) D(1)}
{A(1) B(2) D(2)}
{A(2) B(1) D(1)}
{A(2) B(1) D(2)}
{A(2) B(2) D(1)}
{A(2) B(2) D(2)}
```

Rules 1 to 4 only supply inferences with respect to `E` in the first three of these cases. It may be that some of these fact bases are illegal: for example we might say that the set {`A(2)` and `B(1)`} is illegal because this conjunction of facts cannot be realised in the real world. Eliminating the fact bases containing this unrealisable combination still leaves three fact bases from which nothing can be inferred {`A(1)` and `B(2)` and `D(2)`}, {`A(2)` and `B(2)` and `D(1)`} and {`A(2)` and `B(2)` and `D(2)`}. Preece's definition therefore suggests that this KB is deficient.

Other definitions for completeness include that put forward by Cragen and Steudel [1987]. According to Cragen and Steudel a KB is complete when all possible combinations of logic are addressed by the rules in a decision table, i.e. there are no missing rules. This definition is compatible with the definition used in this work.

Whatever the case, to identify incompleteness an expert is required to identify and hence eliminate illegal sets of facts, since there is no point, or even possibility, in providing for such cases. If out of any of the remaining fact bases nothing can be inferred the rule base can be said to be incomplete, and further knowledge must be supplied and encoded.

We can also derive examples using numeric ranges. Given the fact that an attribute `age` can have a numeric range of between 0 and 110 and two rules:

```
person(X) ∧ age(<12) ⇒ child(X)
person(X) ∧ age(>18) ⇒ adult(X)
```

The rule base can be said to be incomplete because no inference exists if age is greater or equal to 12 and less than or equal to 18. A rule base which is incomplete in this sense will present problems in that there will be cases where the system is unable to offer an answer to the question posed to it. This may not, however, be a deficiency in the KB itself, since it may be that the state of knowledge of the experts is such that they are unable to supply the information that would enable the KB to be complete. For example, we may actually want a 15 year old to be regarded neither as a child nor as an adult. Identification of such deficiencies may well therefore be best used to guide the knowledge elicitation process to close such gaps, or, where the gaps are significant and incapable of being closed, they may indicate that the domain is not really well enough understood to permit the effective use of a KBS.

Soundness

Soundness may be regarded as the complement to completeness. Whereas completeness demands that everything that is true is derivable, soundness demands that everything derivable is true. In our example animal rule base, Rule 7, could be used to show that any animal that is not both a bird and a penguin can fly, supposing that we interpret negation as failure. Thus a consequence of using this interpretation of negation on the rule base would be that, for example, tigers can fly. Clearly the example rule base is unsound under this interpretation.

Often there is a trade off between soundness and completeness. If we attempt to cover every situation we may well introduce rules which are not in fact universally applicable. This tendency is most clearly seen when default rules are used, since here conclusions are drawn in the absence of conclusive information. For example if we consider the following set of PROLOG clauses:

```
flies(X,no):-
    ostrich(X).

flies(X,no):-
    penguin(X).

flies(X,yes):-
    bird(X).

flies(X,yes):-
    bat(X).

flies(X,no).
```

This uses two default rules that all birds except ostriches and penguins fly, and all non-birds except bats do not. This enables us to conclude as to whether an animal not explicitly mentioned can fly, giving us completeness, but is unsound in the case of kiwis and certain insects. Thus the technique of using default rules buys the ability to always reach a conclusion at the price of sometimes (hopefully rarely) producing the wrong conclusions.

8.2.9. Contradiction and Inconsistency

A contradiction in classical logic at its simplest consists of a statement of the form:

$$A \text{ and } \neg A$$

A contradiction can be defined as follows [Lemmon 1965 and Rousset 1988]:

> "A theory is inconsistent if and only if it is possible to derive $\emptyset$ (or A and ¬A for some literal A) from the set of axioms of the theory."

In this work we refer to such a contradiction as a hard contradiction. Such cases tend to be relatively rare in KBSs, as the majority of representations do not permit the explicit drawing of negative conclusions. However, if we have two rules:

```
Rule 1: A(1) ∧ B(1) ⇒  C(1)
Rule 2: A(1) ∧ B(1) ⇒ ¬C(1)
```

where `A` and `B` are attributes and the Arabic numerals values for those attributes the two rules might be said to contradict one another directly, even though there is no hard contradiction, as described above, in this case. What this pair of rules does imply is that `A(1)` and `B(1)` cannot both be true together, since that situation would enable a hard contradiction to be drawn. This, however, does not necessarily represent an error unless we know that `A(1)` and `B(1)` can hold simultaneously. To distinguish this situation from the hard contradiction found in classical logic we refer to this as an inconsistency. We say that an inconsistency occurs when the falsity of some proposition, or conjunction of propositions, is a consequence of the KB whereas it is in fact known that it is possible. In the simplest possible case we may have two rules:

```
Rule 1: A ⇒  B
Rule 2: A ⇒ ¬B
```

Here `¬A` is a logical consequence of the KB. If, however, `A` represents a contingent proposition, something which we know to be sometimes true and sometimes false, this would indicate that our KB is in error. If we consider another example:

```
Rule 1: A ∧ B ⇒ ¬C
Rule 2:     A ⇒ C
```

This system would not be contradictory according to the classical definition although if `A` is true `B` must be false. However, an inconsistency does exist as a contradiction will occur, in a KBS consisting of these two rules, if the user inputs `A` and `B` as true.

Stachowitz and Combs [1987] also refer to this situation as inconsistency; other authors use the terms contradiction, ambiguity or conflict. Stachowitz maintains that a rule base displays inconsistency if it contains two rules with duplicate antecedents but in the consequents a clause is both affirmed and denied. However, it should be noted that this can be a deliberate feature of the KB. If we wish to exclude certain conjunctions of propositions as impossible, that is to impose integrity constraints on the KB, the most convenient way of doing so may well be to write rules of this form.

We can also identify a modification of this situation, where the contradiction is implicit rather than the explicit affirmation and denial of the same literal. If we consider the following two rules:

```
Rule 1: A(1) ∧ B(1) ⇒ C(1)
Rule 2: A(1) ∧ B(1) ⇒ C(2)
```

Again `C` cannot have both the values `1` and `2`, therefore some contradiction must exist. However, again, there is no hard contradiction here although a logical consequence of the KB is that at least one of `A(1)` and `B(1)` must be false. We refer to this situation as a soft inconsistency. This is displayed in our example rule base by RULE 9 and RULE 11 from which, for the same tail propositions, we can establish that `animal` is both a `tiger` and a `lion.` RULE 9 is also inconsistent with RULE 12 according to this definition. Thus we may consider that a soft inconsistency exists when the same set of logical conditions satisfy two or more rules that have different actions.

Agarwal and Tanniru [1991] refer to this type of inconsistency as a potential hard contradiction, waiting to be realised given a suitable fact base. Rousset [1988] defines this type of soft inconsistency as:

> "An RB of a KBS is said to be (softly) *inconsistent if there exists some meaningful initial Fact Base (FB) such that RB,FB/--∅."*

Rousset stresses that the FB must be meaningful - fact bases that cannot occur may rightly be excluded by these *prima facie* inconsistencies - and that this can only be identified by a domain expert which in turn leads Rousset to conclude that consistency checking must involve some interactive mechanism. Preece and Shinghal [1991a, 1991b] consider that a KB that contains an inconsistency of this type is "ambivalent" and Stachowitz and Combs [1987] that it contains a "semantic inconsistency". Preece states that a KB is ambivalent if for some fact base we can infer an illegal set of conclusions and gives the following PROLOG example:

```
graduate(x):-
        enrolled_in(x,y),
        grad_course(y).
```

```
undergrad(x):-
        enrolled_in(x,y),
        undergrad_course(y).

grad_course(60ms).

undergrad_course(63cs).
```

If we know that the set of inferences {graduate(x), undergraduate(x)} is illegal and that a fact base which can lead to this set of illegal inferences is possible, say {enrolled_in(fred,60ms), enrolled_in(fred,63cs)}, then the KB is ambivalent.

In addition we can identify two types of inconsistency and soft inconsistency, namely direct and indirect. All the examples we have considered so far involve just two rules which clash with one another. But, of course, the clash may develop through a chain of rules. For example, if consider the rule base:

```
Rule 1: A(1) ∧ B(1) ⇒ C(1)
Rule 2:        A(1) ⇒ D(1)
Rule 3: D(1) ∧ B(1) ⇒ C(2)
```

Here we have an indirect soft inconsistency in that both `C(1)` and `C(2)` can be inferred from `A(1)` and `B(1)`. In our animals rule base this is illustrated by RULE 10, RULE 11 and RULE 2 and RULE 8. Stachowitz and Combs [1987] also differentiates between direct and indirect inconsistency. Ginsberg [1987] has made a similar observation.

8.2.10. Precision

Precision is specific to systems that produce probabilistic outcomes or deliver qualified judgements. For example MYCIN [Buchanan and Shortliffe 1984] accumulates evidence for a particular hypothesis by a system of certainty factors which act as weightings on evidence and rules. However, as a result of subsumption and rules simply being wrong the accuracy with which this value is calculated can be affected. For example, one rule that subsumes another may cause an error by causing the same evidence to be counted twice. Alternatively the knowledge engineer may have purposely written the rules so that the more restrictive one adds a little more weight to the conclusion made by the less restrictive one. Fixing these problems can only be achieved through "fine tuning" with respect to a set of reliable test cases.

8.3. ERRORS AND ANOMALIES IN FRAME BASED SYSTEMS

In this section we extend the above discussion to the corresponding errors and anomalies that may occur in frame based systems. The discussion is illustrated using a frame base similar to the animals rule base used to illustrated the previous discussion concerning rule based systems. This will help to point out correspondences between the two representational approaches. However, to achieve this correspondence a significant number of (unnecessary) auxiliary slots have had to be included.

Errors that can occur during maintenance of a frame based system can be categorised under the following headings:

- Redundancy.
- Missing slots and frames.
- Misplaced slots and frames.
- Duplication.
- Auxiliary slots and frames.
- Inconsistency and incompleteness.
- Errors related to numeric ranges.
- Errors associated with cardinality.

The animals frame base is given below. The "◇" symbol, taken from the MAUDE KBS development environment, simply indicates a field break. It should be remembered that frame based systems generally display some form of inheritance mechanism. Thus in the example frame base all slots belonging to a super-frame are inherited by its sub-frames. In some cases there is a value for the slot given in brackets. This may be interpreted as a "default" value for that slot. As designed here these values should never need to be cancelled, thus a better interpretation would be that these values are necessary conditions for membership of frames.

The animals frame base is as follows:

```
/* Contains a redundant slot, "habitat". */

Frame: Animals
superFrame: Top Frame
◇ slot laysEggs
◇ slot givesMilk
◇ slot feet
◇ slot skinCover
◇ slot eats
◇ slot habitat

/* Contains no intentional errors. */

   Frame: Mammals
   superFrame: Animals
   ◇ slot type (mammal)
   ◇ slot laysEggs (false)
   ◇ slot givesMilk (true)

/* Contains a misplaced slot, "eyes", and a number of
auxiliary slots with respect to the frames "Tigers" and
"Lions". */

      Frame: Carnivores
      superFrame: Mammals
      ◇ slot type (carnivore)
      ◇ slot eats (meat)
      ◇ slot feet (claws)
      ◇ slot teeth (pointed)
      ◇ slot eyes (pointForward)

/* The frame "Carnivores" contains auxiliary slots to this
frame. */

         Frame: Tigers
         superFrame: Carnivores
         ◇ slot skinCover (Stripes)
         ◇ slot isa (tiger)

/* The frame "Carnivores" contains auxiliary slots to this
frame. */

         Frame: Lions
         superFrame: Carnivores
         ◇ slot skinCover (tawny)
         ◇ slot isa (lion)
```

```
/* Frame cannot be uniquely differentiated from the frame
"Cheetahs" */

         Frame: Leopards
         superFrame: Carnivore
         ◇ slot skinCover (spots)
         ◇ slot isa (leopard)

/* Frame cannot be uniquely differentiated from the frame
"Leopards", i.e. it contains a missing slot. */

            Frame: Cheetahs
            superFrame: Leopards

/* A redundant frame. */

      Frame: Ungulates
      superFrame: Mammals
      ◇ slot type (ungulate)
      ◇ slot feet (hoofs)

/* An auxiliary frame to the frame "Penguins". */

   Frame: Birds
   superFrame: Animals
   ◇ slot flys

/* The frame "Birds" is an auxiliary frame to this frame. */

      Frame: Penguins
      superFrame: Birds
      ◇ slot flys (false)
      ◇ slot isa (penguin)
      ◇ slot eats (fish)

/* Missing frame, the super-frame "Reptiles" is not
defined. */

      Frame: Crocodiles
      superFrame: Reptiles
      ◇ slot isa (crocodile)
```

8.3.1. Redundancy

The concept of redundancy in frame based systems is similar to that for rule based systems. A slot or frame is redundant if it is not used to establish anything that the system is designed to address. In our example frame base the frame `Ungulate` can be considered to be redundant as we have no ungulates in our zoo. Similarly the slot `habitat` in the `Animals` top frame is redundant because it also does not contribute to establishing the identity of any animal in the zoo.

We could argue that frames, other than the top frame, which are connected to super-frames that do not exist are redundant, since they cannot be linked with the rest of the application. However this will, in practice, be more an indication of the presence of missing frames rather than true redundancy. Missing frames are discussed in the following sub-section.

8.3.2. Missing Slots and Frames

A frame based system will contain missing slots if we cannot uniquely identify each frame. There are a number of possible situations where this might occur. Firstly a frame which is a sub-frame of another may not contain an appropriate slot to distinguish it from its super-frame. For example:

```
Frame: A
superFrame: Top Frame
◊ slot a (1)

Frame: B
superFrame: A
```

Here an entity with an attribute `a` which has a value `1` can be instantiated to frame `A` and, through some inheritance mechanism, also to frame `B`. We cannot distinguish between the two. Thus there is simply no purpose in having the frame `B`. In our example frame base this is illustrated by the `Leopards` and `Cheetahs` frames. Inspection of these frames will show that they cannot be uniquely differentiated because the frame for cheetahs has no unique slot to distinguish it from its super-frame. In such a situation we cannot see cheetahs as a sub-frame of leopards - they are just leopards.

Alternatively we may have two identical frames (duplication), not on the same path in the hierarchy. In such a case we will not be able to distinguish between the two or sensibly to assign instances to one rather than the other. This will seriously hamper the operation of a frame based system since the duplicates have different super-frames and sub-frames.

In both cases the situation can be remedied by introducing an additional slot into one of the frames so that they can be distinguished. Alternatively, in some cases, an existing slot may be altered, for example the value that it requires may be changed.

A frame based system will also include a missing frame if a frame is defined as a sub-frame of a frame that does not exist. This is illustrated in our example frame base by the frame Crocodiles which is defined as a sub-frame of the frame `Reptiles`. However, no such frame is defined in the hierarchy. In practice most frame base system development environments will prevent the creation of frames which have a non-existent super-frame; therefore this situation will not usually arise.

8.3.3. Misplaced Slots and Frames

Given the property of inheritance the location of a slot in a frame hierarchy can be highly significant. We can envisage situations where a slot is introduced at a level either too specialised or not specialised enough. Slots should be introduced into the frame hierarchy at the highest point where they will be of use to instantiate an entity to a particular frame, or alternatively where they are required for inheritance by sub-frames. In our example frame base we could argue that the slot `eyes` in the frame `Carnivores` should have been introduced at a higher level in the `Top Frame` on the grounds that all animals are known to have eyes.

We can imagine a similar situation where the sub-frame and super-frame relation between two frames is inverted. We can also conceive of a situation where the hierarchy displays circularity, i.e. a frame is defined indirectly as being a super-frame (or a sub-frame) of itself. This latter situation is again unlikely to occur in practice, however, as most frame based system development environments will not allow this construction. It is worth noting that the frame representation, being more explicitly object centred, does enable these errors in recording knowledge about the ontology of the domain to be recognised more easily and at an earlier stage than do rule based representations where the ontology rather "emerges" from the rule base as a whole.

8.3.4. Duplication

The concept of subsumption does not exist as such in frame based systems. We can, however, envisage a situation where slots and/or frames are duplicates of one another. We have already discussed the effect of the presence of duplicate frames in a frame based system (see section 8.3.2). Where a frame base contains duplicate slots in different frames with a common super-frame, this may indicate that the slot should have been introduced at a higher level and inherited down, or some other flaw in the structure of the hierarchy. Many frame based development environments carry out a number of checks on the frame base when it is compiled. During this process duplicate slots are often detected and the developer advised to this affect.

8.3.5 Auxiliary Frames and Slots

Auxiliary frames, as with auxiliary rules in a rule based system, are included in a frame base to mirror the domain which the system is attempting to model. In our example frame base we include a frame `Birds` although the only bird in the zoo is a penguin therefore the frame could be considered to be irrelevant (or redundant).

Similarly individual frames may include auxiliary slots simply to reflect the domain. For example the frame `Carnivores` contains a number of slots which are not necessary to establish whether an entity is a `tiger`, `lion` or a `leopard`.

As in the case of auxiliary rules, auxiliary frames or slots are not considered to represent an error in this work, since they can have a role in more accurately describing the domain and provide the basis for future extension.

8.3.6. Inconsistency and Incompleteness

It is hard to give as clear cut an analysis of the notions of inconsistency and incompleteness with regard to frame based systems, as the semantics of such system are often not fully specified, and because much of the inference that can give rise to these problems is often implicit in the code that manipulates the structures rather than explicit in the structures themselves. If, however, there is a requirement that frames be exclusive, so that an instance is properly an instance of a single frame, an inconsistency, or incompleteness, occurs if there exists a possible set of facts that would allow an entity to be instantiated to two different frames. This is more acceptable if the two frames are in a super/sub-frame relation, since the higher instantiation is compatible with the lower and can be ignored. If, however, the frames lie on different paths through the hierarchy we either have an inconsistency, if the object is instantiated to both frames, or an incompleteness if we instantiate it to neither.

8.3.7 Errors Associated with Lower and Upper Numeric Ranges

In some frame based systems particular ranges of values that a slot may take may be specified, and be used to validate data supplied for such slots, and to perform a variety of inferences. It is important, however, that these restrictions are applied in a consistent way, and that the range of the slots for lower level frames are strict specialisations of the ranges they inherit, and that ranges between different slots are consistent. If we consider a frame base that contains the following facts:

```
Frame: Person
superFrame: Top Frame
◇ slot age (0-110)

    Frame: Men
    subFrame: Person
    ◇ slot pensionableAge (65-115)
```

Then the frame base will contain an error as the value range restriction for `pensionableAge 65-115` is not included in the value range restriction for `age 0-110` for `Persons`.

8.3.8. Errors Associated with Minimum and Maximum Cardinality

Cardinality in frame based systems refers to the number of values that may be placed in a particular slot. For example in a social security system there may be a slot representing an applicant's spouse which may have a cardinality of one on the assumption that the applicant can have only one spouse at any single moment in time. Again care must be taken that these are of universal applicability rather than simply the normal case. Marriages can be polygamous, and there are three wheeled cars although four is the norm.

8.4. HYBRID SYSTEMS

The KB used in hybrid systems is composed of both a frame base and a rule base. The frame base, often referred to as a class hierarchy, can be used to define the vocabulary for the rule base, i.e. the possible values that slots can take are defined and so limited, and the literals used to construct rules must conform to the restrictions imposed by what is available from the class hierarchy. During compilation the frame base is married together with the rules designed to manipulate it. As a result a number of errors may be discovered. These can be classified as follows:

- Missing values, slots or frame types.

- Unused values, slots or frame types.

8.4.1. Missing Values, Slots or Frames

A value, slot or frame is missing if it appears in the rule base but is not defined in the frame hierarchy, in this case we say that the rule contains an illegal attribute. This situation is directly analogous to that in which an undeclared variable is referenced in a conventional program. In most hybrid KBS development environments this will be discovered during compilation with the result that the compiler will fail. Usually a suitable error message will be displayed to allow the developer to track down the missing item.

8.4.2. Unused Values, Slots or Frames

A slot or frame is unused if it is contained in the frame hierarchy but does not appear in any rule. This will not adversely affect the operation of the existing rule base but may indicate that a missing rule exists or part of a rule is missing. In many cases an attribute will be considered to be both missing and unused because of a typing error where the spelling of a slot identifier or value in the rule base is different to that contained in the frame hierarchy.

8.4.3. Advantages of Hybrid Systems

As can be seen from the above two categories of error, there are certain advantages in a hybrid system. It allows both the ontological knowledge of a domain and the heuristic knowledge of the domain to be represented in a way which is both suitable to the knowledge being represented, and which is explicit, and thus open to checks using the tools we will describe in the next three chapters. Moreover, the kind of cross checking enabled by the comparisons between the ontology that emerges from the rule base and that represented in the class hierarchy provides further safeguards against error.

8.5. SUMMARY

When the section of a KBS which is to be changed has been located and the relevant elements identified (global and local identification), the required maintenance action can then be implemented. As a result errors or anomalies may be introduced. In this chapter we have discussed these errors and anomalies by firstly considering rule based systems and then frame based and hybrid systems. References have been made throughout to existing literature concerning similar errors and anomalies that must be detected during the verification and validation of KBSs. This literature is centred on backward chaining production rule systems thus much of the discussion refers to this type of representation.

In the following three chapters we go on to consider how these errors and anomalies may be detected using existing tools and techniques. Where appropriate, additional tools are suggested.

CHAPTER 9

KBS Verification and Validation systems

9.1. INTRODUCTION

To test for the anomalies and errors identified in the previous chapter we can adopt many of the techniques, methods and devices used for the verification and validation of KBSs. It can be said that this is where KBS maintenance and KBS verification and validation meet. The crucial difference is that KBS verification and validation addresses the entire KBS, while the error checking associated with maintenance activities need only impinge on the section of the KB that has been affected by the change. It is thus appropriate to consider some of the KBS verification and validation systems, that are available or under development, here. Clearly we cannot address all aspects of these systems in a single chapter, therefore interested readers are referred to the references given in the text. A good overview of a number of systems including Suwa's rule checking program, CHECK, INDE and Ginsberg's KB reduction system is given in Lopez [1990]. It should also be noted that many of the systems described are still undergoing further development thus some of the information given here may no longer be correct. In addition the details given for the different systems have been obtained from the authors own experience and from published material. Although the authors believe that all relevant material has been accessed it may be that in certain cases some of the published material available has been overlooked. We therefore apologise in advance for any omissions that may become apparent. Finally, due to the limited amount of space available, we acknowledge that some notable systems have not been included, for example the ART Rule Checker (ARC) [Nguyen 1987], the NASA/Johnson Space Centre's Cross-Reference Style and Verification (CRSV) Tool [Culbert and Savely 1988] and the KES INSPECTOR TOOL [Software Architecture and Engineering Inc. 1983].

In the following two chapters the uses of the systems described in this chapter are illustrated with respect to the possible rule base and frame base errors and anomalies previously identified.

9.2. NORMAL FORM APPROACH TO KBS VERIFICATION AND VALIDATION

Many practitioners consider that KBSs can only be checked at the clausal level. This is firstly because certain forms of inconsistency and subsumption can only be identified at this level and secondly because many different representations, both rule based and frame based can be translated into clausal form using logical equivalences. The most common types of clausal form are Disjunctive Normal Form (DNF) and Conjunctive Normal Form (CNF). One of the best known examples of a KBS verification and validation system that utilises normal forms is MELODIA [Charles 1991] in which rule bases are translated to CNF.

9.2.1. MELODIA

In the MELODIA verification program production rules are translated into CNF form to carry out inconsistency checking. In MELODIA production rules are of the form:

$$A \Rightarrow B$$

Where A and B are conjunctions of disjunctions of elementary expressions and elementary expressions are of the form:

`a R b`

Here `a` and `b` are either attributes or values and `R` is a comparator such as =, <=, <, >, >=, <> etc. Note that attributes are single valued.

Rules are translated into clausal form by first replacing each distinct elementary expression of the form `a R b`, such as `a=b` or `a<b`, by the positive form of a logical variable i.e. a simple literal such as `x`. The opposite expressions of such forms, in the example `a<>b` and `b>=a`, are replaced by the complemented literal $\neg$`x`. Then each rule $A \Rightarrow B$ is translated into clauses. Thus if we have a set of rules:

```
Rule 1: (A1 = TRUE) ∧ (A2 < 0) ⇒ (A3 = 9) ∧ (A4 = BLUE)
Rule 2:     (A5 = 1) ∨ (A2 = 4) ⇒ (A3 < 1)
```

These become:

```
Rule 1: 1 ∧ 2 ⇒ 3 ∧ 4
Rule 2: 5 ∨ 6 ⇒ 7
```

Where `1` equates to `(A1 = TRUE)`, `2` to `(A2 < 0)` and so on. These rules are then converted to CNF as follows:

```
RULE 1
1 ∧ 2 ⇒ 3 ∧ 4
¬(1 ∧ 2) ∨ (3 ∧ 4)                  Implication Elimination
(¬1 ∨ ¬2) ∨ (3 ∧ 4)                 De Morgans Law
(¬1 ∨ ¬2 ∨ 3) ∧ (¬1 ∨ ¬2 ∨ 4)       Associative Law

RULE 2
5 ∨ 6 ⇒ 7
¬(5 ∨ 6) ∨ 7                  Implication Elimination
(¬5 ∧ ¬6) ∨ 7                 De Morgans Law
(¬5 ∨ 7) ∧ (¬6 ∨ 7)           Associative Law
```

We thus end up with four clauses:

```
Clause 1.1: (¬1 ∨ ¬2 ∨ 3)
Clause 1.2: (¬1 ∨ ¬2 ∨ 4)
Clause 2.1: (¬5 ∨ 7)
Clause 2.2: (¬6 ∨ 7)
```

These are denoted as the set `{(¬1 ¬2 3), (¬1 ¬2 4), (¬5 7), (¬6 7)}`. This will be accompanied by a number of exclusion clauses and a set of semantic constraints. The exclusion clauses for the above example are described by the set `{(¬2 ¬6), (¬3 ¬7)}`, because `(A2 = 4)` and `(A2 < 0)` and `(A3 = 9)` and `(A3 < 1)` are incompatible. For the above example there are no semantic constraints. This is thus represented by the empty set `{}`.

The MELODIA program then checks this set of clauses for subsumption and inconsistencies etc.

9.3. DECISION TABLE METHOD

A decision table is a tabular representation of a procedural decision situation, where the state of a number of conditions determines the execution of a sets of actions. Conditions are given along the X-axis and actions along the Y-axis. The aim is to demonstrate the results of an exhaustive set of mutually exclusive combinations of conditions. More succinctly decision tables can be said to be a method of organising and documenting logic in a manner that allows easy inspection and analysis. This approach, widely used in conventional software specification to determine the effect of conditional statements, has been used to facilitate the testing of a set of rules for conditions of ambiguity, redundancy and completeness [Cragen and Steudel 1987, Vanthienen 1991]. One such system, ESC (Expert System Checker) [Cragen and Steudel 1987], is described below. A number of variations on the decision table approach have also been developed, examples include Suwa's rule checking program [Suwa *et al.* 1982] and CHECK [Nguyen *et al.* 1985], which are described in sections 9.3.2 and 9.3.3 below.

A criticism of decision table techniques is that in any realistically sized application the table will grow to unmanageable proportions unless some form of partitioning is implemented whereby only a finite number of condition-action combinations need be considered. A further criticism often leveled at decision table techniques is is that only static checks are involved: no consideration is given to dynamic checking.

9.3.1. Expert System Checker (ESC) Program

ESC [Cragen and Steudel 1987] is a decision table based KBS verification and validation program which checks rule bases for missing rules and values, conflicting pairs and subsumption. A master decision table for the entire KB is first constructed. This is then partitioned into disjoint sets for checking completeness and consistency, reporting discrepancies and missing rules as they are found. Each set is represented as another decision table, with rows indicating logical conditions and columns representing rules. The master decision table is created by parsing the rules and expanding the table as new conditions and actions are found.

One of the problems associated with decision table techniques is that for any realistically sized KB the resulting table quickly becomes unmanageable. This can be avoided by partitioning or splitting the KB into manageable chunks. In the ESC system the splitting of the master decision table is carried out as follows:

1. Separate rules into sub-tables so that they have logical isolation

from other rules i.e. the rules in the set have at least one condition (attribute) in common, and no other rule uses that attribute.

2. Further separate the sub-table so that no rule in a sub-table allocates the value for a condition in another rule in the same table.
3. Repeat for remaining portions of the master table.

Thus if we have three rules:

```
Rule 1:  A(1) ∧ B ∧ C ⇒ D ∧ E ∧ F ∧ G ∧ H
Rule 2:      A(1) ∧ I ⇒ D ∧ H
Rule 3:      A(2) ∧ J ⇒ K
```

Where A is a multi-valued literal and the rest are booleans. The resulting master decision table will be of the form:

CONDITION	RULE 1	RULE 2	RULE 3
A	1	1	2
B	T		
C	T		
I		T	
J			T
ACTIONS			
D	T	T	
E	T		
F	T		
G	T		
H	T	T	
K			T

In this example Knowledge Base (KB) all the rules make reference to values for A, no conditions are set in actions of other rules and thus the table cannot be split any further. The KB is considered to be ambiguous because the fact base {A(1), B, C and I} results in two rules being fired. This is easily identifiable from the table. There are 32 possible combinations of input condition, A can have the value 1 or 2 and the booleans T or F. Rule 1 covers four of those possible conditions and rules 2 and 3 eight each. However, there is some overlap between rules 1 and 2 and hence only a combined total of ten possible conditions are covered. The KB thus covers 18 (10+8) possible fact bases, therefore 14 (32-18) possible fact bases are not covered. The missing fact bases can be used to motivate further rules which need to be added so that the KB is both unambiguous and complete.

9.3.2. Suwa's Rule Checking Program

Suwa's rule checking program is one of the earliest example of a KBS verification and validation program [Suwa *et al.* 1982 and Suwa *et al.* 1984]. It checks for missing rules and values, conflicts, redundancy and subsumption using a decision table technique. It was used successfully on the ONCOCIN system, an EMYCIN-like KBS (for oncology) that uses attribute-value rules. The program checks a rule base in three stages. First the rule base is partitioned into disjoint sets, each set concluding about a single parameter. Then a table is created displaying all possible combinations for condition parameters and resulting action parameters. This table is then checked for conflicts, redundancies, subsumptions and missing rules. Thirdly a table is displayed summarising the errors found. The rule checker assumes that there should be a rule for each possible combination of values of attributes that appear in an antecedent. It hypothesises missing rules based on this assumption. Thus rules that have impossible semantic combinations may be hypothesised. Further, if the number of attributes is large, a very large number of missing rules will be suggested.

For example if we have the following rule set:

```
RULE 1: (A2 T) ∧ (A3 T) ∧ (A4 T) ⇒ (A1 V0)
RULE 2: (A2 F) ∧ (A3 T) ∧ (A4 T) ⇒ (A1 V1)
RULE 3: (A2 F) ∧ (A3 T) ∧ (A4 T) ⇒ (A1 V1)
RULE 4: (A2 F) ∧ (A3 F) ∧ (A4 T) ⇒ (A1 V2)
RULE 5: (A2 T) ∧ (A3 F) ∧ (A4 T) ⇒ (A1 V2)
RULE 6: (A2 F) ∧ (A3 F) ∧ (A4 T) ⇒ (A1 V3)
RULE 7:                   (A2 T) ⇒ (A1 V4)
```

Where `A1` is an attribute that can take values of between `V0` and `V4` and `A2` to `A4` are boolean attributes that can take the values true (`T`) or false (`F`). Rule 7 is a default rule that succeeds whenever `A2` is true. Given the values for attributes `A2` to `A4` there are eight possible combinations, C1 to C8. We can tabulate these and determine what conclusions can be drawn given the above rule base (`T` and `F` values surrounded by parentheses indicate values that are not used by a particular rule):

A2	A3	A4	Combinations	Rule	Value
T	T	T	C1	1	V0
T	(T)	(T)	C1	7	V4
T	(T)	(F)	C2	7	V4
T	F	T	C3	5	V2
T	(F)	(T)	C3	7	V4
T	(F)	(F)	C4	7	V4
F	T	T	C5	2	V1
F	T	T	C5	3	V1
F	T	F	C6	-	-
F	F	T	C7	4	V2
F	F	T	C7	6	V3
F	F	F	C8	-	-

From this table we can conclude that there are no rules for combinations C6 and C8 although these may be illegal combinations and hence the absence of appropriate rules may have been intentional. Two rules, 2 and 3, have the same combinations, C5, and lead to the same value, `V1`. One of them is therefore redundant. Two rules, 4 and 6, with the same combination, C7, lead two two different values, `V2` and `V3`. They therefore contradict one another. Similarly Rules 1 and 7 and Rules 5 and 7 contradict one another. However, as Rule 7 is a default rule designed to succeed whenever the value for `A2` is `T` and no more specific rule has fired, it can be hoped that the rule interpreter running the system will be able to take care of this.

9.3.3. CHECK

CHECK [Nguyen *et al.* 1985 and Nguyen *et al.* 1987] is an automated rule verifier that is also based on ideas about decision tables. It is a precursor of the EVA system described in section 9.6.1. CHECK was developed from Suwa's rule checking program (described above) and operates on KBSs developed using the LES shell. LES employs a combination of goal driven rules and data driven rules and allows rules to contain variables that may be instantiated at run-time. LES also allows the use of certainty factors in its goal-driven and data driven-rules. These are implemented in the same manner as in the EMYCIN system, with a value of +1.0 for definitely true, 0.0 for unknown and -1.0 for definitely false.

LES requires the knowledge engineer to partition rules into sets: thus as with Suwa's rule checker, CHECK operates on a partitioned rule base. Static checks are carried out for redundancy, conflicting rules and subsumption at the local level and global errors in the form of circular chains. Completeness checks to identify missing rules consist of checks for unreferenced and illegal attribute values, unreachable conclusions, dead-end IF conditions and dead-end goals. No consideration is given to dynamic checking.

CHECK operates in the following manner:

1. The antecedent and consequent of every clause of every rule is compared to every antecedent and consequent of every clause of every other rule. The result of each comparison will be that they are either a) different, b) the same (redundancy), c) conflicting (contradiction), d) superseding (subsumption) or e) subceding (subsumption). The results are stored in a two dimensional inter-clause relationship table. The comparison is not straightforward because variables and the ordering of the clauses must be taken into account.

2. The antecedent and consequent of every rule is checked against the antecedent and consequent of every other rule. This process is implemented using the interclause relationship table computed in step 1. The results of this comparison will be the same as those listed for the clause comparisons in 1.

3. The relationships found in 2 are used to compute the relationships among rules. The possible relationships being a) different, b) the same (redundancy), c) conflicting (contradiction), d) sub-set (subsumption) or e) unnecessary (redundancy).

4. Completeness checks for missing rules are made using the table from step 1, i.e. unreferenced and illegal attribute values, unreachable conclusions, dead-end IF conditions and dead-end goals.

5. Two dependency charts are generated. One shows the interaction among data-driven (when) rules and the other the interaction between goal driven rules and the goals. These dependency charts are then used to detect circular rule chains.

An example dependency chart is given in Figure 9.1. This illustrates the dependencies that exist in the following rule list:

```
Rule 1: A ∧ B ⇒ C
Rule 2: D ∧ E ⇒ A
Rule 3:     F ⇒ E
Rule 4:     G ⇒ B
Rule 5:     H ⇒ B
```

If the goal to be determined is C (row 6), from the table we can see that C is dependent on Rule 1 which is dependent on Rules 2, 4 and 5, of which Rule 2 is dependent on Rule 3.

	R1	R2	R3	R4	R5
R1		*		*	*
R2			*		
R3					
R4					
R5					
C	*				

Figure 9.1: A simple rule set and its dependency chart.

9.4. INCIDENCE MATRIX (TABLE) METHOD

The incidence matrix method of KBS verification and validation involves the construction of matrices to determine the number of rules containing a certain variable or combination of variables or the number of variables common to a set of rules. A number of KBS verification and validation systems exist that are based on the development of incidence matrices [Landauer 1990, Agarwal and Tanniru 1991]. Structurely an incidence matrix is very similar to a transposed decision table (see above), except that it uses limited entries. For example given two rules:

```
Rule 1: A(1) ∧ B(1) ⇒ C(1)
Rule 2:        A(2) ⇒ C(2)
```

Where A, B and C are attributes and the Arabic numerals indicate a possible value for those attributes. The incidence matrix is as follows:

	A(1)	A(2)	B(1)	C(1)	C(2)
Rule 1	-1	0	-1	1	0
Rule 2	0	-1	0	0	1

or:

$$\begin{pmatrix} -1 & 0 & -1 & 1 & 0 \\ 0 & -1 & 0 & 0 & 1 \end{pmatrix}$$

Negative numbers indicate possible values for attributes in the antecedent of rules, and positive numbers possible values for attributes in the consequent.

Agarwal advocates that KB checking using the matrices method should be split in to two processes, local checking and global checking. The local checking methods are described in chapter 9. Global checking consists of sub-dividing the KB into sub-networks and carrying out similar checks. Both are described in detail in Agarwal and Tanniru [1991].

9.5. KNOWLEDGE BASE REDUCTION SYSTEMS

The concept of knowledge base reduction, as advocated by Ginsberg [1987], is based upon ideas concerned with solving problems associated with truth maintenance as advanced by de Kleer amongst others, particularly those concepts underlying de Kleer's Assumption-Based Truth Maintenance System (ATMS) [de Kleer 1986]. Ginsberg defines KB-reduction as:

> "A technique whereby for every assertion H that a KB can make one has calculated all possible logically independent and minimal sets of inputs under which the KB will be led to assert H."

The technique requires that that the rules in a KB form a hierarchical network which can be partitioned into levels starting at the leaf nodes. Labels are then computed for every hypothesis and default hypothesis in the KB. A hypothesis is any literal in the consequent of a rule and a default hypothesis is a literal in the antecedent of a rule that negates a hypothesis. A label is thus the set of all minimal logically consistent inputs to establish a hypothesis. This set of inputs is referred to as an environment and the individual inputs as findings. The latter are defined as antecedent literals that are not negated in the consequent of any rule. By comparing labels we can then identify anomalies such as inconsistency, redundancy, auxiliary rules and subsumption.

9.5.1. KB-REDUCER.

KB-REDUCER [Ginsberg 1988] is a KB reduction system for checking all potential inconsistencies and redundancies in rule bases, represented using propositional logic, through the use of a syntactic criterion. Literals involved in the KB are divided into findings (input data) and hypothesis (output data to be deduced). KB-REDUCER computes for each possible conclusion, `C` (hypothesis), the minimal disjunctive normal form of input data (findings) for which `C` can be asserted. Each conjunctive term is an environment for `C`, and the whole disjunction is the label for `C`. The labelling process commences with the lowest level of the rule hierarchy (level 0) and proceeds to the root rules(s) at the end of which labels will have been computed for all possible hypothesis in the rule base. The labels calculated prior to completion of the process are referred to as partial labels. Throughout this labelling process all potential contradictions and redundancies can be detected. KB-reducer assumes the following inference model: inference is monotonic, non-selective, and strongly data-driven.

Lopez gives a description of how labels are computed [Lopez *et al.* 1990]:

1. Let `R` be the current rule that asserts hypothesis `H`.

2. Compute the complete set of minimal environments that satisfy the antecedent part of the rule by taking the logical conjunction of the labels of the literals on its antecedent and minimising the resulting expression (the labels of the antecedent literals of `R` have already been computed because the process follows the level ordering). The KB is assumed to be acyclic thus rules can be partitioned into levels providing a rule ordering in the KB.

3. The set of minimal environments for rule `R` is called the rule-label for `R`. Hypothesis `H` has a partial label, the incomplete label for `H` computed from previous rules in the level ordering.

4. The new partial label for `H` is determined by taking the logical disjunction of the rule label of `R` and the current partial label of H and minimising the current expression.

We can illustrate this process by considering the following example:

```
Rule 1:  P ∨ Q ⇒ R
Rule 2:      A ⇒ B
Rule 3:  B ∧ R ⇒ S
Rule 4: ¬S ∧ C ⇒ T

Findings:             P, Q, A, C
Hypotheses:           R, B, S, T
Default Hypothesis:  ¬S
```

The labels are then:

```
Label  R: P ∨ Q
Label  B: A
Label  S: (A ∧ P) ∨ (A ∧ Q)
Label  T: ¬A ∧ C ∨ (¬P ∧ ¬Q ∧ C)
Label ¬S: ¬A ∨ (¬P ∧ ¬Q ∧ C)
```

At each stage before the new partial label for H is computed (step 4 above), the following tests are made:

1. If the rule label of R consists solely of inconsistent (or invalid) environments the rule R can be eliminated because it can never be fired. For example if we have a label consisting of two environments, $(P \wedge \neg P \wedge \neg Q) \vee (Q \wedge \neg Q \wedge \neg P)$ neither of these can be considered to be consistent.
2. If the rule label is implied by the current partial label of H i.e. every environment of H is a super-set of some environment in the rule label of R, then, since rule R concludes H in every case concluded by the one or more previously processed rules, one or more of the latter may be removed from the KB.
3. The reverse of (3), if the rule label of R implies the current partial label of H, i.e. every environment in the rule label of R is a super-set of some environment of H, then the rule R may be removed from the KB since every case in which it is satisfied is already covered by one or more previously processed rules.

After the new partial label for H has been computed, the following consistency tests are executed. For each hypothesis H a list of conflicting hypotheses is required (negation of the current hypothesis is assumed by default). For every hypothesis `X` that conflicts with `H` a sub-set/super-set test and a union test are made. The sub-set/super-set test determines if there exists any environment in the partial label of `H` that is a sub-set or super-set of any environment of `X`. Such environment is a set of inputs that will lead the KB to assert `X` and `H`. This is a conflicting situation, therefore the environment is flagged and the user notified. The union test computes the union of every environment of the partial label of `H` with every environment of the partial label of `X`. If some of these environments do not violate any semantic constraint, a new conflicting situation is detected because, from these environments, both conflicting hypotheses `H` and `X` can be concluded.

9.6. GENERIC RULE SYSTEMS

Generic rule systems are designed to allow KBSs, using any representation, to be verified and validated by first translating the rules or frames into a generic representation. Two outstanding examples are the EVA system and COVER. Both are described below.

9.6.1. The Expert Systems Validation Associate (EVA)

EVA was developed by a research group headed by Stachowitz and Chang at the Lockhead Artificial Intelligence Center in Austin, Texas. The long range goals of the EVA project, which started in 1986, are to build an integrated set of generic tools to validate any KBS written in any expert system shell [Chang *et al.* 1990, Stachowitz and Chang 1988, Stachowitz and Combs 1987]. EVA is written in PROLOG and consists of a wide range of validation tools that enable the user to check the redundancy, consistency, completeness and correctness of a KBS. EVA can be viewed as a metashell consisting of a unifying architecture that uses a single inference strategy, a single meta-KB and a common language for specifying requirements, constraints and models for domain knowledge. This makes EVA independent of any specific shell.

EVA also incorporates an extended structure checker which tests for synonymy between terms and inheritance information by using metafacts. For example given:

```
Rule 1: human(x)  ⇒ mortal(x)
Rule 2: person(x) ⇒ mortal(x)
```

and the meta-fact that human and person are synonymous, EVA can identify that one of the above two rules is superfluous.

EVA requires translators. It is envisaged by the developers that translators will be available in EVA for every major expert systems shell.

9.6.2. COVER

COVER [Preece and Shinghal 1991a and 1991b] is implemented in PROLOG and C, and runs on Sun workstations. It is designed to check KBS written in a generic rule language. Specific languages used in particular expert system shells must therefore be translated into this generic form. COVER checks for a number of types of anomaly which Preece refers to as the DARC (Deficiency, Ambivalence, Redundancy and Circularity) set of errors. Preece claims that this is the most comprehensive set of formal definitions available. The COVER checking procedure is divided into three phases:

1. Integrity Checking. Unfireable rules, unobtainable data items, unused literals, rules with unusable consequents, circular rule paths and missing values are detected.
2. Rule Checking. Duplicate, subsumed and conflicting rule pairs are detected.
3. Environment Checking. General cases of redundancy and ambivalence (as defined by Preece) are identified.

9.7. PETRI-NET SYSTEMS

Petri-nets are abstract formal representations of information flow often used to illustrate data flow in conventional systems. They can be used to represent the flow of data in KBSs [Agarwal and Tanniru 1991]. The concept of Petri-nets has also been applied to the verification and validation of KBSs [Fidelak and Victor 1989]. One example is the INDE system.

9.7.1 The INDE System

The INDE system [Pipard 1988] operates on KBs formed by rules using the attribute-value formalism with forward chaining. The KB is divided into maximal sub-sets, called concepts, of rules that are mutually exclusive. All attributes are assumed to be monovalued and the concepts are represented using Petri-nets. Tests for inconsistency, incompleteness and non-fireable rules are then made. If there exists a concept where an attribute occurs in the consequent of at least two rules but with different values INDE considers that a possible inconsistency exists. In the Petri-net these will be evidenced by places with more than one input arc with different values. If the union of all the concepts does not include all the rules concluding on the same attribute INDE considers the rule base to be incomplete. If a rule is not included in the union of all the concepts it is considered to be non-fireable.

9.8. INFORMAL METHODS

Many methods of checking KBSs described in this work are dealt with in a formal manner. However, some authors [Cuda and Dolan 1991] claim that many of the properties checked by formal means may be better dealt with by relatively informal techniques based on a particular method of constructing a KB. Cuda and Dolan have developed a methodology, FFAAK, to facilitate such informal techniques.

9.8.1. Feedback Facilitated Automated Acquisition of Knowledge (FFAAK)

FFAAK uses two constructs, knowledge sources and modules. The first is an encoding of knowledge in a particular format coupled with an inference procedure. The second specifies the inputs and outputs for a particular task or sub-task and also includes a set of test cases and a set of test case descriptors. A test case consists of a set of inputs for a particular problem and the correct outputs. The knowledge source is given the inputs of a test case, and the outputs it generates are checked against the known correct outputs. FFAAK produces test cases that cover the range of possible input and output values. A test case descriptor allows a possible range of values to be entered for each input parameter and then forms cases by taking the cross product.

Checks are carried out automatically by testing each new rule as it is entered. FFAAK can detect the following properties:

1. Unfulfillable goals: the situation where the inference procedure can find no value for a goal.
2. Unreachable attribute values: the situation where the inference

procedure cannot find all potential values for an attribute.

3. Unreachable if conditions: the case where the antecedent of a rule may be unfulfillable.
4. Illegal input sets: the situation where a set of input values can be formulated that the KB is not intended to handle.
5. Illegal output sets: the case where an unintended set of values that can be inferred by the KB.

An unfulfillable goal is detected if, as a result of running the test cases a goal does not have a value. Unreachable attribute values and if conditions are detected in a similar way. Illegal input sets are identified by presenting the expert with input sets produced by the test case descriptors. Illegal output sets are checked for by running the widest possible range of test cases and checking the system's output against them.

9.9. CURRENT RESEARCH

There is currently a great deal of further research activity concerning the verification and validation of KBSs in addition to the continuing development of the systems already described. It is appropriate therefore to mention some of the more notable projects here that have not been covered by the foregoing text, namely VALID, VIVA, ACKNOWLEDGE and KADS-II.

VALID is an ESPRIT-II project specifically concerned with methods and tools for KBSs. The objective is to develop a tool-box based on a common representation with which validation concepts can be defined and analysed. There are several strands to the project:

- The definition of a KBS quality manual, with special attention to validation actions during the different phases of KBS life-cycles.
- A general model in which validation issues can be defined.
- A Common Conceptual Representation (CCR) in which most KBSs can be expressed.
- The definition of a Validation Meta-language (VETA) to provide the abstract mechanisms to build validation tools.

Three validation tools are currently under development as part of the project:

- WITNESS. Tool to manage comments from the validators of a KBS.

- CURRICULUM CV. A query language for use by the knowledge engineer when inspecting the KB.
- CONTROLLER. Tool to check the integrity constraints associated with input and output data.

The project was due to complete in December 1991.

VIVA is another ESPRIT project, partly following on from the VALID project, scheduled to start in June 1992. The aim of the project is to produce a set of tools that allow off-line validation, on-line validation (testing), interpretation of anomalies found and KB refinement. VIVA is the only specific project dealing with KBS validation in ESPRIT III.

The ACKNOWLEDGE project is primarily concerned with the efficient acquisition of knowledge. However, validation is considered in the context of knowledge acquisition methods, generic problem-solving techniques and knowledge transformations and integration. A number of validation tools have been developed including KVAT which validates knowledge in a core KB. The ACKNOWLEDGE project was scheduled to finish in January 1992.

The aim of KADS-II is to provide an advanced and comprehensive methodology for integrating KBS development. It is based on the work carried out in KADS-I (see section 5.3), extending the current methodology to cover the full development life cycle, from project definition, through, system development, to the subsequent maintenance of the system. Greater emphasis will be given to quality control, hence techniques for verification and validation are expected to be developed.

9.10. SUMMARY

In this chapter we have described a number of KBS verification and validation techniques, tools and systems. Although specifically aimed at KBS verification and validation the errors and anomalies that these systems are designed to discover are the same as those we wish to avoid as the result of a KBS maintenance session.

The techniques, tools and systems discussed are grouped under a number of headings:

- Normal form systems, e.g. MELODIA.
- Decision table methods, e.g. ESC, Suwa's rule checking program and CHECK.
- Incidence matrix methods.

- Knowledge base reduction, e.g. KB-REDUCER.
- Generic rule systems, e.g. EVA and COVER.
- Petri-net techniques, e.g. the INDE system.
- Informal methods, e.g. FFAAK.

We also briefly reviewed a number of systems that form part of current research projects.

In the following two chapters we illustrate the use of the techniques, tools and systems discussed here to detect the errors and anomalies found in rule and frame based systems as identified in the previous chapter.

CHAPTER 10

Checking for Rule base Errors and Anomalies

10.1. INTRODUCTION

In chapter 8 the errors and anomalies that can occur in a rule base as a result of a maintenance session were identified, namely:

- Redundancy.
- Dead end rules.
- Missing rules.
- Subsumption.
- Auxiliary rules.
- Circular rule sets.
- Incompleteness.
- Inconsistency.

In this chapter the currently available tools, techniques and systems that exist to detect these errors and anomalies are discussed. Where gaps in these tools are identified, further possible tools are suggested. Most of the existing tools discussed have been taken from the verification and validation systems introduced in the previous chapter and the maintenance tools associated with the MAUDE development environment. The discussion of the methods used by these tools is based on the authors' own experiences and from information gleaned from published material. The authors appreciate that some of this published material may now be out of date and therefore it should again be noted that any criticism directed towards the techniques concerned may no longer be applicable.

10.2. REDUNDANCY (MISSING LINKS)

We have defined a redundant rule as a rule that plays no part in establishing a root proposition. Further, we identified two types of redundancy, absolute redundancy and partial redundancy. A rule is absolutely redundant if it has no "upward link" to a root proposition, associated with a particular task. A rule is partially redundant if the value that the head proposition establishes is not used to establish a root proposition although the attribute or predicate name does appear in the antecedent of another rule. We also identified a situation whereby a literal occurring positively in one rule and negatively in another cancelled itself out; that literal being referred to as an irrelevant literal.

10.2.1. Redundancy Checking Using Static Inspection

The simplest method of identifying redundancy is by static inspection using some appropriate rule base viewing tool. If we consider the Datamap viewing tool described in section 7.12 with respect to local identification of the elements in the KB that will require attention, and the following example rule base:

```
Rule 1: (B (1)) ∨ (C (2)) ⇒ (A (1))  [The Root Rule]
Rule 2: (D (1)) ∧ (E (2)) ⇒ (B (1))
Rule 3: (D (1)) ∧ (E (1)) ⇒ (B (1))
Rule 4: (F (1)) ∨ (G (2)) ⇒ (C (2))
Rule 5: (D (1)) ∧ (H (1)) ⇒ (I (1))
Rule 6: (J (1)) ∧ (H (1)) ⇒ (B (2))
Rule 7: (K (1)) ∨ (L (1)) ⇒ (H (1))
```

Where upper case letters represent attributes (or object slots) while the Arabic numerals represent values for those attributes (or slots). The set of possible values for each attribute is given by {1 2}.

At the rule-attribute level the resulting Datamap will be of the form given in Figure 10.1 (rules with negated heads are not shown). From the figure it can quickly be seen that Rule 5 displays pure redundancy. The head attribute I is not upwardly linked to the root attribute and it does not itself represent a root attribute. If we now examine the Datamap at the clause-proposition level as depicted in Figure 10.2 (clauses with negated heads are not shown) we can see that clause 6.1 is also redundant. Further inspection shows that this is the only clause derived from Rule 6. If all the clauses derived from a rule are redundant then we can state that the rule from which they are

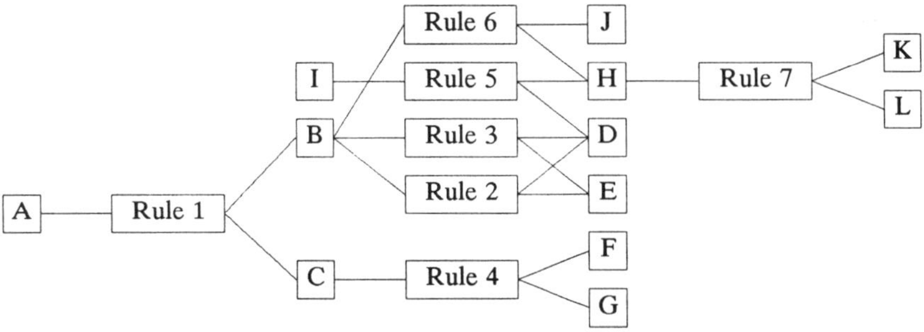

Figure 10.1: Rule-attribute Datamap depicting pure redundancy.

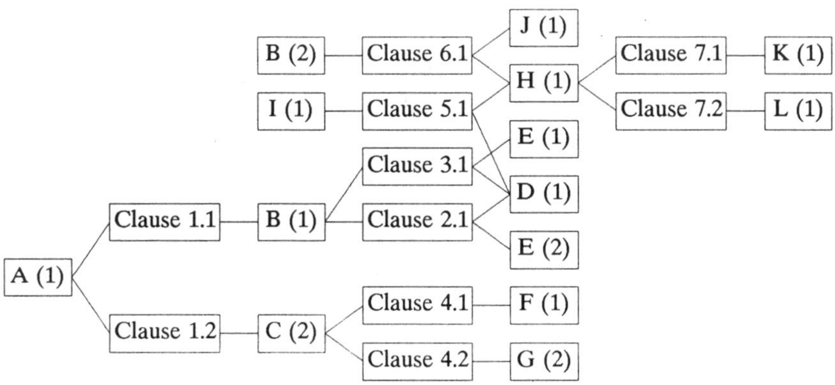

Figure 10.2: Clause-proposition Datamap depicting partial redundancy.

derived is also redundant (pure redundancy). Rule 6 in our example therefore displays partial redundancy. Further inspection of Figure 10.2 shows that clauses 7.1 and 7.2 are used only to establish `H(1)`, which itself is required only by the redundant rules 5 and 6. If we remove these redundant rules, rule 7 will be rendered redundant also. Close inspection also reveals that the literal `E` is irrelevant (remember that `E(1)` is equivalent to `¬E(2)`).

Static inspection techniques supported by viewing tools are very useful for small rule bases and rule bases capable of being partitioned into relatively small independent units. The technique is not, however, viable for more realistically sized rule bases, unless the rule base can be partioned so as to display only a tractable amount of the rule base at any given time. Such tools also require a certain amount of skill on behalf of the user. Further, given the rule-attribute and clause-proposition Datamaps in Figures 10.1 and 10.2, only a very astute observer would detect the presence of the irrelevant literal `E` in Rules 2 and 3.

10.2.2. Redundancy Checking Using Rule Base Folding

The disadvantage of static inspection techniques to identify redundancy are firstly that they require a considerable amount of user interaction and secondly that success depends on the skill and judgement of the observer. Some automation, especially for large rule bases, is therefore desirable. This can be achieved using a number of techniques. One such technique is referred to as rule base folding.

The technique is based on the following premise; for a rule not to be redundant it must eventually fold into a root rule. In other words, with the exception of the root rule, the head of each rule in a KB must also appear in the tail of at least one other rule in the the KB. If we consider the set of rules given in the previous sub-section `(H (1))` folds into Rules 5 and 6, `(C (2))` into Rule 1, `(B (1))` into Rule 1 and `(A (1))` is the head proposition; however, `(B (2))` and `(I (1))` do not appear in the tails of any other rules and therefore Rules 5 and 6 can be declared to be redundant. As in the case of static inspection, once Rules 5 and 6 are removed this will reveal that Rule 7 is redundant also.

The success with which rule base folding can be achieved depends on our ability to compare literals before the system is executed. In some representations it may not be possible to consider values for attributes at all in which case only pure redundancy can be detected using this method. Where values can be compared difficulties may be encountered where the possible value for an attribute cannot be known in advance. For example if we have an attribute `age` which can have a value range of between (say) 0 and 120 for a particular `person` the precise value for the attribute can not be known until appropriate instantiations have been made. Where values such as ranges cannot be fully matched it must be assumed that they may match given some suitable input, i.e. no redundancy exists. We can illustrate this by considering the following two rules designed to determine whether a person is a teenager or not:

```
Rule 1: (person (name)) ∧ (age (13-19)) ⇒
                   (teenager (true)) [Root Rule]
Rule 2: (person (name)) ⇒ (age (0-120))
```

We cannot establish with certainty that Rule 2 folds into Rule 1, since it may be impossible in practice to instantiate the attribute `age` to the critical range of values: however, we typically will give such cases the benefit of the doubt and assume that the attribute can take the required value. Rule base folding also requires the inclusion of some mechanism whereby the system can distinguish between a root rule and a rule that is truly redundant because its head it not required for the task which the system is designed to perform.

Finally it should also be noted that rule base folding simply proves that a path exists from each rule in the rule base to another rule in the rule base. It gives no indication of the correctness of this path, or whether the path forms part of a cycle.

10.2.3. Redundancy Checking Using EVA

The principle behind the rule base folding technique described above is utilised in the EVA system [Chang *et al.* 1990] where redundant rules are referred to as containing unreachable literals. EVA uses QUINTUS PROLOG rules which operate using a backward chaining inference mechanism. Unreachable literals are defined as consequent literals of a rule or facts which do not appear in the antecedent of any other rule. Unreachable literals will therefore never be used. Thus if we have a simple PROLOG rule base, designed to respond to queries of the form `animal(X,Y)` :

```
/* Rules */

animal(X,tiger):- skinCover(X,stripes).
type(X,carnivore):- eats(X,meat).

/* Facts */

skinCover(peter,stripes).
skinCover(peter,fur).
eats(peter,meat).
```

Here the literals `type(X,carnivore)` and `skinCover(peter,` `fur)` are considered by the EVA system to be unreachable (redundant). The literal `eats(peter,meat)` may be considered to be indirectly unreachable (redundant), since it can only be reached through a call to `type` which will not in practice *be* called.

10.2.4. Redundancy Checking Using Incidence Matrices

If we have a rule base consisting of two rules, for example:

```
Rule 1: A ∧ B ⇒ C
Rule 2: D ∧ E ⇒ A
```

Where the letters `A` to `E` represent elements of a KB, we can produce a matrix which indicates the elements present in each rule:

	A	B	C	D	E
Rule 1:	1	1	1	0	0
Rule 2:	1	0	0	1	1

This can be displayed as an *incidence* matrix:

$$\begin{pmatrix} 1 & 1 & 1 & 0 & 0 \\ 1 & 0 & 0 & 1 & 1 \end{pmatrix}$$

If we multiply an incidence matrix by the transpose of itself:

$$\begin{pmatrix} 1 & 1 & 1 & 0 & 0 \\ 1 & 0 & 0 & 1 & 1 \end{pmatrix} \begin{pmatrix} 1 & 1 \\ 1 & 0 \\ 1 & 0 \\ 0 & 1 \\ 0 & 1 \end{pmatrix} = \begin{pmatrix} 3 & 1 \\ 1 & 3 \end{pmatrix}$$

The resulting matrix shows the common elements contained in the rules in the KB:

	Rule 1	Rule 2
Rule 1	3	1
Rule 2	1	3

If a rule does not share an element with one other rule in the KB we can consider it to be redundant (absolute redundancy). Thus if we add the rule:

```
Rule 3: F ⇒ G
```

to the rule base and multiply the previously derived incidence matrix for Rules 1 and 2 with the transpose of the incidence matrix for Rule 3:

$$\begin{pmatrix} 1 & 1 & 1 & 0 & 0 & 0 & 0 \\ 1 & 0 & 0 & 1 & 1 & 0 & 0 \end{pmatrix} \begin{pmatrix} 0 \\ 0 \\ 0 \\ 0 \\ 0 \\ 1 \\ 1 \end{pmatrix} = \begin{pmatrix} 0 \\ 0 \end{pmatrix}$$

The resulting matrix contains only zeroes and hence Rule 3 can be said to be redundant.

Where the resulting matrix shows that a new rule shares only one element with one or more rules in the KB this is a good indication that it is a dead end rule as discussed further in section 10.3 below. Alternatively the new rule may be either a root rule or a leaf rule.

10.2.5. Irrelevant Literals

Irrelevant literals can only be detected by comparing rules. This process can be very much simplified if the rule base is translated into some clausal form. We can illustrate this by considering the MELODIA system [Charles 1991]. If we have two rules:

```
Rule 1:  (B ∧ C) ∨ D ⇒ A
Rule 2: E ∨ (C ∧ ¬B) ⇒ A
```

These translate into the following four clauses:

```
Clause 1.1: ¬B ∨ ¬C ∨ A
Clause 1.2: ¬D ∨ A
Clause 2.1: ¬E ∨ A
Clause 2.2: ¬C ∨ B ∨ A
```

When the clauses are in this standard form they can be most easily manipulated by rewriting them alphabetically, and making the ∨ implicit:

```
Clause 1.1a: (A ¬B ¬C)
Clause 1.2a: (A D)
Clause 2.1a: (A E)
Clause 2.2a: (A B ¬C)
```

Once in this form, it is straightforward to detect clauses which are identical save for a single literal which occurs positively in one clause and negatively in the other. Any such literal is irrelevant and can be removed. This would result in the clauses:

```
Clause 1.1b: (A ¬C)
Clause 1.2b: (A D)
Clause 2.1b: (A E)
Clause 2.2b: (A ¬C)
```

We can now see that 1.1b and 2.2b are identical, and so we could remove one of them (absolute subsumption). If we now wished to return to the original form, this would suggest that the rules be combined into the single rule:

```
Rule 3: D ∨ C ∨ E ⇒ A
```

The conveniently manipulable standard form used by MELODIA is also convenient for a variety of other checks as described in Charles

[1991]. Some of these will also be discussed in subsequent sections of this chapter.

10.3. DEAD END RULES (MISSING LEAVES)

Dead end rules are defined as rules whose antecedents do not represent leaf propositions and cannot be matched to a consequent in another rule. As such dead end rules may be considered to be the complement of redundant rules. The presence of dead end rules in a rule base often indicates that it contains missing rules, since the dead end rule does contain helpful information, but is not properly integrated with the rest of the application.

10.3.1. Dead End Rule Checking Using Static Inspection

For small rule bases dead end rules can be easily identified using a rule base viewing tool of some description. Again the Datamap described earlier provides a useful example. If we consider a set of rules:

```
Rule 1: (B (1)) ∧ (C (1)) ⇒ (A (1))
Rule 2: (B (1)) ∧ (C (2)) ⇒ (A (2))
Rule 3: (E (1)) ∨ (D (1)) ⇒ (B (1))
Rule 4: (E (2)) ∨ (F (1)) ⇒ (C (1))
```

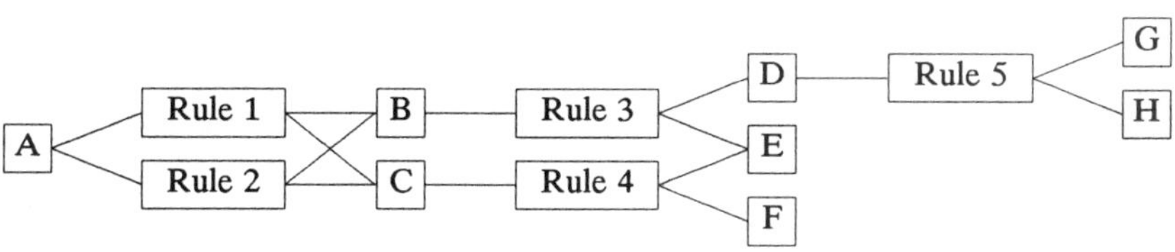

Figure 10.3: Rule-attribute Datamap showing a dead end rule.

These can be displayed using the Datamap tool (Figure 10.3). Inspection of Figure 10.3 quickly allows us to identify possible leaf propositions. To determine whether they actually are leaf propositions requires us to inspect the mechanism for instantiating these propositions. Depending on the representation and inference strategy used this may, for example, involve determining whether these attributes can be

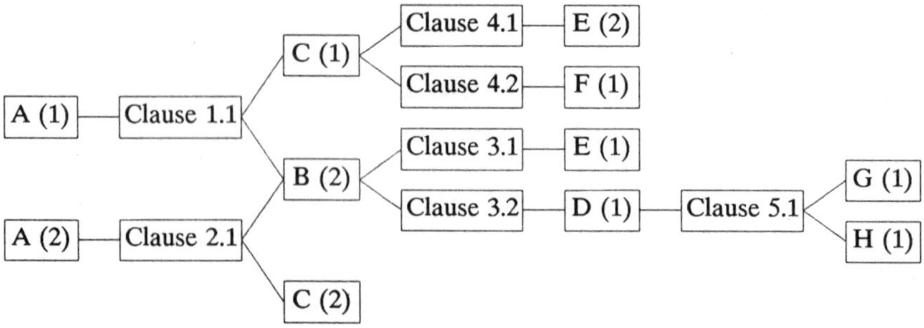

Figure 10.4: Clause-proposition Datamap showing a dead end rule (Clause).

be asked of the user, or whether they are contained in a separate fact base, or obtainable from an external database, or whatever. Let us assume that we discover that `G`, `H` and `E` are leaf propositions, which can have their values supplied from some external source, and that `F` is not. Rule 4 is therefore a dead end rule, either because there exists a missing rule to establish F or because F should have been declared a leaf proposition, with a specified means of obtaining a value for it.

Reference to the lower level proposition-clause Datamap (Figure 10.4) shows that Rule 3 contains a proposition, `C(2)`, which is a potential leaf proposition which was not revealed at the attribute-rule level, since although one value for the attribute, `C(1)`, can be supplied by lower level rules, `C(2)` cannot. Further, if the representation used defines all the possible values that each attribute in a proposition can have, we will be able to compare the values required with those defined. If some of these values can neither be supplied by the rule base nor obtained externally further maintenance will be required.

10.3.2. Dead End Rule Checking Using Rule Base Unfolding

We have described how redundancy in a rule base can be detected using a technique referred to as rule base folding. As dead end rules can be considered the complement of redundant rules it seems natural that they can be detected using a complementary technique, rule base unfolding. This is indeed the case. We can state that a rule base contains a dead end rule if every rule in the rule base does not unfold into only leaf propositions the truth of which can be ascertained by direct reference to an external source such as a fact base or the user. In other words each condition contained in the tail of every rule in a rule base must either (a) be contained in the head of another rule in the rule base or (b) represent a leaf condition, ascertainable from some external source.

As with the rule base folding technique rule base unfolding simply shows the existence of a path from each rule in the rule base to one or more other rules contained in the rule base, it does not in any way verify the correctness of this path.

10.3.3. Dead End Rule Checking Using EVA

A similar concept, to the rule base folding technique described above, is used in the EVA system [Chang *et al.* 1990]. In the EVA system dead end rules are defined as production rules, the antecedent of which can never be satisfied because they contain a literal which cannot be matched with a fact or literal in the consequent of any rule. Thus if we have a simple production rule base:

```
Rule 1: A ∧ B ⇒ C
Rule 2: D ∧ E ⇒ A
```

Where `D` and `E` are literals intended to represent facts in the data base. In this case Rule 1 is a dead end rule because the literal `B` is not contained in the consequent of any rule and is not a fact in the database. Notice that this definition excludes the possibility of externally supplied data, since all facts are considered part of the KB itself. Thus dead end rules identified in EVA can be removed either by adding rules to solve the antecedent, or by adding facts to satisfy the antecedent.

10.4. MISSING RULES

Where redundancy or dead end rules are discovered this may indicate that the rule base is missing one or more additional rules. The tools to detect redundancy and dead end rules have already been described, and action to remedy defects identified by them may in turn result in missing rules being discovered. Missing rules may also exist where a rule base is considered to be incomplete. The possible tools that can be used to test for incompleteness are discussed later in this chapter, in section 10.8.

```
1. Select first rule in rule base.

2. Select first proposition in antecedent of rule.

3. Attempt to match proposition with propositions in
   antecedent of other rules.
   a) If match successful and more propositions in
      antecedent select next proposition and repeat 3.
   b) If match successful and no more propositions in
      antecedent then 4.
   c) If match unsuccessful then 6.

4. Select first proposition in consequent of rule.

5. Attempt to match proposition with propositions in
   consequent of other rules.
   a) If match successful and more propositions in
      consequent select next proposition and repeat 5.
   b) If match successful and no more propositions in
      antecedent then ABSOLUTE SUBSUMPTION EXISTS.
   c) If match unsuccessful then 6.

6. Select next rule in rule base.
   a) If no more rules then END.
   b) Otherwise repeat 2.
```

Table 10.1: Absolute subsumption algorithm.

10.5. SUBSUMPTION

A subsumed rule is a rule that need not play any part in establishing a root proposition but, unlike a redundant rule, it *is* linked to a root proposition. In the previous chapter we identified three types of subsumption:

1. Absolute Subsumption (Duplication): The rule base contains two or more rules which are identical.
2. Complex Subsumption: The rule base contains one or more rules that are a more specialised form of some other rule.
3. Compound Subsumption: The rule base contains a group of rules that represent a more specialised case of another group of rules (where one of the groups of rules must consist of at least two rules while the other may consist of only a single rule).

The tools and techniques that can be used to detect these different types of subsumption are discussed in the following sub-sections.

10.5.1. Absolute Subsumption (Duplication)

Testing for absolute subsumption can be achieved by straightforward comparison of the the consequents and antecedents of individual rules. It must be remembered that duplication will still exist if two rules contain the same propositions, in the antecedent or consequent part of the rules, but in a different order. Some consideration must also be given to the possibility of absolute subsumption existing between more than two rules. A suggested algorithm to detect absolute subsumption is given in Table 10.1.

10.5.2. Complex Subsumption Checking Using Incidence Matrices

The following description of KB checking for subsumption using incidence matrices is based on an example given by Agarwal and Tanniru [1991]. Given two rules:

```
Rule 1: A(1) ∧ B(1) ⇒ C(1)
Rule 2:        A(2) ⇒ C(2)
```

Where A, B and C are attributes and the numerals indicate a desired value for these attributes. The incidence matrix is as follows:

	A(1)	A(2)	B(1)	C(1)	C(2)
Rule 1	-1	0	-1	1	0
Rule 2	0	-1	0	0	1

or simply:

$$\begin{pmatrix} -1 & 0 & -1 & 1 & 0 \\ 0 & -1 & 0 & 0 & 1 \end{pmatrix}$$

A -1 is used to indicate an input and a +1 an output from a rule. If we now carry out some maintenance on this rule base and add the following:

```
Rule 3: B(1) ⇒ C(1)
```

We can test the resulting KB using matrix multiplication. Agarwal advocates that local testing (testing of each individual new rule against each individual existing rule) takes place first. We first construct a "row vector" for Rule 3:

$$\begin{pmatrix} 0 & 0 & -1 & 1 & 0 \end{pmatrix}$$

```
Rule 3   0    0   -1    1    0
```

Multiplication of the incidence matrix derived for Rules 1 and 2 by the transpose of this vector gives:

$$\begin{pmatrix} -1 & 0 & -1 & 1 & 0 \\ 0 & -1 & 0 & 0 & 1 \end{pmatrix} \begin{pmatrix} 0 \\ 0 \\ -1 \\ 1 \\ 0 \end{pmatrix} = \begin{pmatrix} 2 \\ 0 \end{pmatrix}$$

Each row of the resulting column vector (the output vector) corresponds to an existing rule in the rule base and indicates the number of elements that are shared by the new rule and the existing rules. If two values are now considered:

$S(i)$ = The total number of antecedent conditions and consequent actions that appear in a rule i.

$O(i)$ = The value of the ith row in the output vector corresponding to rule i.

Then (where rule k represents a new rule):

If $S(i)>O(i)$ and $O(i)=S(k)$ then rule i is subsumed by the new rule k.

If $S(i)=O(i)$ and $O(i)<S(k)$ then rule i subsumes the new rule k.

If $S(i)=O(i)=S(k)$ then rule i is duplicated by the new rule k.

In our example $S(1)=3$, $S(2)=2$ and $S(3)=2$ and $O(1)=2$ and $O(2)=0$. Thus by applying the above, Rule 1 is subsumed (complex subsumption) by the new Rule 3 because $S(1)>O(1)$ and $O(1)=S(2)$, $2>0$ and $2=2$.

Alternatively if we add a rule:

```
Rule 4: A(2) ⇒ C(2)
```

Then:

$$\begin{pmatrix} -1 & 0 & -1 & 1 & 0 \\ 0 & -1 & 0 & 0 & 1 \end{pmatrix} \begin{pmatrix} 0 \\ -1 \\ 0 \\ 0 \\ 1 \end{pmatrix} = \begin{pmatrix} 0 \\ 2 \end{pmatrix}$$

Here S(1)=3, S(2)=2, S(4)=2, O(1)=0 and O(2)=2 and thus we can deduce that Rule 4 is a duplicate of Rule 2 (absolute subsumption) as S(2)=0(2)=S(4) (2=2=2).

10.5.3. Complex Subsumption Checking Using KB-Reduction

Using Ginsberg's KB-Reduction method [Ginsberg 1987] a KB is considered to contain subsumption (redundancy) if:

1. The rule label for R is more general than the current (partial) label for H. Since R concludes H in every case concluded by one or more previously processed rules, one or more of the latter may be removed from the KB.
2. The rule label for R implies the current label for H. Rule R may be removed from the KB since every case in which it is satisfied is already covered by one or more previously processed rules.

Rule R is the rule for which a label has just been computed and H is the hypothesis asserted by that rule. Thus if we consider an example, given the following three rules:

```
Rule 1: P ∧ S ⇒ R
Rule 2:     P ⇒ Q
Rule 3:     Q ⇒ R
```

The labels derived from Rules 1 and 2 will be:

```
Label for R: P ∧ S
Label for Q: P
```

The label for R when Rule 3 is included is then:

```
Label for R: P
```

This new label for R is a more general label for the hypothesis than that previously calculated ($P \wedge S$), thus subsumption exists and Rule 1 can be removed from the KB.

10.5.4. Complex Subsumption Checking by Examining Clauses

In section 8.2 it was established that in a KBS that operates at a clausal level individual clauses can be subsumed by other clauses without the rules from which they are derived subsuming one another. If we consider the following example:

```
Rule 1:         B ∨ C ⇒ A
Rule 2: (B ∧ D) ∨ E ⇒ A
```

These then translate into the following clauses:

```
Clause 1.1:     B ⇒ A
Clause 1.2:     C ⇒ A
Clause 2.1: B ∧ D ⇒ A
Clause 2.2:     E ⇒ A
```

Here Clause 1.1 subsumes Clause 2.1: however, Rule 1 does not subsume Rule 2, since otherwise the effects of clauses 1.2 or 2.2 would be lost. Thus it is suggested that the identification of subsumption - even in KBS that do not use an exclusively clausal form of representation - is best implemented at this clausal level of representation, so that these partly subsumed rules can be detected.

We can define a set of "rules" to identify subsumed clauses. These are given in Table 10.2. The operation of these rules can be illustrated by applying them to the following examples to show that in each case Clause A is either a duplicate of Clause B (absolute subsumption) or that Clause A Subsumes Clause B (complex subsumption).

```
1. (Clause A Subsumes Clause B) if
      (Compare Head is true)
      and
      (Compare Body is true)))

2. (Compare Head is true) if
      (The Head of Clause A is identical to the Head of
         Clause B)
      or
      (The Values for the Head Attribute in A are a sub-set
         for the Values in the Head Attribute in B)

3. (Compare Body is true) if
      (The body of Clause A is identical to the body of
         Clause B)
      or
      (The Propositions in the body of Clause A are a
         sub-set of the Propositions in the body of Clause
         B i.e. A is more general)
      or
         ((The Values of the Attributes in the body of
            Clause A are a superset of the Values in the
            corresponding Attributes in the body of
            Clause B)
         and
            (The Attributes in the body of Clause A are a
               sub-set of the Attributes in the body of
               Clause B)
            or
            (The Attributes in the body of Clause A are
               identical to the Attributes in the body of
               Clause B))
```

Table 10.2: Rules to detect subsumption at clausal level.

```
Clause A: B(1) ∧ C(1) ⇒ A(1)
Clause B: B(1) ∧ C(1) ⇒ A(1)

Clause A: B(1) ∧ C(1) ⇒ A(1)
Clause B: B(1) ∧ C(1) ⇒ A(1 2)

Clause A:        B(1)) ⇒ A(1)
Clause B: B(1) ∧ C(1) ⇒ A(1)

Clause A:         B(1) ⇒ A(1)
Clause B: B(1) ∧ C(1) ⇒ A(1 2)
```

```
Clause A: B(1 2) ∧ C(1 2) ⇒ A(1)
Clause B:     B(1) ∧ C(1) ⇒ A(1)

Clause A: B(1 2) ∧ C(1 2) ⇒ A(1)
Clause B:     B(1) ∧ C(1) ⇒ A(1 2)

Clause A: B(1) ∧ C(1 2) ⇒ A(1)
Clause B:   B(1) ∧ C(1) ⇒ A(1)

Clause A: B(1) ∧ C(1 2) ⇒ A(1)
Clause B:   B(1) ∧ C(1) ⇒ A(1 2)

Clause A:        B(1 2) ⇒ A(1)
Clause B: B(1) ∧ C(1) ⇒ A(1)

Clause A:        B(1 2) ⇒ A(1)
Clause B: B(1) ∧ C(1) ⇒ A(1 2)
```

However, it should be noted that where:

```
Clause A: B(1) ∧ C(1 2) ⇒ ...
Clause B: B(1 2) ∧ C(1) ⇒ ...
```

Clause A does not subsume Clause B.

The rules given in Table 10.2 can thus be used to automatically identify absolute and complex subsumption with respect to clauses derived from a set of rules. The rules can be summarised informally by stating that a clause A subsumes a clause B if the head of A is at least as "strong" as the head of B, and the body of A is no "stronger" than the body of B.

10.5.5. Compound Subsumption Checking Using MELODIA

In the MELODIA verification program [Charles 1991] a rule which is affected by compound subsumption is referred to as "redundant". Charles considers a rule base (RB) to contain redundancy (compound subsumption) if a rule (R) exists such that the set of rules {RB - R} is equivalent to the set {RB}. Thus if we have a set of rules:

```
Rule 1:     A ⇒ B ∧ E
Rule 2: A ∨ C ⇒ B
Rule 3: A ∧ D ⇒ E
```

Rule 3 is redundant because `E` can be deduced just from `A` by Rule 1.

MELODIA detects redundancies in a rule base by first converting the rule base into Conjunctive Normal Form (CNF) and then eliminating redundant literals, irrelevant literals and subsumed clauses. Charles considers that a clause is subsumed by another if all literals in the second clause are also contained in the first, i.e. a clause `(A ∨ B ∨ C)` will be subsumed by a clause `(A ∨ B)`. If all the clauses derived from a rule are eliminated then the rule is declared to be redundant. If only some clauses are eliminated then the rule is declared to contain redundant premises or conclusions. We can illustrate this be considering the rule base given above. This translates into the following CNF clauses:

```
Clause 1.1: (¬A ∨ B)
Clause 1.2: (¬A ∨ E)
Clause 2.1: (¬A ∨ B)
Clause 2.2: (¬C ∨ B)
Clause 3.1: (¬A ∨ ¬D ∨ E)
```

Clause 1.1 and 2.1 are the same and so one of them is redundant and can be removed. Further Clause 3 is subsumed by either Clause 1.1 or Clause 2.1 so can also be removed. Thus either Clauses 1.1 and 3 or Clauses 2.1 and 3 can be removed. We could therefore say that Rule 3 is redundant. However, Charles claims that the solution is not to remove Rule 3 from the rule base but to resolve the redundancy by either eliminating B from Rule 1 or A from Rule 2. This suggests that deciding how to resolve subsumption - as against simply identifying its existence - is not entirely straightforward, and will often depend on some view as to how the RB should be structured, or some expert view of the domain.

10.6. AUXILIARY RULES

The existence of auxiliary rules in a KB is not always considered to represent an error in this work. However, should we wish to detect auxiliary rules, an interesting approach is to determine whether a rule can be constructed that subsumes some two other rules in the rule base (compound subsumption) without adversely affecting the operation of the rest of the rule base. If so, one of the two rules can be considered to be an auxiliary rule and both can be replaced with the newly formed subsuming rule. We can illustrate this by considering the following set of rules:

```
Rule 1:         B ∧ C ⇒ A
Rule 2:         D ∨ E ⇒ B
Rule 3: F ∨ (G ∧ H) ⇒ C
```

Assuming that A is not a proposition required elsewhere in the KB we can create a rule that subsumes Rule 1 and 2:

```
Rule 4: (D ∨ E) ∧ C ⇒ A
```

From this we can determine that Rule 2 is an auxiliary rule, since B is now used to represent the truth of the disjunction D ∨ E. We can continue the example (assuming B is also a proposition not required elsewhere in the KB) so that Rule 3 is subsumed by replacing C in Rule 1 by the antecedent of Rule 3:

```
(D ∨ E) ∧ (F ∨ (G ∧ H)) ⇒ A
```

This can be somewhat simplified by rewriting it in a standard form:

```
Rule 5: (D ∨ E) ∧ (F ∨ G) ∧ (F ∨ H) ⇒ A
```

Even so, in this trivial example, it quickly becomes apparent that as auxiliary rules are removed one by one the remaining rules become more and more complex. It is for this reason that auxiliary rules can be considered to be a desirable facet of a rule base and not necessarily to represent an error. Moreover, the complexity of a rule depends on whether it is viewed from the standpoint of a *reader* or of the *rule interpreter*. The simplification, in terms of the number of predicates represented by the above rewriting may well ease the task of the rule interpreter, and of applying maintenance tools. This trade off between the needs of the expert, who needs to be able to read the rules to validate the system, and the needs of the system itself, is a further instance of the advantages that can come from working with a number of equivalent forms of the KB. This approach is exploited most fully when an intermediate representation accessible to the expert is used to communicate with the expert, and then mechanically compiled into the form most suitable for the inference engine of the target system (see section 6.9).

10.7. CIRCULAR RULE SETS

As discussed in section 8.2.7, whether the presence of circular rule sets represents an error or not depends on how the rule based will be used. In a forward chaining system values for attributes will be set according to data supplied to the system. Thus if the values of the literals lying on the cyclic path can all be externally supplied, the cycle may be beneficial, since it allows those not so supplied to be deduced - provided there is no subsequent attempt to reset the value of the externally supplied literal. In a backward chaining system, in contrast, such circularity may well lead to a non-terminating loop.

In section 8.2.7 we identified two types of circularity, direct and indirect. Thus:

DIRECT CYCLE:

```
Rule 1: A ∨ B ⇒ A
```

INDIRECT CYCLE:

```
Rule 2: C ∧ D ⇒ B
Rule 3: B ∨ F ⇒ D
```

We will discuss methods of detecting such cycles in the following sections.

10.7.1. Circular Rule Set Checking Using Static Inspection

By using a rule grapher such as the Datamap the presence of circularity is self evident simply by static inspection of the rule base. If we consider the above rule base this will appear, at the attribute-rule level, as shown in Figure 10.5. If this figure is compared with previous illustrations of the Datamap (Figures 10.1 and 10.3) it is clear that this Datamap is significantly different in that the connectors can be traced round to form a circuit, i.e. the rule base displays circularity. Again,

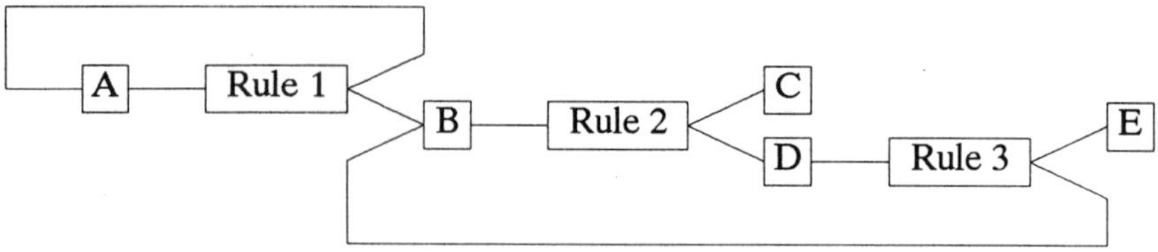

Figure 10.5: Rule-attribute Datamap depicting indirect and direct circularity.

the ease of spotting such cycles in this way will vary according to the size and complexity of the Datamap which in turn will be dependent on the degree of complexity displayed by the KB under consideration.

10.7.2. Circular Rule Set Checking Using EVA

It is impractical to determine whether a KBS will always terminate given any set of input values. However, we can test whether a KBS contains rules that lead to an infinite cyclic path. This can be done by constructing inference paths consisting of lists of rule names or numbers [Chang *et al.* 1990]. If we consider the procedure:

```
Rule 1: (X parent Y) ⇒ (X ancestor Y)
Rule 2: (X parent Y) ∧ (Y ancestor Z)
                ⇒ (X ancestor Z)
```

Using backward chaining we can construct a number of inference paths:

```
(Rule1)
(Rule2,Rule1)
(Rule2,Rule2)
```

Rule 1 represents the base case, and so only paths ending in Rule 1 will terminate. The third inference path in the above list indicates that a loop may exist, since attempts to reach the base case will again result in the same three possibilities, of which only the first two reach the base case. Thus the above inference may or may not terminate, depending on whether there will in fact be a call to the base case. If no base case exists a cyclic path will result.

In the EVA system a meta-predicate "derive" is used to determine possible inference paths such as those listed above. These paths can then be inspected. In the above example, if no terminating case, represented by a single element list, was present a non-terminating cycle would exist.

10.8. INCOMPLETENESS

Incompleteness was defined in chapter 8.2.8 as the situation where possible legal fact bases exist from which nothing can be inferred. To determine whether a given fact base is legal or not will usually necessitate reference to a domain expert. The presence of incompleteness in a rule base indicates that rules are missing, or that domain knowledge is not sufficient to deal with every possible case. Incompleteness implies that for certain cases the KBS will be unable to arrive at a solution, i.e. an uninformative "no conclusion" [Cragen and Steudel 1987] will be returned to the user. Another aspect of this is soundness. A rule base is unsound if given a legal fact base a false inference can be made, i.e. the result is untrue. Clearly both completeness and soundness are desirable properties, but as was remarked when defining these concepts, there may be a trade-off between them.

10.8.1. Incompleteness Checking Using EVA

The EVA system includes a tool to check for completeness of a rule base, i.e. that there are no missing rules or facts [Chang *et al.* 1990]. A rule base is complete if an output can be produced for every possible combination of input. Since in a relistically sized rule base there are a large number of input combinations it is impossible to check all possible cases. Chang suggests the use of completeness constraints. A completeness constraint specifies a pattern for a complete sub-set of schemas, facts and rules in a rule base. Thus if the maintenance engineer notices that there is a rule involving a range of values of an attribute of an object, then there must exist other rules involving complementary ranges of values for the same attribute of the same object otherwise some rule is missing.

10.8.2 Incompleteness Checking Using Incidence Matrices

Agarwal and Tanniru [1991] consider that a rule base displays incompleteness if:

1. There exists certain legal combinations of parameter-value pairs which are not contained in the antecedent of an existing rule, or
2. There are certain legal consequent values which are not present in the consequent of any rule.

This form of incompleteness can be discovered using their incidence matrices method as follows. If we (again) consider the following two rules used in the example given in section 10.5.2 above:

```
Rule 1: A(1) ∧ B(1) ⇒ C(1)
Rule 2:        A(2) ⇒ C(2)
```

Where `A`, `B` and `C` are attributes which can, in this case, take the values `1` or `2` we have four possible inputs, `A(1)`, `A(2)`, `B(1)` and `B(2)`. The incidence matrix of this rule set is than as follows:

	A(1)	A(2)	B(1)	B(2)	C(1)	C(2)
Rule 1	-1	0	-1	0	1	0
Rule 2	0	-1	0	0	0	1

Note that `B(2)` has an entry of `0` for both Rule 1 and Rule 2. However, we have four possible inputs, `A(1)`, `A(2)`, `B(1)` and `B(2)`. We can construct a "condition test matrix" where each row in the test matrix corresponds to a combination of the antecedent inputs, with a `+1` entry for the corresponding consequent value. We have labelled the four possible combinations of input C1 to C4. Thus:

	A(1)	A(2)	B(1)	B(2)	C(1)	C(2)
C1	-1	0	-1	0	1	0
C2	-1	0	0	-1	0	0
C3	0	-1	-1	0	0	1
C4	0	-1	0	-1	0	1

If we now multiplying the incidence matrix with the transpose of the "condition test matrix" we get:

$$\begin{pmatrix} -1 & 0 & -1 & 0 & 1 & 0 \\ 0 & -1 & 0 & 0 & 0 & 1 \end{pmatrix} \begin{pmatrix} -1 & -1 & 0 & 0 \\ 0 & 0 & -1 & -1 \\ -1 & 0 & -1 & 0 \\ 0 & -1 & 0 & -1 \\ 1 & 0 & 0 & 0 \\ 0 & 0 & 1 & 1 \end{pmatrix} = \begin{pmatrix} 3 & 1 & 1 & 0 \\ 0 & 0 & 2 & 2 \end{pmatrix}$$

In the resulting output matrix the rows correspond to the rules 1 and 2 and the columns to the possible combinations of input `C1` to `C4`, Thus:

	C(1)	C(2)	C(3)	C(4)
Rule 1	3	2	1	1
Rule 2	2	1	2	2

The matrix actually indicates the number of shared elements between each input combination and each existing rule.

Now recall the values S(i) and O(i) given in section 10.5.2:

S(i) = The total number of antecedent conditions and consequent actions that appear in a rule i.

O(i) = The value of the ith row in the output matrix. Where a number of columns exist in the output matrix this indicates that we are considering a number of "additional rules" or, as in this case, possible input combinations.

In our example S(1) = 3, S(2) = 2, S(C1) = 3, S(C2) = 2, S(C3) = 3 and S(C4) = 3; and O(1/C1) = 3, O(1/C2) = 1, O(1/C3) = 1 and so on. Also recall that:

If S(i)>O(i) and O(i)=S(k) then rule i is subsumed by rule k.

If S(i)=O(i) and O(i)<S(k) then rule i subsumes the rule k.

If S(i)=O(i)= O(k) then rule i is duplicated by the rule k.

Here we assume that k represents an input combination. Thus:

Input Combination C1.

S(C1) = O(1/C2) = S(1) (3 = 3 = 3)

C1 is a duplicate of Rule 1.

Input Combination C3.

S(C3) > O(2/C3) (3 > 2)

O(2/C3) = S(2) (2 = 2)

C3 is subsumed by Rule 2.

Input Combinations C4.

S(C4) > O(2/C4) (3 > 2)

O(2/C4) = S(2) (2 = 2)

C4 is subsumed by Rule 2.

Condition C2 is not duplicated or subsumed and so the rule base can be said to be incomplete since no outcome is specified for the combination {`A(1), B(2)`}.

10.8.3. Soundness

Checking for soundness requires that each possible input configuration is tested and the result presented to a domain expert so that he/she can ascertain whether the result is valid or not. For most KBSs this sort of exhaustive testing is not possible unless the KB can be partitioned into relatively independent and tractable modules. Moreover, since whether an inference is sound or not is largely a matter of content, there is little scope for the mechanisation of the process: potential problems need to be considered by an expert. Soundness is thus more related to testing than to the detection of structural problems in the KB.

10.9. INCONSISTENCY

In section 8.2.9 we argued that hard contradictions in the strictly logical sense will not typically occur in KBs which use production rules, Horn Clause logic or frames. However, it is quite possible for a rule base to produce contradictory results when presented with a given fact base. We referred to this as an inconsistency and said that an inconsistency occurs when some proposition or disjunction of propositions is a consequence of a KB when it is known that its negation is possible, so that a contradiction will arise if a fact base negating that proposition is supplied by the user. We also identified a situation, which we referred to as a soft inconsistency, where, as a result of a given set of inputs, a non-Boolean attribute can take more than one value.

To carry out exhaustive tests for inconsistency all possible fact bases applicable to a particular KBS must be generated, and executed in the system to see whether they give rise to a contradiction. However, for any realistically sized rule base this is not possible. Thus the various methods for testing for inconsistency, as described in the following sub-sections, include some technique to circumvent this problem.

10.9.1. Inconsistency Checking Using KB-Reduction

Using Ginsberg's KB-Reduction method [Ginsberg 1987] a KB is considered to contain a soft inconsistency if two conflicting hypotheses exist and a legal environment in the label for one is a sub-set of a legal environment in the other. If we consider the following three rules:

```
Rule 1: A ⇒ ¬R
Rule 2: P ⇒ Q
Rule 3: Q ⇒ R
```

The labels for the hypotheses ¬R and R will be:

```
Label for ¬R: A
Label for  R: P
```

A soft inconsistency will exist because a contradiction will result if we assert both A and P, provided that the conjunction $A \wedge P$ is meaningful.

10.9.2. Inconsistency Checking Using EVA

Chang [Chang *et al.* 1990] considers that a KBS is inconsistent if we can derive contradictory conclusions from it and gives the following example:

```
fact1: car(c).
fact2: new(c).
fact3: big(c).
fact4: broken(c).

rule1: car(X),broken(X) ⇒ bad(X).
rule2: car(X),new(X),big(X) ⇒ expensive(X).
rule3: car(Y),bad(Y) ⇒ not expensive(Y).
```

This KB permits both expensive(c) and not expensive(c) to be derived.

To detect inconsistency Chang has defined a predicate, `incompatible`, as a goal for the EVA logic checking program. Thus:

```
incompatible(B, not B)
```

In the above example `B` and `¬B` can be instantiated to both expensive(c) and not expensive(c). This method, as pointed out by Chang, requires a specific input of initial facts. To detect "inconsistencies" for any possible set of input facts templates to represent a general set of input facts need to be asserted. Thus:

```
car(C).
new(N).
broken(B).
big(G).
```

We can then show that both expensive(X) and not expensive(X) are possible if C, N, B and G are instantiated to X. Using these fact templates it is possible to enable the maintenance engineer to be prompted with incompatible sets of predicates even in the absence of any facts. Such sets can then be examined to see whether they represent a set which *should* be compatible: it may be that the set genuinely represents a situation that cannot occur.

Chang extends this method to cover cases where two different predicates are deemed incompatible by the knowledge engineer. For example instead of `not expensive(c)` we might prefer to write `cheap(c)`. This would make rule 3 of the example KB:

```
rule3: car(Y), bad(Y) ⇒ cheap(Y).
```

Given this interpretation, an inconsistency exists if a set of facts can lead to the conclusions expensive(X) and cheap(X). Chang uses the `incompatible` predicate to prove this also. However, the method does rely on someone constructing these "negative constraints" to record pairs of incompatible predicates.

10.9.3. Inconsistency Checking Using MELODIA

For the MELODIA verification program [Charles 1991] Charles defines inconsistency using the following illustration. Given the following two rules:

```
Rule 1: A>0 ∧ B<0 ⇒ C=3
Rule 2:       A=5 ⇒ C=2
```

and the fact base:

```
(A=5, B<0)
```

two conflicting facts, `C=3` and `C=2` are inferred.

In the MELODIA system the strategy for detecting such inconsistencies is to generate from the KB, in the Conjunctive Normal form (CNF) used by MELODIA, all the minimal consistent initial fact bases which lead to a contradiction during inference. These initial fact bases can then be said to be inconsistent with the KB. In order to find these fact bases MELODIA looks for sub-sets of initial literals inconsistent with the KB (an initial literal is a literal associated with an initial elementary expression, that is one that can be supplied externally to the KBS). This is done by reducing the KB by eliminating non-initial literals between clauses. Each step of the reduction process consists of applying the following three operations:

1. Elimination of Pure Non-Initial Literals. If a literal is such that its negation does not appear in the KB in clausal form it is said to be pure. All clauses containing pure non-initial literals are thus removed.
2. Elimination of Non-Initial Variables. This is achieved by combining clauses that contain both x and ¬x (where x is a non-initial variable) and thus eliminating x.
3. Elimination of Tautologies and Subsumed Clauses. Tautologies are clauses containing both x and ¬x. A clause is subsumed by another clause if all literals in the second clause are also in the first clause.

The reduction process continues until the resulting set of clauses contains only initial literals. If the resulting set of clauses is empty or contains only exclusion clauses then any consistent initial fact base is consistent with the KB and the KB is proven to be consistent (an exclusion clause is a clause that describes incompatible sets of facts supplied by the domain expert). Otherwise the resulting set of clauses provides us with the potential set of inconsistencies in the KB. These clauses are referred to as initial constraints. The user must then examine each constraint to determine whether the contradiction might occur or not. If they cannot occur they can be added to the list of exclusion clauses. Any remaining initial constraints indicate that the KB is inconsistent.

The operation of this process can best be illustrated by considering an example (based on Charles 1991). Given the following set of two rules:

```
Rule 1: (A1=TRUE) ∧ (A2<0) ⇒ (A3=9) ∧ (A4=BLUE)
Rule 2:     (A5=1) ∨ (A2=4) ⇒ (A3<1)
```

We rewrite these rules using Arabic numerals to represent each distinct literal and clauses as lists where each literal is separated by a logical or (∨). We then number the literals as follows:

```
1   A1 = TRUE
2   A2 < 0
3   A3 = 9
4   A4 = BLUE
5   A5 = 1
6   A2 = 4
7   A3 < 1
```

The above two rules then translate in to four CNF clauses and two exclusion clauses (2 and 6 cannot both be true, nor can 3 and 7):

```
Clause 1: (-1 -2 3)
Clause 2: (-1 -2 4)
Clause 3: (-5 7)
Clause 4: (-6 7)
Clause 5: (-2 -6)
Clause 6: (-3 -7)
```

The reduction procedure is as follows:

1. Elimination of Pure Non-initial Literals. The negation of literal 4 does not appear in the Clausal KB therefore Clause 2 can be eliminated (the negations of literals 3 and 7 do appear).
2. Elimination of Non-Initial variables. There are two remaining non-initial literals, 3 and 7, If we select literal 3 (because it only appears in two clauses) the elimination process is as follows. If `x` is the literal to be eliminated we can say the that-clausal KB consists of the set of clauses {P∧N∧R} where `P` is the conjunction of clauses containing `x`, `N` is the conjunction of clauses containing ¬x and `R` is the conjunction of clauses containing neither `x` or ¬x. The elimination of `x` is achieved by replacing `P∧N` by `P*N`, where `P*N` is the set of clauses obtained by combining each clause of `P` with each clause of `N`. This process is, of course, akin to standard resolution. The clauses obtained by this combination is the disjunction of the literals in each clause except the variable `x`. Thus:

```
P = {(-1 -2 3)}
N = {(-3 -7)}
R = {(-1 -2 -7)}

P * N = {(-1 2 7)}        :Clause 7
```

   This eliminates clauses 1 and 6 in favour of Clause 7 and so the clausal KB now consists of the following four clauses:

```
Clause 3: (-5 7)
Clause 4: (-6 7)
Clause 5: (-2 -6)
Clause 7: (-1 -2 -7)
```

3. Elimination of Tautologies and Subsumed Clauses. There are no tautologies or subsumed clauses.

We now repeat the process to eliminate the literal 7. This results in the set of clauses:

```
Clause 5: (-2 -6)
Clause 8: (-1 -2 -5) [from 1 and 7]
Clause 9: (-1 -2 -6) [from 4 and 7]
```

Clause 5 can now be removed because it is subsumed by Clause 9 and we have:

```
Clause 8: (-1 -2 -5)
Clause 9: (-1 -2 -6)
```

Neither of these represent exclusion clauses and so therefore we can say that the KB is inconsistent, since a user might well wish to assert e.g. `A1 = TRUE`, `A2 < 0` and `A5 = 1`, which would give rise to contradictory values for `A3`.

10.9.4. Soft Inconsistency Checking Using MELODIA (Hidden Theorems)

Charles [1991] refers to a soft inconsistencies as "hidden theorems". MELODIA detects hidden theorems by identifying the literals L where a set of clauses {KB, ¬L} is inconsistent. If we have a set of rules:

```
Rule 1: (E1 > 3) ⇒ (E2 = True)
Rule 2: (E1 < 4) ⇒ (E2 = True)
```

This will produce a set of clauses:

```
Clause 1: (1 2)
Clause 2: (-3 2)
```

and the exclusion clause:

```
Clause 3: (-1 3)
```

Literal `2` is a theorem because the fact `2` is can always be deduced when the exclusion clause is not violated. This can be shown if we resolve Clauses 1 and 3 to get `(2 3)`, and this resulting clause with Clause 2 to get the single literal `(2)`.

10.9.5. Inconsistency Checking Using Decision Tables

A decision table is a tabular representation of a procedural decision situation, where the state of a number of conditions determines the execution of one of a set of actions. Rules are given along the X-axis and conditions and actions along the Y-axis. The aim is to demonstrate the result of the exhaustive set of mutually exclusive combinations of conditions. Since for any realistically sized KBS the number of combinations will mean that this is not possible, some form of partitioning of the rule base will be required. A number of researchers (such as Cragen and Steudel [1987] and Vanthienen [1991]) have attempted to use decision table techniques to detect inconsistencies in KBSs.

If we consider the following set of rules:

```
Rule 1:  A ∧ B ⇒ C ∧ ¬D
Rule 2: E ∧ ¬F ⇒ A ∧ ¬G
Rule 3: ¬G ∧ H ⇒ B
```

We can draw up a table:

CONDITIONS	Rule 1	Rule 2	Rule 3
A	T	-	-
B	T	-	-
E	-	T	-
F	-	F	-
G	-	-	F
H	-	-	T
ACTIONS			
A	-	T	-
B	-	-	T
C	T	-	-
D	F	-	-
G	-	F	-

If as a result of a given input an action can be both true and false we can consider that the KBS contains an inconsistency. Consider, for example the attempt to add a rule:

```
Rule 4: A ∧ B ∧ H ⇒ D
```

In this case action `D` can be both true and false as a result of asserting {`A(T) B(T) N(T)`}.

Note that the above rule base contains conjunctions only. To incorporate disjunctions the rule base must be converted to a suitable normal form.

10.9.6. Inconsistency Checking Using Theorem Proving

The most direct approach to detecting contradictions and inconsistency is to immediately apply a theorem proving technique to the rule base. If any theorems at all are proved, they will represent a potential inconsistency, and if both some literal and its negation are provable, this will represent a contradiction.

Suppose we have the following rule base:

```
Rule 1: P ∨ ¬S
Rule 2: Q ∨ ¬P
Rule 3: R ∨ ¬P
```

and we wish to add the following clause:

```
Rule 4: ¬Q ∨ ¬R
```

We can now explore the logical consequences of adding this rule using the following standard logical consequences:

```
1.  A ∨ B, ¬A ⊢ B
2.  A ∨ B, ¬B ⊢ A
3.  ¬A ∨ B, A ⊢ B
4.  A ∨ ¬B, B ⊢ A
5. A ∨ ¬B, ¬A ⊢ ¬B
6. B ∨ ¬A, ¬B ⊢ ¬A
7. ¬A ∨ ¬B, A ⊢ ¬B
8. ¬A ∨ ¬B, B ⊢ ¬A
```

The ⊢ ("turnstile") symbol here should be reads as "given as assumptions ... we may validly conclude ...". Thus in logical consequence 1 we would read given as assumptions `A` or `B` and not `A` we may validly conclude `B`. Using these standard equivalences we can assert each literal in the rule we wish to add in turn and determine the consequences of that literal. When we have asserted all the literals in the rule the intersection of these consequences will be the consequences of the rule as a whole. Where we have several rules, we can perform this for each rule in turn until the consequences of the complete set of new rules have been determined.

To return to our example: we can test for contradiction by determining the effect of asserting first ¬Q, then ¬R, and then using the union of the values of each literal that remain possible after the inference to give the consequences of the disjunction ¬Q ∨ ¬R as a whole. The result can be drawn up in the form of a Logical Consequence Table as shown in Table 10.3. In this case no contradiction occurs although there is a potential inconsistency in that ¬P and ¬S are both consequences of Rules 1-4).

		Rule 4		
	(I)	¬Q	¬R	(I+4)
P	T/F	F (2)	F (3)	F
Q	T/F	F	T/F	T/F
R	T/F	T/F	F	T/F
S	T/F	F (1)	F (1)	F

Table 10.3: Logical consequence table (1).

Suppose we now wish to make the addition of a further rule:

```
Rule 5: S ∨ P
```

Then asserting each attribute for this rule in sequence we produce a Logical Consequence Table as shown in Table 10.4, where the initial rule set is I plus Rule 4. When we assert S, P is proven to be true (T) from Rule 1. Q is then proven to be true (T) from Rule 2 and R from Rule 3. However, now Rule 4 can fire allowing us to conclude that R (or Q) is false (F). Thus by asserting S a contradiction results. However, this does by itself not invalidate Rule 5 which states S ∨ P since if P can be true then the rule may still be correct. But on asserting P, Q and R are again shown to be true from Rule 2 and Rule 3 respectively, and again according to Rule 4 if R is true then Q must be false and if `Q` is true then `R` must be false. Therefore a contradiction also results when `P` is asserted. A contradiction thus results from the attempt to add Rule 5 to the rule base, since both arms of the disjunct lead to a contradiction.

		Rule 5		
	(I+4)	S	P	(I+5)
P	F	T (1)	T	F
Q	T/F	X	X	X
R	T/F	X	X	X
S	F	T	T/F	T/F

Table 10.4: Logical consequence table (2).

It should be noted, however, that this approach to inconsistency detection assumes that the unaltered part of the KB is known not to contain any contradiction, and that any consequences as to possible truth values are recorded in the column representing the initial state, otherwise it would be necessary to verify the entire rule base, which would be an over-lengthy task.

10.9.7. Inconsistency Checking Using COVADIS

The COVADIS system is an inconsistency checking system based on constraint propagation techniques designed to operate on KBSs developed using the MORSE shell [Rousset 1987, 1988]. The shell uses forward chaining with attribute-value rules. It generates, from a rule base, the specifications of all fact bases from which $\emptyset$ (absurdity) can be deduced. These are then presented to a domain expert to determine whether they are meaningful or not. If a fact base is not considered meaningful the expert is interactively asked to express why it is not meaningful in the form of some integrity constraint.

Given an example rule base:

```
Rule 1:              (A2 T) ∧ (A3 T) ⇒ (A1 T)
Rule 2: (A2 T) ∧ (A5 T) ∧ (A6 <8) ⇒ (A4 F)
Rule 3:  (A2 T) ∧ (A5 T) ∧ (A7 T) ⇒ (A1 T)
Rule 4:             (A1 T) ∧ (A6 <6) ⇒ (A4 T)
```

We can show that given the fact base `A2=T`, `A3=T`, `A5=T`, `A6=<6`, and `A7=T` that `A4` can have the both the values `T` and `F`. The expert is then presented with this fact base and asked to determine whether this is meaningful. If not the expert is asked to provide an integrity constraint. Perhaps, for example, the expert's knowledge of the domain tells him that if `A5` is true, then `A6` must be at least 7. If the fact base is meaningful the rule base is considered to be inconsistent (contradictory).

COVADIS generates the fact bases as follows [Lopez *et al.* 1990]:

1. Initial attributes are propagated in the rules forming contextual facts. A contextual fact is:

   `(ATT=VAL)[CONTX]`

   that is, the attribute `ATT` takes the value `VAL` when `CONTX` is satisfied. `CONTX` is a Boolean expression in disjunctive normal form.

2. The contextual facts `(ATT=VAL)[CONTX]` are propagated in those rules where there are antecedents referring to `ATT` as soon as `CONTX` is saturated, that is as soon as all the rules concluding `ATT=VAL` have been fired. If the antecedent clause is satisfied by `VAL`, a new contextual fact is created. The context of this new contextual fact is computed by "anding" the context of the different antecedent clauses.

3. The propagation mechanism includes special rules given by the integrity constraints (implicit and explicit) from which "false" can be obtained. In particular the implicit integrity constraints of no contradiction (`A` and `¬A`), and of monovalued attributes are considered.

4. The propagation phase stops as soon as either an integrity constraint is fired or no more rules can be fired, in which case no inconsistencies have been detected. In the former case, the context

is displayed to the expert. If the fact base is judged to be meaningful, the rule base is inconsistent, and must be corrected. If the fact base is not meaningful this cannot be regarded as a defect in the KB and so the propagation process is reactivated.

10.9.8. Inconsistency Checking Using MAUDE

The MAUDE inconsistency tool is intended to assist the maintenance engineer by eliminating any possibility of a single inconsistent "put" being sent to the end user at run time. It operates by examining the rules affecting the slot under consideration to see if the head propositions of the compiled clauses can be combined to create a contradiction. If they are co-tenable then no contradiction can follow from that particular combination. If they are not co-tenable then the tail propositions are examined. If they include a non-cotenable group then the contradiction cannot occur and the combination is discarded. If the contradiction is still possible the tail propositions are unfolded into the clauses of the rules that affect their slots and the process repeated. A combination which the system cannot eliminate is reported to the maintenance engineer for inspection and possible amendment. In most cases the reasons why the set offered are not co-tenable will be obvious to the domain expert, but where a genuine inconsistency exists the information can be used as the starting point to explore the KB, using the Datamap and other facilities in the MAUDE environment.

10.9.9. Inconsistency Checking Using Ayel's Inconsistency Checker

Once a KB grows to a reasonable size, its combinatorial properties mean that it is impossible to construct all the deductive fact bases to check it for inconsistency. Ayel therefore suggests that a conceptual model for consistency of the KB is required [Ayel 1988]. The conceptual model defines the structure of the KB and the checks for its consistency. The static consistency of the KB can then be verified by confirming that the available knowledge conforms to this model. Dynamic inconsistencies, those which involve both factual and deductive knowledge, are then checked using protocols aimed at directing and focusing the search. These protocols are developed by reference to domain experts. This will not guarantee that the KB is dynamically consistent but will reduce the likelihood of inconsistencies existing. Ayel goes on to suggest that this model is the group of instantiations to which the greatest number of constraints can be attached, e.g. a set of classes and objects in a fact base. Consistency is then expressed as conformity to this conceptual model. The following checks on single attributes are proposeed:

1. Checks on legal values to ascertain whether for each object in the class the values that attributes can have belong to the set of values for each attribute.
2. Checks on prohibited values to see if they can be associated with any attribute for a given object.
3. Checks on the upper and lower limit of the cardinal number of sets of values for an attribute.
4. Checks on the make up of the set of values e.g. sets of simultaneously contradictory values.

Checks about several attributes include:

5. Mutually exclusive attributes, "no one can have the same person for father and mother."
6. Integrity constraints, "a midwife cannot be a man".
7. Symmetry (completion mechanisms), if we know "Paul is Bob's parent" we should also know that "Bob is Paul's child".

Integrity constraints and completion mechanisms may also cross over from one class to an other. Ayel maintains that these checks define consistency in the conceptual model.

To check for dynamic inconsistencies of a rule base Ayel suggests, as we cannot construct all possible deductive factual bases, the identification of potential inconsistencies is the most that can be looked for. However, it would also be impractical to construct all potential inconsistencies. Thus those potential inconsistencies which have the "greatest chance" of giving rise to a dynamic inconsistent must be selected. Ayel calls these relevant potential inconsistencies. It is then necessary to prove that these inconsistencies may arise. Potential inconsistent situations are identified by looking for prohibited values, going over the upper limit of a cardinal number, simultaneously contradictory values and the violation of the integrity constraints. These can be limited by concentrating on inconsistencies that do not involve many variables and/or entities. Alternatively a given group of entities can be concentrated on. To determine relevant potential inconsistencies specific knowledge concerning the entities which may play a role in the presence of a dynamic inconsistency is required. To try and prove the selected relevant potential inconsistencies, Ayel uses a problem solver.

Ayel suggests a protocol for consistency checking composed of:

1. Technical limits to control the construction of potential

inconsistencies.

2. Specific knowledge to indicate the entities which may or may not play a role in the description of a consistency.
3. Heuristics to define the relevance of a potential inconsistency.
4. A relevance limit to select the most relevant potential inconsistencies.
5. Heuristics to limit the construction of potential inconsistencies deduced by using backward chaining rules.
6. A heuristic to stop the problem-solver and signify the failure of the inconsistency detector.

10.10. SUMMARY

In this chapter we have looked at a number of tools that have been constructed to detect errors and anomalies in rule based systems. There are two chief stumbling blocks to all the tools: first that as a KB grows to a size where such tools become necessary, the resources needed to apply them become daunting. The second problem is that many of the situations detected by the tools are not clear cut errors: whether there is a problem or not depends on whether or not some combination of facts can meaningfully be supplied to the system, or whether some consequence is desirable or undesirable. These issues are not capable of automatic resolution - unless we insist on an exhaustive specification of integrity constraints in advance, which would present an even greater burden to the expert than examining the candidate problem fact bases produced by the system. Even in a system like MELODIA, where detection of structural problems is relatively efficient, the need to construct the exclusion clauses is very domain knowledge dependent.

Such tools therefore are useful aids, alerting the maintenance engineer to potential problems, but these problems invariably need detailed investigation, in co-operation with a domain expert.

CHAPTER 11

Checking for Frame Base Errors and Anomalies

11.1. INTRODUCTION

In this chapter we discuss the methods and tools that may be applied to detect the errors and anomalies that may result in a frame based system as a result of the implementation of some maintenance action. In comparison to the tools available to check Knowledge Based Systems (KBSs) which use a rule based representation the number of methods and tools available for frame based systems is very limited. There are a number of reasons which help to explain why less effort has been devoted to developing these sort of tools for frame based representations than has been the case with respect to rule based representations. Firstly there is a lack of a formally precise understanding of the methods and techniques that are required to build frame base systems. In practice those of a very formal disposition, who are keen to investigate more formal methods of constructing and verifying Knowledge Bases (KBs), have tended to be drawn towards rule rather than frame based representations. Moreover, the environments available for the construction of frame representations have tended to be more sophisticated, allowing for many errors to be trapped at encoding time rather than waiting for the knowledge base to be complete, as must be the case where the KB consists of a number of interacting rules. Finally much of the inferencing - which is a major source of anomaly in rule based systems - is implicit in a frame system, since it is buried in the code which manipulates the representation. Much of what follows is therefore theoretical only, and cannot be illustrated by reference to currently existing systems.

In chapter 8 the errors and anomalies that may result after some maintenance has been implemented on a frame based system were discussed. These can be summarised as follows:

- Redundancy.
- Missing slots and frames.
- Misplaced slots and frames.
- Duplication.
- Auxiliary slots and frames.
- Inconsistency and incompleteness.
- Errors related to numeric ranges.
- Errors associated with cardinality.

We consider each of these individually in the following sections. At the end of this chapter we also consider hybrid systems which make use of both frames and rules for representing different aspects of the system.

11.2. REDUNDANCY

A frame or slot in a frame based system is considered to be redundant if it plays no part in reaching the goal which the system is designed to establish. Thus to establish whether individual frames and slots within frames are redundant or not will require a certain amount of domain knowledge. The most straightforward option is for a domain expert statically to inspect individual frames and comment on the relevance of these frames and the slots they contain. Viewing tools may be used to assist in this task, but there is little scope for further automation or any possibility of dispensing with the need for a domain expert, since the actual use of slots is typically implicit in the code which manipulates the system.

11.3. MISSING SLOTS AND FRAMES

A frame based system contains missing slots if two frames cannot be distinguished from one another. This may be because two frames are duplicates of one another or because a sub-frame does not contain a slot (or slot value) to distinguish it from its super-frame. Missing frames are not normally detected at compilation time: however, a tool to detect duplication in a frame based system is not hard to envisage. A missing slot (or slot value) in a super-/sub-frame relation is harder to identify although we can search the frame base for frames which have no slots associated with them, a sure indication that a missing slot exists.

Missing frames arise when there are frames which are not connected, through the frame hierarchy, to a higher level frame, because some intermediate frame which should tie them into the hierarchy has been omitted. Missing frames are usually detected at compilation time with the result that the compilation fails. Alternatively such frames may be discovered, prior to compilation, using static frame base inspection tools such as a frame base browser or grapher (see section 11.4 below) or using a specific missing frame identification tool.

11.4. MISPLACED SLOTS AND FRAMES

A frame is misplaced if it appears in the wrong place in the frame hierarchy, i.e. it may be too specialised or not specialised enough. To determine where a frame should be located in the hierarchy will require a certain amount of domain knowledge. Assistance can be obtained from tools such as frame browsers or graphers which graphically display the frame hierarchy. These are utilities for displaying the frame hierarchy together with any entities that have been instantiated to frames. If we consider the following example frame base:

```
Frame: A
superFrame: Top Frame
◊ slot ...

Frame: B
superFrame: A
◊ slot ...

Frame: C
superFrame: B
◊ slot ...

Frame: D
superFrame: B
◊ slot ...

Frame: E
superFrame: B
◊ slot ...

Frame: F
superFrame: C
◊ slot ...
```

```
Frame: G
superFrame: E
◊ slot ...

Frame: H
superFrame: E
◊ slot ...
```

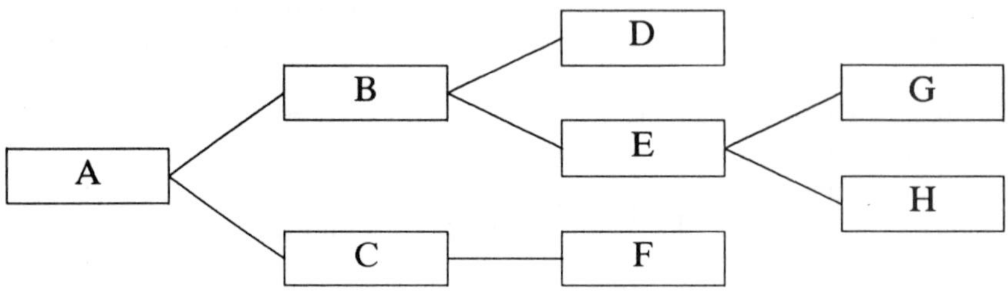

Figure 11.1: Frame hierarchy browser.

We can display this in the form of a graph as shown in Figure 11.1. This can then be inspected for (say) inverted super- and sub-frames, for example frames `C` and `F` may be inverted. Again this relies on some feel for the structure of the domain which can only be supplied by a domain expert. It should be stressed that the ordering of frames in the hierarchy is both an important and non-trivial matter. If the ontological knowledge of the domain expert is to be properly captured, decisions have to be taken, and need to be correct. Choices are not always easy: is "pensioner" a higher or lower level concept than "woman"? The answer may even vary with the application under consideration. Whether the right choices are made will rely heavily on the knowledge engineer's skill in capturing fully the knowledge of the expert.

Another alternative to this purely visual inspection is for a frame hierarchy navigation tool to be used to identify inverted super- and sub-frames. This will allow the user to step up or down the frame hierarchy, displaying the value of particular attributes and the associated values, until, in the case of stepping up, the point at which the attribute is introduced into the hierarchy, or in the case of stepping down the point at which the values of the attribute become specialised to a point range, is reached. Consideration will be required as to whether stepping down is best done in a breadth or depth first fashion. The primary purpose of frame hierarchy navigation tools is to assist in the identification of the appropriate point at which to introduce a new frame within an existing frame hierarchy.

We should also mention attribute sub-set identification tools here which can also support the appropriate location of a new frame within an existing frame hierarchy. Given a list of attributes the tool should be able to identify the lowest existing frame(s) which possess a sub-set of those attributes. This should then be the best place to add the new frame to the hierarchy. Additionally, given a frame the tool should be able to determine the highest existing frame(s) whose attributes are a super-set of that frame. This will determine the proper sub-frames.

11.5. DUPLICATION.

Duplicate frames have already been discussed (see section 11.3), but we should also consider duplicate slot values. The existence of duplicate slots with the same required value, but contained in two different frames, in a frame based system indicates that the slot should perhaps have been introduced at a higher level, or that an intermediate frame is needed. A simple tool can be envisaged to examine and compare individual slots in different frames.

11.6. AUXILIARY FRAMES AND SLOTS

As in the case of KBSs that use a rule representation, auxiliary frames and slots in frame based systems are not considered to represent an error in this work. However, using suitable viewing tools, the presence of auxiliary frames can be detected and their relevance then considered. Auxiliary frames are represented by nodes in a frame hierarchy which do not represent leaf nodes but where no furcation takes place. For example in Figure 11.1 the frame representing the entity `C` can be considered to be an auxiliary frame. Auxiliary slots can only be identified by careful inspection of individual frames and with the assistance of a domain expert. Sometimes they may be a simple error, but more usually they will reflect a view as to the structure of the domain ontology, or represent provision for the eventual extension of the hierarchy when a furcation will be introduced.

11.7 INCONSISTENCY AND INCOMPLETENESS

In a frame based system inconsistency can only be fully established by considering all possible legal fact bases and determining what conclusions can be drawn. If legal fact bases exist from which no conclusion can be drawn because a number of possibilities exist which, given the fact base, cannot be distinguished, missing slots can be said to exist. Again to determine whether a fact base is legal or not will usually require the intervention of a domain expert.

A different approach would be to adapt and make use of the tools that exist for finding inconsistency and incompleteness in rule based systems. Given a frame representation, it is always possible to translate this into a set of rules, although doing so may call for the exercise of judgement in the interpretation of particular links. Once such a translation had been made, any of the tools described in the preceding chapter could be used to perform the necessary checks.

11.8. ERRORS ASSOCIATED WITH LOWER AND UPPER NUMERIC RANGES

Some errors associated with numeric ranges can only be discovered by inspecting the slots pertaining to the attribute for which the range has been defined. If, however, ranges are specified for slots in sub-frames they must be encompassed by the range given in the slots of super-frames which introduce the attribute in question. In most frame based systems this sort of incompatibility associated with numeric ranges is identified during compilation with the result that the compilation fails. Hopefully a suitable error message will be output to the user when this occurs.

The EVA system [Stachowitz and Combs 1987] described in section 9.6.1 includes a semantics checking module which has two main functions: checking the KB for violations of semantic constraints and checking the semantic constraints for internal consistency and agreement with other meta constraints. Checks for lower and upper numeric ranges are included under this heading of semantic checking.

11.9. ERRORS ASSOCIATED WITH MINIMUM AND MAXIMUM CARDINALITY

Again errors in cardinality can often only be identified by inspecting the slots which reference this cardinality. The process of comparing these slots may of course be automated and a "cardinality checking" tool developed, to present cardinalities to the expert, and to check for consistency of definitions with super-frames.

Amongst the semantic checks to be addressed by the semantic checking module that forms part of the EVA system [Stachowitz and Coombs 1987], Stachowitz also identifies the need to check the minimum and maximum cardinality of sets, relations and schemata.

11.10. HYBRID SYSTEMS

In this section we shall consider detection of the errors and anomalies that can occur in hybrid systems. Particularly:

- Missing values, slots and frames.
- Unused values, slots and frames.

Values, slots and frames that appear in the rule base but not in the frame hierarchy should be detected during compilation into the target representation when the frame hierarchy and rule base are married together. Facilities should be included in the compiler for error messages to appear and the relevant rule highlighted thus allowing the user to identify the missing values, slots and frames readily and, if desired, to add them to the frame hierarchy. For example if we attempt to compile the following frame hierarchy:

```
Frame: Thing1
slot a literal (1 3)
slot b literal (1)
slot c literal (1)

Frame: Thing3
slot h literal (1)
```

And then try to load a set of rules of the form:

```
Rule 1: Thing1 a(2) if Thing1 b(1) and Thing1 c(1)
Rule 2: Thing1 a(1) if Thing1 b(1) and Thing1 d(1)
Rule 3: Thing2 e(1) if Thing2 f(1) and Thing2 g(1)
```

We will discover that slot `a` has a missing value `(2)`, slot `d` does not exist and that the entire frame `Thing2` is missing.

In the above example the frame hierarchy also has a value for slot `a(3)`, which is unused, and an unused attribute (slot) `h` in the frame `Thing3` which is itself an unused frame. The unused attribute can be identified using an appropriate unused slots tool such as the INSPECTOR tool described below in section 11.10.1. The fact that the frame hierarchy contains a superfluous frame is also quickly apparent by invoking a frame hierarchy browser of some sort. There is no simple mechanism for detecting unused attribute values.

The simple example given here illustrates the value of giving a separate description of the ontology of the domain in the form of a frame hierarchy instead of simply allowing the ontology to emerge from the heuristic knowledge encoded in the form of rules. The possibility of this kind of "cross check" can show up deficiencies in either the frame hierarchy or the rules, but where these are not in step, there is something wrong which needs to be fixed by changing or extending one of them.

It should, however, be appreciated here that a frame hierarchy may contain unused values, slots or frames either so that the KB remains isomorphic with the source, or more importantly in anticipation of future change. It may well be advantageous to record the ontology of the domain as fully as possible, without reference to the specific task enshrined in the rule base.

11.10.1. INSPECTOR

There are a number of tools available that can be used to detect unused or missing slots in hybrid systems. One such tool is INSPECTOR [Software Architecture and Engineering Inc. 1983]. This is a support tool designed to be used on KBSs developed using the Knowledge Engineering System (KES) expert system shell. INSPECTOR identifies all unattached attributes e.g. attributes that are not contained in the antecedent or consequent of any rule. However, this situation may not necessarily represent an error as the attribute, although not used in the current version of a particular KBS, may have been included with an eye to future maintenance.

11.11. SUMMARY

This section on tools available to assist in the maintenance of frame representations has been somewhat briefer than that describing the tools available for rule based representation. This in part represents the comparative paucity of tools that have been developed for maintaining such systems and in part the greater emphasis that has been placed on tools for the initial construction of frame based systems. Although these development tools are outside the scope of this book, they are none the less useful in preventing the occurrence of some of the errors that may occur during the development of frame based systems.

CHAPTER 12

Verification, Validation and Testing

12.1. INTRODUCTION

Verification and validation is an integral part of the development of any software system and this includes Knowledge Based Systems (KBSs). It also has a considerable bearing on maintenance, particularly corrective maintenance. Comprehensive verification and validation throughout the development of a KBS can substantially reduce the amount of future corrective maintenance that may be required. This has been observed by many authors, for example O'Leary [1991]. Verification and validation must also be implemented on completion of a maintenance session. The significant difference between this type of verification and validation and that carried out earlier in the development cycle is that it need only impinge on the section of the KB that is affected by the change. We refer to this section of the KB as the jeopardised rule or frame set. However, this does assume, firstly that the rest of the KB is correct and secondly that the affected section of the KB can be identified.

There are many definitions of verification and validation, reviews of these definitions are given in Satre and Massey [1991] and Balci and Sargent [1984]. In this work the definitions, with respect to traditional software systems, originally proposed by Boehm [Boehm 1981] and adopted elsewhere [Sommerville 1989, Pressman 1987] have been adopted for application to KBSs. Boehm's definitions are:

Verification: "Are we building the product right?"

Validation: "Are we building the right product?"

Thus verification is the process of checking that the system meets the requirements definition/specification and validation is the process of checking that the system actually does what the customer wants.

With regard to KBSs, where (in most cases) no meaningful requirements specification exists, the process of verification described in these terms becomes meaningless. Some authors disagree with this statement arguing that to test a KBS some sort of requirements specification is essential [Geissman 1988, Green and Keyes 1987]. Geissman goes on to argue that such a specification exists because expert systems are problem orientated and therefore allow the specification of the attributes of an acceptable or correct solution and that from these attributes a series of testable statements can be produced. Regardless of whether a requirements specification for a KBS can be derived or not, in this work we have defined KBS verification as the process of checking that the system's operation is right, i.e. that results are arrived at in the correct manner. KBS validation is then the process of checking that the system does what the user expects it to do, i.e. the result is correct. Verification is usually implemented throughout the development cycle while validation takes place, given an incremental KBS development life-cycle paradigm, at the end of each iteration.

There are many other definitions for KBS verification and validation. For example O'Leary and O'Keefe [1989] define KBS verification and validation as follows:

Verification: "Proving that an Expert System has the properties of consistency, completeness and correctness."

Validation: "Determining whether a KB is an effective encoding of the knowledge and behaviour of the expert."

Whatever the case in this work, verification is concerned with the internal mechanisms of the KBS and can be addressed by the techniques described in earlier chapters. Validation is traditionally carried out by running test cases and interacting with human experts in such a manner that the expert can state objections to the conclusions, to the use of the rules or to the operation of the system. This is still considered to be the most convincing "proof" of correctness, where a KBS is considered to be correct if its behaviour is not detectably inadequate.

As a result of validation testing a certain level of confidence in a KBS can be obtained. This can be expressed as a percentage of the system's success rate with respect to the test cases to which the KBS has been subjected. The accuracy of the final percentage obtained will thus hinge on the choice and number of test cases. The test cases should reflect the entire input domain and not just the most obvious section of it.

The testing of KBSs, compared to traditional software systems, is hampered by two principal difficulties. Firstly, problems are encountered because most of the program flow and control in KBSs is hidden. Secondly the nature of KBSs means that exhaustive testing is impractical. Constantine and Ulvila [1990] have identified a number of further difficulties that may be encountered when testing KBSs:

- In many cases issues concerning testing are not raised early enough in the KBS development process.
- In a resource constrained environment it is difficult to carry out thorough testing.
- Often what a KBS should do is not clearly defined or made explicit.
- Testing is often hindered by the complexity of the Knowledge Base (KB) and the lack of tools for static analysis.
- The domain experts used during knowledge analysis are often no longer available when the system testing stage is reached.

Some of these difficulties are also encountered when testing traditional software systems.

In this chapter the testing techniques available and associated software support tools are discussed. These are discussed in the following sections.

12.2. KBS TESTING TECHNIQUES

A number of testing techniques to validate expert systems have been developed, any one or more of which may be adopted by the KBS developer or maintenance engineer. Many of these are analogous to traditional software testing techniques. Some of the more common are discussed here. Firstly testing techniques can be classified as being either black box or white box. Black box testing considers input and output only. A KB, part of it or individual rules are tested by supplying appropriate input data and then examining the output. The test is successful if the output is correct. The test cases are generally developed intuitively, an approach that is time consuming, requires a domain expert and is prone to errors where the test cases defined do not address the appropriate elements within the KB. However, black box testing is currently the most common testing technique used for KBSs. White box testing is the reverse of black box testing and focuses on the internal structure of the encoded knowledge. In traditional software systems this is typified by path testing where a set of inputs are supplied to a piece of code and the paths and sub-paths through the code that result examined. In KBSs this involves examining the internal operation and structure of rules. For example we will be interested in what instantiations are made when a rule is fired and, often more importantly, what instantiations are not made.

Alternatively we can classify testing techniques as being either static or dynamic. Static testing examines the KBS as text or code. Many of the techniques described in previous chapters involve static examination of code e.g. redundancy and subsumption checking. As the name implies dynamic testing is the reverse of static testing. Dynamic testing involves evaluating a system during its actual execution. Many black box techniques may also be described as dynamic testing techniques. The Interactive Test Case Construction (ITCC) Tool described below in section 12.5.2 can also be considered to be a dynamic testing technique.

During development (and after a maintenance session has taken place) testing can be carried out at different levels, at the local level, at the sub-system level and globally. Local testing involves checking individual rules against other individual rules in the KB. Local testing is analogous to unit testing in traditional software systems. It cannot be carried out in isolation as it assumes that errors occur in pairs of rules. A criticism of local testing is that this is clearly an unrealistic assumption. Examples of this type of testing include the simple and complex subsumption identification methods described previously.

Sub-system testing requires that the KBS be decomposed into sub-systems, or groups of rules, enabling the performance of each sub-system to be observed individually. This has a number of advantages:

- Testing can be incorporated into the development cycle.
- Sub-systems can be tested more easily since they are less complex and more manageable.
- Error detection is simplified since errors are localised.

The disadvantages of sub-system testing are:

- It may not be possible to observe the input-output of the sub-system.
- Successful testing of each individual sub-system does not validate the overall system since integration may introduce errors due to incorrect interaction between sub-systems.

Sub-system testing is analogous to module testing in traditional software systems.

Global testing involves checking the rule base as a whole. Global testing is similar to acceptance testing in traditional systems where scenarios are run on a completed system to show that it operates to the satisfaction of the user. Unit, sub-system and global testing techniques may all also be categorised as being either black box or white box techniques.

It is also worth considering a number of more specific techniques in this section, namely:

- Third Party Testing.
- Thread Testing.
- Field Testing.

These techniques may again be considered to be either black box or white box and their implementation static or dynamic at the various different levels within a KBS.

The concept behind third party testing is that the software engineers and domain experts involved in developing a KBS have a vested interest in the success of the product and, intentionally or unintentionally, may influence the nature of the testing to encourage positive results. The Prospector expert system was tested by comparing its output with that of the experts used to develop the system [Gashing 1979], with the result that the validation of the system can best be described as being of dubious value. Third party testing thus maintains that testing should be carried out by personnel who had no involvement in the development of the system as this will result in more rigorous and impartial testing. Third party testing also has its parallels in traditional software verification and validation.

Thread testing involves the identification of unique cases with all their characteristics. For example in the case of a KBS to identify animals in a zoo, such as that given in chapter 8, a single thread would be that connecting the rules to establish that (say) `animal isa tiger`. Threads that deal with similar instances can then be grouped together with a complete set of test cases to ensure that the necessary fine distinctions have been made. These groupings are sometimes referred to as builds and can form an important part of some development methodologies [Micco 1988]. Each build represents a stand alone system that forms a module in a larger system.

The concept of field testing was developed as a result of evidence that many KBSs are tested in laboratory conditions. The disadvantage of this is that such conditions do not reflect the actual working conditions in which the system will be expected to operate. Advocates of field testing maintain that systems can only be tested fully by allowing them to be operated by the end users in the surroundings that the end users will use them in. From the developer's viewpoint there are also some additional advantages. Firstly it places the burden of testing on the user. Secondly acceptable performance ranges are obtained implicitly, since users will cease to report on problems when acceptable performance ranges are reached. Field testing was used extensively in the case of R1/XCON subsequent to its implementation [Brachant and McDermott 1984]. However, it should be noted that field testing is only possible for noncritical applications.

Finally in this section we should also mention model testing. An essential part of verification and validation is also testing of the domain model on which the KBS is based. This can involve:

- Analytical validation: checking each part of the model.
- Synoptic validation: checking that an acceptable output is achieved for each of a set of inputs and total model performance.

12.3. TESTING USING A DATABASE OF CASES

As observed in the introduction to this chapter, on completion of a KBS maintenance session it is only necessary to test the section of the KBS that is affected (directly or indirectly) by an implemented change, i.e. the jeopardised rule or frame set. In some cases this may be very far reaching. Techniques exist to identify this extended sub-set of KBS elements; these were considered in chapter 7. However, to avoid the identification of this sub-set a number of systems, such as GARVENES1 [Compton *et al.* 1988] and EXPERT and ENYCIN [Buchanan *et al.* 1983], utilise a database of what can be described as corner stone cases. Every time a change is made to the KBS these cases are run to ensure that the correct interpretation is still arrived at. A criticism of this approach, however, is that very often a great number of unnecessary test cases are run. Moreover the corner stone cases will need to be maintained, for example we may be required to include a previously overlooked situation and hence the corner stone cases may need to be expanded to cover this situation.

12.4. RULE GROUPING

KB testing can be very much simplified if the KB is decomposed into groups of associated rules. By using rule grouping methods the use of validation criteria can be improved upon by modularising rules based on some domain specific semantics and performing analysis on these individual groups as necessary.

Roberts and Hall [1991] categorise different methods of rule grouping. They suggest that there are two basic types of organisation:

1. Quiescent Characterisation Organisations (QCO): Rule organisations which group according to static properties of the rules. These can be further broken down into types:
   (a) Syntactic (pattern match) groupings based on the rule condition part, rule conclusion part or conclusion-condition matching.
   (b) Semantic groupings based on some relationship like properties, entities, objects or situations.
2. Dynamic Characteristics Organisations (DCO). Rule groupings formed during system execution according to system performance such as distance/time relationship between rules, e.g. how close in time one rule fires with respect to another. This can be used, typically, to reduce the computational overhead of computing rule matches.

Rule grouping using these methods may be carried out manually or using some form of automation.

12.5. VALIDATION (TESTING) TOOLS

There exist a number of tools that can be used to assist in the testing of KBSs. We can categorise these tools according to the following classification:

- Test case generators.
- Test case analysis tools.

Test case generators allow the user to develop suitable test cases. They range from simple editors to automatic test case generators. A number of these are described in the following sub-section. Test case analysis tools can be inspection tools, such as tracers and graphers, or more sophisticated tools, some of which are discussed below. Tracers and graphers and other inspection tools allow the user to examine the inference process either as it takes place or on completion. Many of the tools that belong to this latter class of tools have already been discussed in chapter 7, where their use in identifying problematic elements in a KBS (local identification) that required maintenance was considered. Examples include inference tracing tools, also sometimes referred to as rule tracers, which are used to inspect the sequence of rules fired to establish a proposition. Essentially this is achieved by providing a record of all the rules that were activated to arrive at a conclusion. However, no indication is given of which body variables had an impact on the conclusion and which did not. This information can, however, be obtained using interactive test case construction techniques. Interactive test case construction has not yet been discussed in this work and is thus considered extensively in section 12.5.2 below.

12.5.1. Test Case Generation and Analysis Tools

Currently the most usual way of validating a KBS in practice is to run test cases and to compare the result produced by the system to those produced in "real life". If a conflict arises some further maintenance will be required. To this end it will be necessary to be able to identify the rules fired to reach a conclusion in each case. This is usually achieved by storing the identifiers of all the rules that have been fired to establish a proposition. Where a correct conclusion is not reached the identifiers of the rules fired to reach what ever conclusion was reached can then be retrieved. If this process is implemented for a large number of test cases the results can be compared and any similarities in the path taken in each case identified. If in a batch of (say) 100 test cases 10 cases fail to produce the expected result, it may be that on inspection of the execution path through the KB certain similarities exist. For example the same rule may have been fired in all 10 failed test cases but not in the remaining 90, thus indicating that this rule may be the source of error. To this end test case monitoring tools may be used to identify such problematic rules. These are used to compare groups of execution paths representing test cases from a standard set of test data that have failed to reach a satisfactory conclusion. Tools of a similar type are the past case analysis tools. These are used to compare execution trails for a number of cases to determine the frequency with which (a) particular slots are set to particular values, (b) particular rules are activated and (c) instances of particular objects occur.

When testing a KBS the example cases used to develop a system should of course not also be used to test it as the system would undoubtedly be able to solve these. Often the number of additional test cases available to a development team is limited therefore it is necessary to contrive additional test cases. This can be a difficult and time consuming task that can be alleviated by using a test case generator. There are many examples of these. The EVA system [Chang *et al.* 1990] has two types of test case generator, a structure based generator (white box) and function based generator (black box). The first utilises a rule flow diagram to represent the KB and generates test cases to activate every rule in the graph at least once. The second utilises the input-output specification for the KBS. Alternatively the manual generation of test cases may be assisted through a menu driven utility such as that utilised by the IBM 9370 information system KB verification process [Roscoe 1988].

To assist in the generation of test cases we can also envisage tools that will allow the user to browse previous test cases. These test case browsers can be made more efficient by providing the maintenance engineer with the capability to identify test cases with particular properties.

12.5.2. Interactive Test Case Construction

A major difficulty in constructing test cases is the need to specify fully a case for presenting it to an expert system. This means that features are specified without reference to the path that the inference will follow, and so there is no assurance that the most fruitful path will be taken.

In this sub-section we give a detailed study of a tool, which we have termed the Interactive Test Case Construction (ITCC) tool [Coenen and Bench-Capon 1992b], which was specified as part of the MAKE project. The tool allows the initial partial construction of test cases which can then be filled out with further detail according to the results shown when the partial test case is run. More generally the tool can be considered to be a rule base simulation tool. Rule base simulation is concerned with the graphical animation, also referred to as "peopling", of the rule base so that the user is able to observe visually the rule base while inferencing takes place and to interact with it so that the inferencing process can be guided along a particular route. The animation of the rule base thus involves the asserting of instances of entities and values for attributes associated with a particular test case, after which inferences can be made and inspected by working from the leaf propositions up to the root propositions. Alternatively the execution trail can be traced from the top down, i.e. from a desired root proposition to the associated leaves.

The ITCC tool described here is superimposed on a rule grapher such as the Datamap tool described in section 7.12. We will illustrate the operation of this tool by considering the following (deliberately flawed) example MIR rule base designed to establish whether `personA` is the `cosister` of `personB`:

```
RULE 1
(personA cosister personB)
iff
(personA sister personB)
and
(personB sister person A)

RULE 2.
(personA sister personB)
iff
(personA sex female)
and
(personC == personD)
    when
        (personA hasParent personC)
        and
        (personB hasParent personD)
```

Note that Rule 1 contains a `when` (relational) proposition. These rules translate into the following CMIR clauses:

```
CLAUSE 1.1
(personA cosister personB)
if
(personA sister personB)
and
(personB sister personA)

CLAUSE 1.2
(not personA cosister personB)
if
(not personA sister personB)

CLAUSE 1.3
(not personA cosister personB)
if
(personB sister personA)
```

```
CLAUSE 2.1
(person A sister personB)
if
(personA sex female)
and
(personC == personD)
and
(personA hasParent personC)
and
(personB hasParent personD)

CLAUSE 2.2
(not personA sister personB)
if
(not personA sex female)

CLAUSE 2.3
(not personA sister personB)
if
(not personC == personD)
and
(personA hasParent personC)
and
(personB hasParent personD)
```

Note that the `when` proposition translates into an additional conjunction.

Figure 12.1 shows a proposition-clause Datamap for the example rule base. Recall that, due to the CMIR clausal form used for the target representation, all propositional furcations represent conjunctions, while clausal furcations represent alternatives (disjunctions). Thus any two or more propositions branching out from a clause are conjoined, while any two or more clauses branching out from a proposition represent disjunctions. In other words we can identify "and" and "or" connectors from the Datamap.

To animate a rule base we must "people" it by creating instances of entities and by asserting propositions to establish attribute values for those entities. This may be implemented interactively by clicking on propositions for which the user wishes to supply an instance. To this end a number of types of proposition need to be identified. For our example we need consider only two:

PREDICATIONS. Single entity propositions, for example `personA sex female` where the single entity is `personA`.

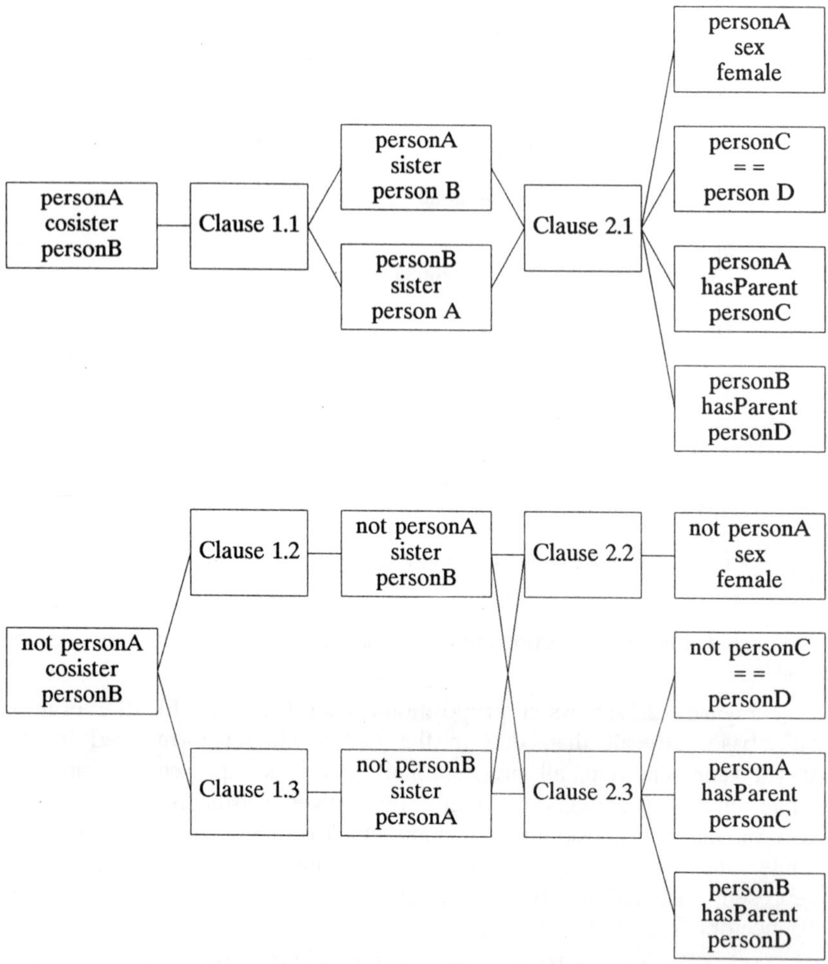

Figure 12.1: Proposition clause animated Datamap (1).

RELATIONS. Dual entity propositions, for example `personA cosister personB` where the entity pairs are `personA` and `personB`.

When peopling the rule base the following requirements are relevant:

1. Provision for the users to be able, if they so desire, to select a

particular instance from a list of existing instances (if there are any) applicable to the class of object under consideration.

2. The ability to prevent users from asserting a particular instance where this will contradict previous assertions. For example if the proposition `mary sex female` has been asserted then users should be prevented from asserting a contradictory proposition such as `not mary sex female` (assuming that in both cases `mary` refers to the same instance).
3. An indication of instances that have already been associated with a proposition.

When starting with an unpeopled rule base there will be no existing instances of entities available from which the user may make suitable selections. The user must therefore create the required instances. This is achieved by clicking on a proposition we wish to assert. The result will be empty menus of the form illustrated in Figure 12.2 (a) and (b) depending on the type of proposition selected. The user can now enter an instance for the proposition in question by typing into the box. In the case of a relational proposition both boxes must be completed.

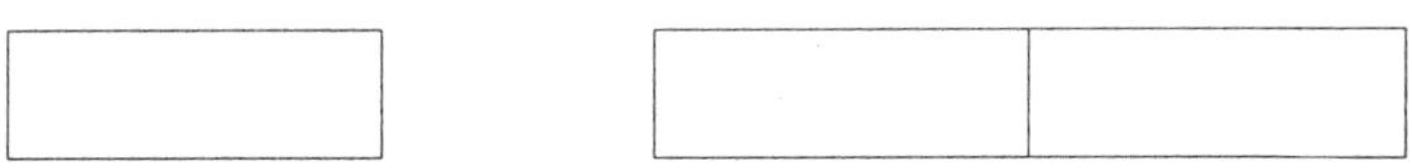

(a) Predication *(b) Relation*

Figure 12.2: Proposition menus (1).

For example if we were to click on the proposition `personA sex female` we could (say) enter the instance `mary` into the empty menu displayed. The effect of this would then be to assert the proposition `mary sex female`. We could create another instance for the same proposition, by clicking on it again. This time a menu of the form given in Figure 12.3(a) would appear, note that `mary` now appears in this menu indicating that this instance already exists and has been associate with the attribute-value `sex female`. Another instance can now be created, say `ann`, by typing into the empty box again. The effect of this is to assert the proposition `ann sex female`. We can also assert propositions using existing instances. For example if we click on the proposition `personA hasParent personC` relation a menu of the form depicted in Figure 12.3(b) would result. The bracketed instances

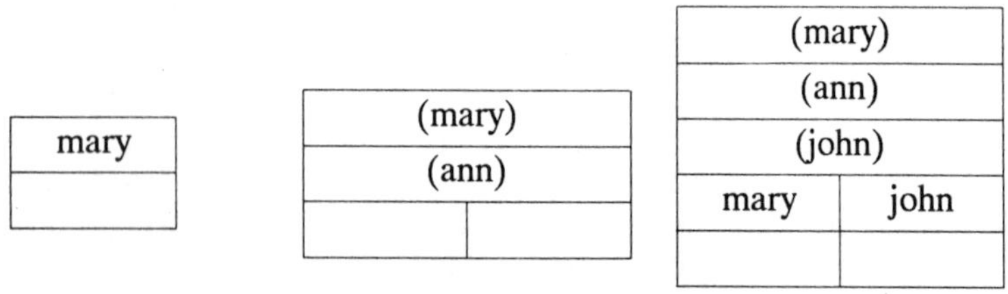

(a) personA sex female *(b) personA hasParent personC* *(c) personA hasParent personC*

Figure 12.3: Proposition menus (2).

indicate that these instances exist and that they have been bound to other propositions in the rule base but not the proposition presently under consideration, i.e. they are possible candidates for the subject(s) of the selected proposition. We can either select one or more of these existing instances or create further new instances by typing into the empty blocks. The first will be instantiated to `personA` and the second to `personC`. For example we may select `mary` from the list of existing instances for the entity `person` and instantiate it to `personA` and create a new instance, `john`, and instantiate it to `personC`. The effect of this will be to assert the proposition `mary hasParent john`. If we clicked on the `personA hasParent personC` proposition again the proposition menu will now be of the form given in Figure 12.3(c). Similarly we can assert the proposition `ann hasParent john`.

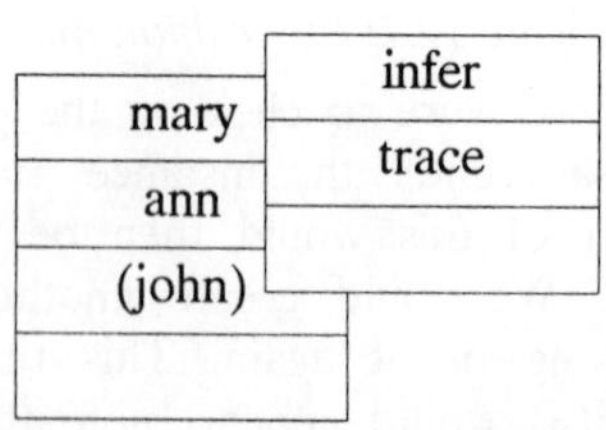

(a) personA sex female

Figure 12.4: Proposition sub-menu.

In this manner the rule base can be peopled interactively with a complete or partial set of test data. In the above illustration this has been carried out from the leaf propositions. It is suggested that this is the approach that will most closely match the normal operation of the KB. However, instances can equally well be created by clicking on other propositions in the KB, if other aspects of the behaviour of the KB need to be investigated.

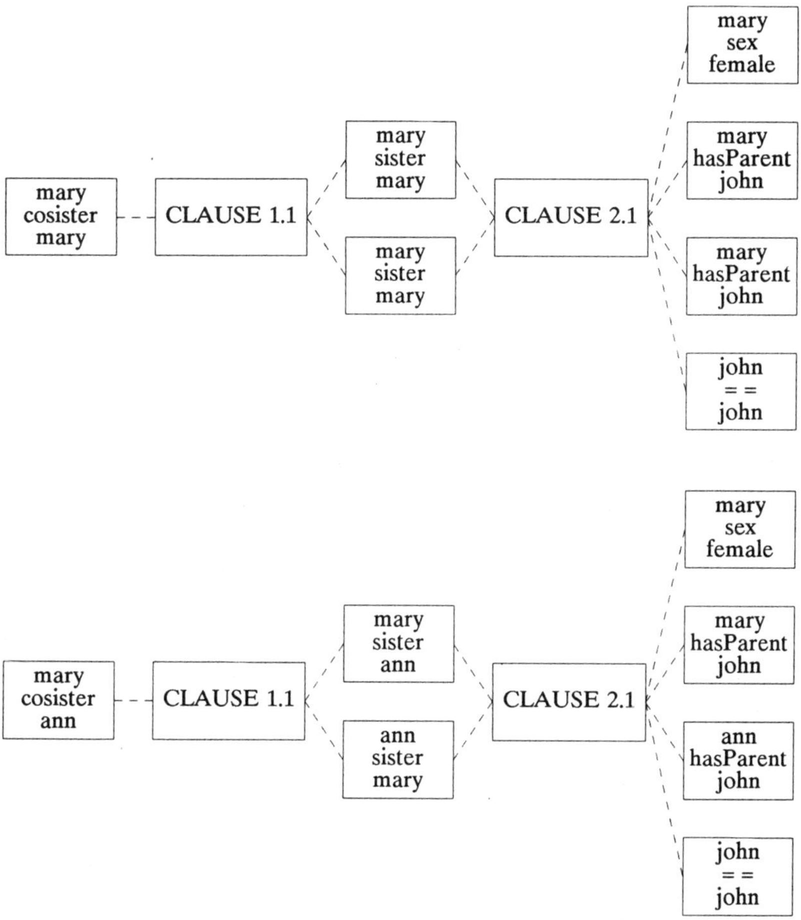

Figure 12.5: Proposition-clause Datamap.

Inferencing.

Inferencing can take place at any time, although to be effective at least one proposition must have been asserted. The inferencing process uses the inference engine that forms part of the KBS under consideration thus no additional control is required, i.e. the MAUDE inference engine in this case. The user proceeds as follows. First a subject for the inference must be selected by clicking on a proposition which references an entity of the type desired. A proposition menu will appear from which an instance for the desired entity can be selected. This instance then becomes the subject of the proposed inference. If we now drag right a sub-menu will appear listing a number of options including an inference option. The effect of selecting the inference option is that inferences are attempted with respect to the selected subject and the propositions asserted to date. The inference trail or trails are indicated on the Datamap, either leading up to a root proposition or until the inference cannot continue any further due to the absence of necessary information. In the latter case further propositions can be asserted as necessary in the same manner as described above.

For example if we wish to select `mary` as the subject of our inference we may click on the proposition `personA sex female`, select the instance `mary` from the resulting proposition menu and then drag right and select the infer option (Figure 12.4). A Datamap of the form shown in Figure 12.5 will result (clauses with negated heads are not shown). Note that where applicable instance names have been instantiated and that the inference trail is highlighted by a "dashed" line. The Datamap immediately shows a flaw in the KB in that a person can be a cosister of themselves: this is clearly not the intention. At first glance the problem might appear to be located in Rule 1, but if we look a little further along the graph we can see that the problem is actually located in Rule 2, since `mary sister mary` is itself undesired. We can now inspect Rule 2, using the Datamap facilities (see section 7.12). From this it then becomes clear that Rule 2 requires an additional proposition:

```
RULE 2.
(personA sister personB)
iff
(personA sex female)
and
(personC == personD)
    when
        (personA hasParent personC)
        and
        (personB hasParent personD)
and
(personA \== personB)
```

Tracing

Whereas inferencing is a bottom up approach to inspecting the KB, tracing is the reverse top down approach, i.e. from root to leaf propositions. Before tracing can be implemented a start proposition, not necessarily a head proposition, must be selected as the point at which the trace is to commence. This is carried out in a similar manner as described above by selecting a proposition, identifying an instance and then dragging right and selecting the trace option from the resulting sub-menu (Figure 12.4).

The tracing facility clearly indicates the inference path that would have to be followed to establish the start proposition. Unlike the infer option no account is taken of whether the user has asserted any propositions along the route: the aim is to indicate what propositions need to be asserted to establish an end goal. Further, during the operation the Datamap is pruned so that irrelevant branches are not shown.

The pruning process is implemented by removing "nullified" propositions and clauses from the Datamap. In its simplest form a nullified proposition is a proposition which cannot be true. If we consider the following two propositions:

```
(Entity Attribute true)
(not Entity Attribute true)
```

where the entity and attribute referred to are both the same, and if we know that the first proposition is "true" then the second must be "false". If we required our trace to start at the first proposition the second would be irrelevant and therefore considered to be nullified. A nullified clause in turn is one for which at least one body proposition is nullified (clauses consist of conjuncted propositions). Nullified propositions and clauses do not appear in the Datamap when implementing the trace option. This greatly enhances the clarity of the trace as the inference trail is demonstrated free of the clutter of rules and clauses irrelevant to the situation under consideration. To determine whether a proposition or clause is nullified or not the following "rules" must be applied starting with the nullification of the start proposition for the trace.

RULE 1: If a nullified proposition appears in the body of a clause and the clause is disjuncted with a sibling clause nullify the clause and any other propositions in the body but not the head proposition.

RULE 2: If a nullified proposition appears in the body of a clause and the clause is not disjuncted with a sibling clause nullify the clause and any other propositions in the body or the head proposition.

RULE 3: If a nullified proposition appears in the head of a clause nullify the clause and the body propositions unless a body proposition is also located in the body of another clause which has not been nullified.

Rules 1 and 2 are first used to prune clauses and propositions located above the nullified inverse of the start proposition and Rule 3 the section of the Datamap below the nullified inverse of the start proposition. These rules are applied repeatedly to a clause list, clause by clause, until a "clear run" is attained. The nullification process proceeds both up and down the Datamap towards both the root and leaf propositions.

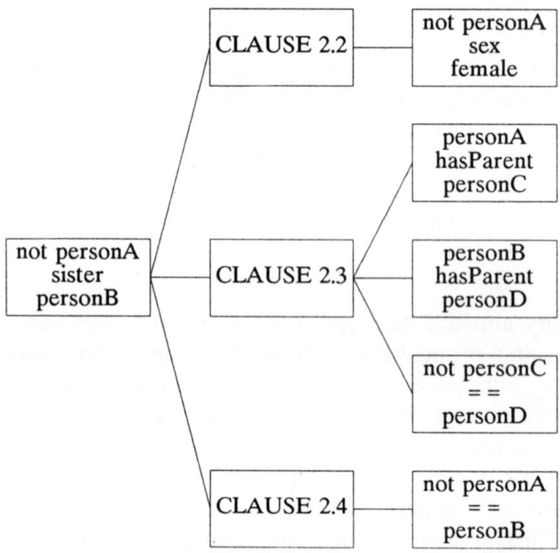

Figure 12.6: Inference trace.

If, for example, we wish to start the trace from the proposition `not personA sister personB` we click on it, select an instance, and then drag right ad select the trace option from the associated submenu (Figure 12.4). The resulting Datamap is depicted in Figure 12.6. Note firstly that the execution trail leads all the way down to the leaf propositions required to establish the root proposition: unlike the infer option this will occur regardless of whether the intervening propositions have been asserted or not. Secondly note that the Datamap has been pruned by ignoring irrelevant branches.

The pruning process will start with the nullification of the inverse of the start proposition `personA sister personB`. Clauses 2.1 will then be nullified according to Rule 3. Where applicable, by repeated application of Rule 3, the entire branch leading down from a nullified start proposition will be nullified and hence not depicted in the Datamap.

A rule base simulation tool to animate and illustrate the behaviour of a KBS such as described here may be used:

1. Where a test case has produced some wrong result either because some unexpected conclusion has been drawn, or because some desired conclusion has not been drawn.
2. To ensure that, given some data, some particular conclusions are drawn and/or some other particular conclusions are not drawn.
3 To explore the KB, perhaps to determine the effect of a particular rule, i.e. what consequences flow from a rule on an assertion or set of assertions, or what assertion or set of assertions would license a particular conclusion.

More specifically, given one or more assertions, the user will be able to determine one or more of the following:

1. What inferences can be drawn.
2. What inferences cannot be drawn.
3. What inferences lead to a particular conclusion.
4. What further assertions will be of interest in exercising the KB.

These can all be done using the infer and trace facilities described above. The ability to handle and present negative results is of particular practical significance.

In some cases it may still be desirable to load part or all of a test case before commencing interaction so that whole cases can be provided at the outset, rather than asserting each proposition individually using the peopling method described above. Partial cases can be constructed using an editor and then loaded into the ITCC tool where appropriate inferencing and tracing can then take place. The case can then be extended or modified in the light of the result.

12.6. JEOPARDY TOOLS

In the introduction to this chapter it was suggested that the significant difference between the verification and validation carried out as part of a KBS development process and that implemented on completion of a maintenance session was that in the latter case only a sub-set of the KB would require consideration, the jeopardised sub-set. There was a proviso to this in that we must be able to identify this sub-set. In the following sub-section we consider a tool, also specified as part of the MAKE project [Coenen and Bench-Capon 1992a], to identify rules jeopardised by rule changes.

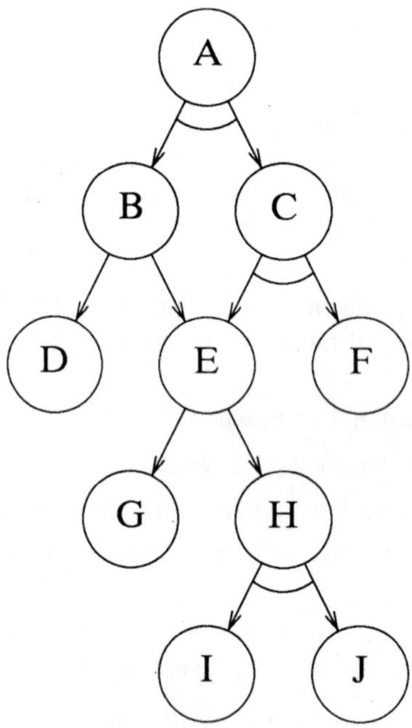

Figure 12.7: AND-OR tree for rule base prior to maintenance.

12.6.1. MAUDE Jeopardised Rule Sub-set Identification

As a result of a maintenance session in which some rule base maintenance has been carried out the set of rules which will require verification and validation will comprise three identifiable types:

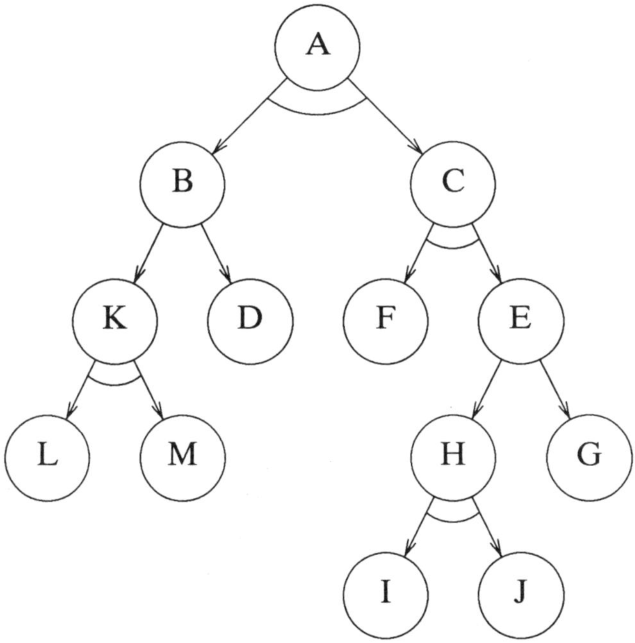

Figure 12.8: AND-OR tree for rule base after maintenance.

1. New rules, i.e. rules that have been added to the KB.
2. Modified rules, i.e. existing rules that have been modified.
3. Compromised rules, i.e. existing rules that are affected by the modification or removal of a rule immediately above them in the KB structure.

These rules can be identified by comparing the KB after maintenance has taken place with the KB in its original form as follows:

- A new rule = a rule in the revised rule base whose head does not feature in the original rule base (this assumes that the rule base does not contain procedures which share the same head and are fired according to some strategy).
- A modified rule = a rule in the revised rule base whose head does appear in the original rule base but whose tail, in its entirety, does not.

- A compromised rule = a rule in the revised rule base whose head appears in the tail of a modified rule prior to its modification or in the tail of a rule that has been deleted.

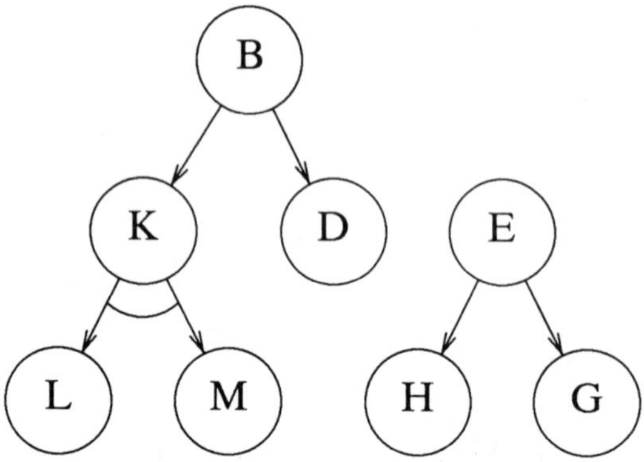

Figure 12.9: The jeopardised rule set.

The above definitions also require a definition for deleted rules:

- A deleted rules = a rule in the original rule base whose head does not appear in the revised rule base.

The operation of this identification techniques using the above definitions can best be illustrated using an example. If we consider the rule base illustrated by the AND/OR Tree in Figure 12.7, which comprises the following rules:

```
Rule 1.1: B ∧ C ⇒ A
Rule 1.2: D ∨ E ⇒ B
Rule 1.3: E ∧ F ⇒ C
Rule 1.4: G ∨ H ⇒ E
Rule 1.5: I ∧ J ⇒ H
```

We may carry out some maintenance on this rule base so that the new rule base (Figure 12.8) consists of the following 6 rules:

```
Rule 2.1: B ∧ C ⇒ A
Rule 2.2: D ∨ K ⇒ B
Rule 2.3: E ∧ F ⇒ C
Rule 2.4: G ∨ H ⇒ E
Rule 2.5: I ∧ J ⇒ H
Rule 2.6: L ∧ M ⇒ K
```

According to the above criteria the jeopardised rule set will be of the form:

```
Rule 2.6: L ∧ M ⇒ K
Rule 2.2: D ∨ K ⇒ B
Rule 2.4: G ∨ H ⇒ E
```

Rule 2.6 because its head does not appear in the original rule set therefore it is a new rule, Rule 2.2 because its tail, in its entirety, does not appear in the original rule base therefore it is a modified rule; and Rule 2.4 because its head is contained in the tail of the modified Rule 2.2, prior to its modification, i.e. in the tail of Rule 1.2, therefore it is a compromised rule. The jeopardised rule set is given in Figure 12.9. Note that Rule 2.5 which branches off Rule 2.4 is not included in the jeopardised rule set as this part of the rule base will not require any post maintenance verification and validation.

12.7. EFFECTIVENESS OF TESTING

There are a number of methods where by the effectiveness of testing can be measured. One method is to employ statistical techniques, sometimes referred to as quantitative validation, to compare expert system performance against either test cases or human experts. O'Keefe *et al.* [1987] review three of these:

- Paired T-tests.
- Hotelling's one-sample T-test.
- Simultaneous confidence intervals.

Alternatively we can consider the coverage of our testing techniques. In traditional software systems this refers to the percentage of statements or branches in a piece of code which have been executed by test cases. These percentages are often referred to as TERs (Test Effectiveness Ratios) where:

$$TERn = \frac{\textit{number of program compoments exercised at least once}}{\textit{total number of program components}}$$

Statement testing corresponds to TER1, branch testing to TER2 and so on. With reference to KBSs, coverage refers to the percentage number of rules or clauses that have been executed. From this the maintenance engineer can determine whether the test cases run fully explore the KB or not. For example we could consider the following:

TER1 = Every rule executed at least once.

TER2 = Every clause executed at least once.

However, we must be clear as to what we mean by "executed".

12.8. SUMMARY

In this chapter we have discussed the verification and validation of a KBS after a maintenance session has taken place. We consider a number of testing techniques which we broadly classify as being either black box or white box, or alternatively, static or dynamic. We also consider a tool to identify the jeopardised sub-set of rules in a rule based system on which verification and validation should be implemented.

Most of the remaining discussion is devoted to a suggested Interactive Test Case Construction (ITCC) tool, which was specified as part of the MAKE project. ITCC allows:

- Interactive construction of test cases.
- Run time viewing of the inference process.
- Ability to influence the inference process by editing test cases.
- Opportunity to examine the rule base using the Datamap facilities.

During the final verification and validation process it may be that a need for further maintenance is detected in which case the maintenance methodology outlined in this work (see section 4.1) dictates that the process should be repeated. If successful the maintenance process ends with the testing phase described here. The only maintenance topic that has not been considered in this work so far is the management of the maintenance process. This is discussed in the following and final chapter of this book.

CHAPTER 13

Management of Maintenance

13.1. INTRODUCTION

In this chapter we shall look at a number of issues relating to the management of a Knowledge Based System (KBS) in operation, concentrating, as is in keeping with the rest of this book, on the management of maintenance. The issues we shall address include configuration management, quality assurance and evaluation. Each of these is discussed in the following sections. We then devote a section to a discussion of a methodology to assess the effectiveness of maintenance tools and techniques such as those we have described in this work. This centres around a *maintainability metrics*. To evaluate the effectiveness of particular tools, this could be applied to both maintenance activities using the tools and techniques described and without this benefit so as to provide control information. Further, so that information concerning the maintenance of a KBS can be collected and collated, a *maintenance change log proforma* is suggested.

There are also a number of tools, which can best be described as housekeeping tools, that have a bearing on KBS maintenance but do not fit comfortably into any of the chapters in which specific classes of tools were discussed. These include data dictionaries, thesauruses and syntax and semantics checkers. A brief section is therefore devoted to these tools at the end of this chapter.

13.2. CONFIGURATION MANAGEMENT

Configuration management can best be defined as being about managing changes to systems in such a way that any version of any system supplied to a customer can be reproduced from its component parts [Chard 1990]. All software is subject to change ranging from minor alterations to significant changes which require that large parts of the existing system be rewritten. To be able to overcome the problems of managing change in an environment requires:

- That every component of the system is uniquely identifiable.
- The upkeep of records of every change and what components were supplied to each and every customer.

Configuration management systems provide the necessary control and recording capability for these requirements.

Configuration management is applicable to both traditional software systems and KBSs. In conventional systems modules are developed by different people, and at different times. Similarly many KBSs consist of a number of KBs, each of which may have been developed by different members of a development team at different times. In both cases it is important to keep careful track of the history and provenance of the various components.

To manipulate such multiple KBs a configuration management facility suggests itself to prevent mishaps and to lead to better control of the KBS development process and subsequent maintenance. Such a facility is described in Prerau *et al.* [1990] where a meta-level utilities knowledge base is discussed that contains information concerning the KBs under development as part of a KBS and which supervises the saving and loading of KBs and their associated files. The MAUDE development environment [Coenen and Bench-Capon 1992a], described in chapter 5, allows individual sections of a KB to be linked and displayed on a grapher so that an overall picture of the components of a system during and after its development can be obtained.

13.3. QUALITY ASSURANCE

Quality assurance is a management function that should be applied throughout the development cycle. It includes:

1. Testing methods and tools.
2. Formal reviews.
3. Control of documentation and record keeping.
4. Methods for measurement and reporting.
5. Adherence to specified methodologies, standards and techniques.

Conventional software engineering has come up with a number of attributes which are considered desirable for software, and hence provide the dimensions against which quality may be measured. When the development is started, targets for these attributes should be agreed, and the role of quality assurance is to check that these levels are, in fact attained, and to take remedial action when the system falls short. We shall now consider a number of these attributes.

13.3.1. Correctness

Correctness refers to the extent which the software satisfies its specification, and fulfils the objectives of the customer. This is, of course, the mosts important aspect, since if the software is not correct, then it is of little importance how good it is with respect to other considerations. Proving that the software is correct with respect to its design specification is somewhat easier that proving that it meets the needs of the customer.

In conventional systems, the issue of correctness can often be clear cut since there will normally be a precise definition of the input that the system should accept and the output that should result from the inputs. The situation can be rather less clear in the case of KBS however. We recognise that human experts are not infallible, and we may therefore be prepared to tolerate a less that perfect performance on the part of the KBS. In extreme cases, where experts disagree, there may even be no universally accepted answer that the KBS can aspire to. This being so, correctness for a KBS may be relative, and there should be some agreed level of performance which, if attained, will be considered acceptable.

13.3.2. Reliability

The reliability of software can be defined as a measure of how well it provides the services expected of it by the end users without malfunction. By malfunctions in this context is not meant so much the provision of incorrect answers, as the system behaving in an unexpected or inappropriate way - "crashing" and "hanging". The reliability of traditional software systems is measured using statistics such as failure rate and number of faults discovered. Software reliability models, for example SMERFS (Statistical Modeling and Estimation of Reliability Functions for Software), are applied to conventional software systems to compute such statistical quantities. It has been suggested [Barrett 1990] that such models can be applied with little modification to KBSs.

13.3.3. Efficiency

Efficiency refers to the amount of computing resources and code required by the software to perform its functions. This will manifest itself in two chief ways. First there is the hardware which is required to run the system. Typically the target hardware will be laid down at the outset of development. If the system is to be run on stand alone hardware this provides a hard constraint, and the main importance is the impact that the required hardware will have on the cost of the system. If the system is to run on a machine also used by other systems, it is important that it does not seize a disproportionate amount of the resource, so that the performance of these other systems degrades.

Response time is also critical, and is a major determinant of the acceptability of the system to its users. Again, some target response times should be indicated in the requirements definition for the system, but these are notoriously difficult to estimate for KBS.

13.3.4. Integrity

This feature refers to the extent to which access to the software and data by unauthorised persons can be controlled. In a conventional system it is clearly important that data cannot be corrupted, whether by accident or malicious design. In the case of a KBS there is a further complication in that there is not the same clear distinction between the data of the system and the knowledge which will be used to manipulate it. Who can amend the rules of the system, and under what circumstances, is an important issue, and care needs to be taken that the KB cannot be changed without proper control.

13.3.5. Usability

Usability concerns the amount of effort required to learn, operate, prepare input for and interpret the output from the system. Again this may present particular problems for KBSs since such systems have fewer well established conventions than standard software systems. In particular the interpretation of the output from such systems can often give rise to difficulties amongst non-expert users, and much current research is directed towards improving the explanation capabilities of KBSs. The uncertainty concerning the look and feel of the final system, and as to what can be provided, is one of the main reasons why prototyping has proved so popular in the KBS area.

13.3.6. Maintainability

This relates to the amount of effort required to locate and fix errors in the system, and depends on such things as a relevant structure, appropriate decomposition and complete documentation. The special problems relating to the maintenance of KBS need no discussion here, as they have been the prime concern of the previous chapters. Under this heading we should also consider flexibility, which refers to the effort required to modify operational software, that is to carry out perfective and adaptive maintenance.

13.3.7. Testability

Testability refers to the amount of effort that is required to test the software to give an assurance that it can perform the required functions. Again we have discussed testing KBSs in a previous chapter. One element of the design which is of particular importance is the way in which the system is decomposed during development. In general, the greater the extent to which the system can be decomposed into small, relatively self-contained elements, the easier it is to test. We have already seen that this can be critical for KBs because of the combinatorial explosion that takes place as they increase in size. This feature can thus be promoted if thought is given to sensible partioning of the KB at an early stage.

13.3.8. Portability

This concerns the effort required to transfer software to different hardware and/or software configurations. This can be an important consideration where the system is intended to have a long life, since hardware becomes obsolete and operating systems are continually upgraded. It has received little attention so far with regard to KBSs, since there are very few systems which have been long lived enough for this to become a pressing problem.

13.3.9. Reusability

Reusability applies to the extent to which software can be used in applications other than those for which it was originally constructed. In particular, when dealing with KBSs one needs to consider both the flexibility of the inference engine, which may be able to manipulate other KBs to perform different tasks, and the flexibility of the KB itself, the extent to which it can be adapted for use in solving other tasks in the same domain.

13.3.10. Interoperability

Interoperability concerns the interface that can be made between the system and other systems in the organisation with which it would be useful to exchange information. Thus many KBS applications could make extensive use of the data held on conventional systems in the organisation. Again it is important to consider these issues early so that the desired interfaces can be specified and the system constructed with a view to this mode of operation.

13.4. EVALUATION

When embarking on the development of a system it is essential to state the expected costs and benefits on that system. The costs will be the quantifiable costs of purchase of hardware and the resources expended on building the software, together with the costs of introducing the system into the organisation, and the costs of keeping it operational. The benefits may also be quantifiable in terms of savings of money or of time, or they may relate to the more intangible factors such as improvements in quality or customer satisfaction. When the project is complete it is also important that it be evaluated in the light of these original estimates so that the actual costs and benefits realised can be compared with those that were expected.

This need for evaluation is no less true of KBSs, although very often we find that there are rather more intangible factors involved and so the evaluation is correspondingly less precise. Often too, there is not the same degree of explicit statement of the expected costs and benefits at the outset of a KBS development, and so there is no fixed point with which to compare the results achieved.

More specific questions that can be posed of a KBS relate to how well its performance compares with a human expert. One approach is to adapt the famous Turing test. The Turing test was originally proposed as a way of determining whether a system could be said to be intelligent or not, and basically involved an impartial observer attempting to distinguish responses from the system being tested from those of a human control. In the case of expert systems, the test would be to see whether responses to questions in the domain received from the system could be distinguished from those of a domain expert. The key element is that the observer should not know which responses came from the system and which from the expert, so that bias can be eliminated. Such tests have been used to evaluate both MYCIN and

ONCOCIN (Buchanan and Shortliffe 1984). Similarly INTERNIST/CADUCEUS [Pople 1982], another well known medical KBS, was evaluated by comparing its diagnostics against those published on selected cases from the medical literature. This is a rather stringent test, and in practice of course a KBS may be useful enough without rising to the heights of emulation of expert performance.

Lopez summarises a number of evaluation measures [Lopez *et al.* 1990]. He divides such measures into two classes:

1. Measures concerning structure and contents.
2. Measures concerning functionality.

Measures belonging to the first group are obtained by examination of the KB and include measures of structural elements, intelligibility, comprehensibility and complexity measures of time and space. The second group requires information concerning the behaviour of the KBS and includes measures of execution efficiency, reasoning efficiency, correct reasoning, precision, sensitivity analysis, robustness, utility and transferability.

13.5. EVALUATING KBS MAINTENANCE TOOLS

In this section we pass from considering the evaluation of the KBS itself to the evaluation of tools designed to support its maintenance. As we have seen in the earlier chapters of this book, tools designed to assist the maintenance of KBS are still undergoing development and refinement. For this reason we will suggest here a means by which we can evaluate such tools in a practical setting.

It is suggested that, wherever possible, KBS maintenance should be evaluation using test data that has been derived from actual changes which have or should be implemented. These changes can be gathered together and classified according to the maintenance action required. To this end Swansons's maintenance categorisation scheme [Swanson 1976] can be adopted (see section 1.2.6); namely:

1. Corrective maintenance (e.g. as a result of a bug report).
2. Perfective maintenance (e.g. as a result of a user request).
3. Adaptive maintenance (e.g. as a result of a change in the source data).

Maintenance tools can then be used to implement, verify and

validate the changes. Control can be provided by implementing the same changes without using any tools. It is essential that a number of example changes to address each type of maintenance action be implemented using a variety of maintenance engineers selected from the personnel who will eventually be maintaining a system. This will serve to weed out any variance in the ability of individuals to implement changes which will be subject to their knowledge of the system. The results can then be analysed according to a "maintainability metrics". This will result in a numeric evaluation of each tool. The metrics should be applied to each example addressing an element of the maintenance classification scheme. Further the metrics should be applied to the implementation of the example change both with and without the use of tools to support the maintenance effort. Finally a change log proforma is suggested so that any maintenance activity can be collected and fed into the evaluation. A schematic of this test procedure is given in Figure 13.1.

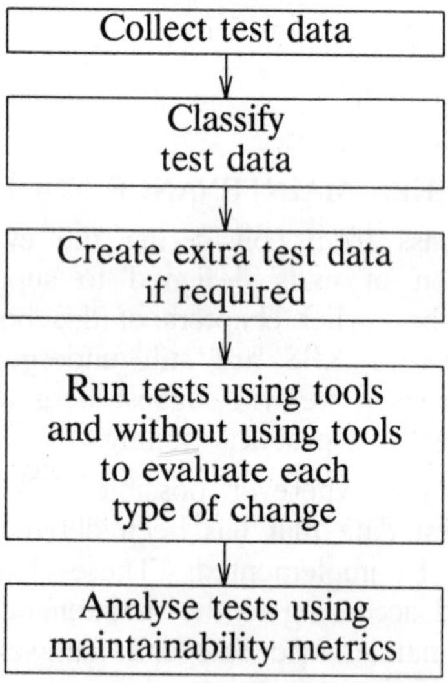

Figure 13.1: Maintenance tool test procedure.

Maintainability Metrics

The enhanced KBS maintainability resulting from the use of maintenance tools is difficult to quantify. However, it can be assessed indirectly by considering attributes of the maintenance activity that can be measured. Gilb suggests a number of maintainability metrics for traditional software systems that relate to the effort expanded during maintenance [Gilb 1979]. These can be adapted to fit KBS applications by considering the following maintenance attributes:

1. Total recovery time: Time spent from start of initial problem recognition to end of global testing.
2. Problem recognition time: Time required to identify the nature of the change; adaptive, corrective or perfective.
3. Problem analysis time: Time required to identify the type of change according to the above classification and identify where in the KB it should be implemented i.e. where in the frame hierarchy or rule base.
4. Change specification time: Time required to change the specification for the KB (where an intermediate representation is used).
5. Active correction time: Time required to compile the changed specification.
6. Local testing time: Time required to test the changed rule or section of frame hierarchy.
7. Global testing time: Time required to test the system after the change has been implemented.

Each of the above metrics can be recorded without great difficulty in (say) hours and decimals of hours. Such data will provide the project team with an identification of the efficiency of the proposed tools. It should be noted that during a maintenance session there may be several periods of time slot covering each of the above. For example, as a result of local testing it may be that the maintenance engineer will required further change specification and active correction time.

Other factors that may be used to define the efficiency of the tools are:

8. Ease of use: The ease with which the maintenance engineer can use the tools.
9. Confidence in result: A measure of the correctness of a KBS after maintenance has taken place.

The above are subjective attributes of KBS maintainability. It should be possible to allocate a value between 0 and 1 to indicate ease of use where 1 equates to very highly rated and 0 to very poorly rated. Similarly it should be possible to apply confidence levels between 1 and 0 to a KBS after maintenance has been carried out. For example we

MAINTENANCE ATTRIBUTE	VALUE	WEIGHTING	QUANTUM
TOTAL RECOVERY TIME	TIME (hrs)		
PROBLEM RECOGNITION TIME	TIME (hrs)		
PROBLEM ANALYSIS TIME	TIME (hrs)		
CHANGE SPECIFICATION TIME	TIME (hrs)		
ACTIVE CORRECTION TIME	TIME (hrs)		
LOCAL TESTING TIME	TIME (hrs)		
GLOBAL TESTING TIME	TIME (hrs)		
EASE OF USE	NUMERIC (0-1)		
CONFIDENCE IN RESULT	NUMERIC (0-1)		
		TOTAL	

Figure 13.2: Maintainability metrics.

may have a much higher degree of confidance in the correctness of a system after successfully running appropriate KBS anomaly and error detection tools than if these tools were not available.

The metrics listed above can be combined together in a single metrics as illustrated in Figure 13.2. The weightings to be applied are of course subjective and may have to be refined to fit a particular application.

Maintenance Proforma

So that details for the maintainability metrics can be collected a change log must be completed by the maintenance engineers whenever a maintenance session is taking place. So as not to place any undue additional burden on the engineer this need not be very extensive. A suggested format for this log is given in Figure 13.3. Note that if two or more maintenance attributes cannot be separated they should be bracketed together for quantification purposes.

Maintenance Change Log Proforma

Name [ ] Date [ ]

Change requested by [ ]

1) Type of Maintenance Change
(Adaptive, Corrective, Perfective) [ ]

2) Maintenance Classification
(M1 ... Mn) [ ]

3) Maintenance Attributes

Total Recovery Time (hours)	
Problem Recognition Time (hours)	
Problem Analysis Time (hours)	
Change Specification Time (hours)	
Active Correction Time (hours)	
Local Testing Time (hours)	
Global Testing Time (hours)	
Ease of Use (numeric 0-1)	
Confidence in Result (numeric 0-1)	

NOTE: If Maintenance Attributes cannot be separated, two or more may be bracketed together for quantification purposes.

Figure 13.3: Maintenance change log proforma.

13.6. HOUSEKEEPING TOOLS.

The term "housekeeping" with respect to software engineering refers to the activities which ensure that the development and maintenance of a system is consistent. There are a number of tools which can be used to this end. The most common are data dictionaries, thesauruses and syntax and semantics checkers.

When adding new rules it is desirable, wherever possible, to use existing rules and slots rather than create new ones. A useful tool to assist in the identification of appropriate existing rules and slots is a data dictionary, whereby existing rules and slots can be identified by entering keywords. Data dictionaries have been used as an important software development support tool to aid in the design of conventional systems for some time. For example in database systems [Sprague and Carlson 1982], and as a quasi-formal method of describing the content of information items in Data Flow Diagrams [Pressman 1988].

Data dictionaries can also be used in the development of KBSs. For rule based systems the data dictionary would include, for each entry, the head of the rule, the heads of any rules from which it may be fired and the heads of any rules which it in turn may fire, plus any additional information which the software engineer considers relevant. Such a dictionary will be indexed according to the head of the rule, and so this should therefore be carefully selected so that it accurately describes the function of the rule. In the case of frame based systems the data dictionary should include the frame name, the slots immediately associated with the frame and (possibly) their slot values, the super-frame or frames to which it belongs as further attributes may be inherited from these frames and any sub-frames that branch of it, again because slot values will be passed down the frame hierarchy. For hybrid systems the frame hierarchy may serve many of the functions of a "data dictionary" for the rule based part of system.

The concept of using data dictionaries for KBS maintenance has been promoted by a number of researchers, such as Jansen and Compton [1989]. Jansen has developed a Knowledge Dictionary Tool to facilitate the documentation and maintenance of KBSs which operate using production rules. The dictionary is used to record heuristics and their component parts, facts and rule actions so that it can be used to determine the usage of any part of the knowledge hence simplifying the addition of extra rules and checking the effect of such rules.

With respect to KBS development and maintenance the use of a thesaurus will ensure that one particular spelling for (say) an attribute or a rule head is adhered to by adopting it as the internal version regardless of other spellings. Standard approximate word-matching functions will identify most common or nearly common names to assist in preparing a thesaurus.

Under the heading of housekeeping tools we should also consider syntax checkers. Regardless of the development method used the knowledge represented by a KBS must be entered into the system following some structure. In the case of some development shells this may be a very simple syntactic structure akin to natural language.

Alternatively if the KBS is implemented directly using an expert system "language" such as LISP or PROLOG very strict syntactic rules must be followed. A considerable amount of maintenance (and development) time is wasted correcting trivial semantic errors such as missed brackets and commas or simple "typos". To some extent this can be alleviated by the use of suitable editors, though it is hard to envisage a technique whereby typing errors can be avoided completely.

Usually the maintenance engineer will modify or add rules using some sort of editor. Most expert system shells have editors "built in". These editors tend to use standard editor routines and allow the user to alter rules and frames without the need to learn the high level language in which the shell is implemented. This representation is then loaded into the target representation. During this process semantic checks are carried out. This is a facility included in the MAUDE KBS development system [Coenen and Bench-Capon 1992a] which highlights rules and frames that are incorrect due to, for example, missing brackets or misspelled object and attributes names. The latter are identified by comparison with the class hierarchy which must be loaded first. Other editors incorporate manual checking facilities. For example the editor supplied with the INTERLISP used on XEROX expert system work stations has a facility to inspect bracket pairing [Xerox 1985]. Some systems incorporate template editors. Template editors provide the maintenance engineer with a mechanism for constructing forms based on existing forms. This will then dictate the style and enforce uniformity and control.

13.7. SUMMARY

In this final chapter we have given a very brief overview of some of the issues that concern the management of a KBS development. It is still the case that KBS technology is not yet sufficiently mature for it to be possible to be very prescriptive, but we have drawn attention to some of the points that must be considered. The relative wealth of material relating to these matters for conventional systems has only resulted from twenty years of experience of engineering conventional software. We believe that it is now time to take the idea of engineering KBSs with equal seriousness, and as this is done, and KBSs becomes a routine part of the Information Systems armoury, it is to be expected that a similar body of conventional wisdom will emerge.

BIBLIOGRAPHY.

This bibliography does not constitute a complete catalogue of the work relevant to the maintenance of knowledge based systems. However it does contain all the items referred to in the text and a number of additional works which the authors hope will also be of interest.

Agarwal, R. and Tanniru, M. (1990). Systems Development Life-Cycle for Expert Systems. Knowledge Based Systems, Vol 3, No 3, September, p170-180.

Agarwal, R. and Tanniru, M. (1991). A Petri-Net Based Approach for Verifying the Integrity of Production Systems. Knowledge-Based Systems Verification, Validation and Testing, Workshop Notes from the 9th National Conference on Artificial Intelligence, AAAI-91, Anaheim CA, 17 July.

Aiken, M.W. and Sheng, O.L. (1990). Nexpert Object. Expert Systems, February, p54-57.

Alexander, J.H., Freiling, M.J., Shulman, S.J., Rehfuss, S. and Messick, S.L. (1987). Ontological Analysis: an On-going Experiment. International Journal of Man-Machine Studies, Vol 26, No 4, 473-486.

Alford, M. (1985). SREM at the Age of Eight: The Distributed Computing Design System. (IEEE) Computer, Vol 18, No 4, p35-46.

Allen, L.E. and Saxon, C.S. (1987). Some Problems in Designing Expert Systems to Aid Legal Reasoning. Proceedings First International Conference on Artificial Intelligence and Law, Boston, May, ACM Press, p94-103.

Ayel, M. (1988). Protocols for Consistency Checking in Expert System Knowledge Bases. Proceedings ECAI, Munich, 1-5 August, p220-225.

Bachant, J. and McDermott, J. (1984). R1 Revisited: Four Years in the Trenches. AI Magazine, Vol 5, No 3, p21-32.

Balci, O. and Sargent, R.G. (1984). A Bibliography of the Credibility and Validation of Imulation and Mathematical Models. Simuletter, Vol 15, No 3. p15-27.

Barrett, B.W. (1990). A Hypothetical Application of the Statistical Modeling and Estimation of Reliability Functions for Software (SMERFS) to Knowledge-Based Systems (KBSs). Expert Systems with Applications, Vol 1. No 3, p281-289.

Becker, L.A., Green, P.E., Duckworth, J., Bhatnagar, J., and Pease, A. (1989). Evidence Flow Graphs for VV&T. Paper presented at IJCAI-89 Workshop on Verification, Validation and Testing of Knowledge-Based Systems, Detroit, MI.

Bellman, K.L. (1990). The Modeling Issues Inherent in Testing and Evaluating Knowledge-Based Systems. Expert Systems With Applications, Vol 1, No 3, p199-215.

Bench-Capon, T.J.M. (1990). Knowledge Representation: An Approach to Artificial Intelligence. Academic Press, London.

Bench-Capon, T.J.M. and Coenen, F.P. (1991a). Practical Applications of KBS to Law: The Crucial Role of Maintenance. In van Noortwijk, C., Schmidt, A.H.J. and Winkels, R.G.F. (eds), Legal Knowledge Based Systems, Aims for Research and Development, Koninklijke Vermande BV, Lelystadt, Netherlands, p5-17.

Bench-Capon, T.J.M. and Coenen, F. (1991b). The MAKE Project: Maintenance Tools FOR Knowledge Based Systems. In Liebowitz, J. (ed), Expert Systems World Congress Proceedings, Pergamon Press, Vol 3, p1030-1036.

Bench-Capon, T.J.M. and Coenen, F.P. (1991c). Exploiting Isomorphism: Development of a KBS to Support British Coal Insurance Claims. Proceedings Third International Conference on AI and Law, Oxford, ACM Press, pp 62-68.

Bench-Capon, T.J.M. and Coenen, F. (1992). The Maintenance of Legal Knowledge Based Systems. AI Review, Vol 6, p129-143.

Bench-Capon, T.J.M., Coenen, F. and Dunne, P. E. S. (1992). Integrating Legal Support Systems Through Document Models. Expert Systems with Applications, Vol 4, p355-362.

Bench-Capon, T.J.M., Coenen, F., Paton, R., Nwana H. and Shave, M. (1991). Two Aspects of the Validation and Verification of Knowledge Based Systems. European Workshop on the Verification and Validation of Knowledge Based Systems, EUROVAV-91, Cambridge, 22-24 July.

Bench-Capon, T.J.M. and Forder, J.M. (1991). Knowledge Representation for Legal Applications. In Bench-Capon, T.J.M. (ed), Knowledge Based Systems and Legal Applications, Academic Press, p245-264

Bobrow, D.G. and Winograd, T. (1977). An Overview of KRL, A Knowledge Representation Language. Cognitive Science, Vol 1, No 1, p3-46.

Boehm, B.W. (1981). Software Engineering Economics. Prentice Hall.

Boehm, B.W. (1988). A Spiral Model of Software Development and Enhancement. IEEE Computer, Vol 21, No 5, p61-72.

Booch, G. (1986). Object Oriented Development. IEEE Transactions Software Engineering, SE-12, No 2, p211-221.

Boose, J. and Bradswaw, J. (1987). Expertise Transfer and Complex Problems, Using AQUINAS as a Knowledge Acquisition Workbench for Expert Systems. In Addis, T., Boose, J. and Gains, B (eds), Proceedings of the Knowledge Acquisition for Knowledge-Based Systems Workshop, Banf, Canada.

Borgida, A., Greenspan, S. and Mylopoulos, J. (1985). Knowledge Representation as the Basis for Requirements Specification. (IEEE) Computer, Vol 18, No 4, p82-91.

Brachman, R.J. (1985). "I Lied about the Trees" or, Defaults and Definitions in Knowledge Representation. AI Magazine, Vol 6, Part 3, p80-93.

Brachman, R.J., Fikes, R.E. and Levesque, H.J. (1983). KRYPTON: A Functioned Approach to Knowledge Representation in Brachman, R.J. and Levesque, H.J. (eds), Readings in Knowledge Representation, Morgan Kaufman.

Brachman, R.J., Gilbert, V.P. and Levesque, H.J. (1985). An Essential Hybrid Reasoning System: Knowledge and Symbol Level Accounts of KRYPTON. Proceedings IJCAI-85.

Bratko, I. (1986). PROLOG Programming for Artificial Intelligence. Addison-Wesley.

Bratley, P., Fremont, J., MacKaay, E. and Poulin, D. (1991a). Coping With Change. Proceedings of the Third International Conference on Artificial Intelligence and Law, Oxford, 25-28 June. ACM, p69-76.

Bratley, P., Poulin, D. and Savoy, J. (1991b). The Effect of Change on Legal Applications. In Karagiannis, D. (ed), Database and Expert System Applications, Springer-Verlag, p436-441.

Brown, D. and Mayfield, T.P. (1990). ALDACS: A Knowledge-Based System to Assist Power Plant Operation. In Addis, T. and Muir, R.M. (eds), Research and Development in Expert Systems VII, Cambridge University Press, p116-124.

Buchanan, B.G., Barstow, D., Bechtel, R., Bennet, J., Clancey, W., Kulikowski, C., Mitchell, T. and Waterman, D.A. (1983). Constructing an Expert System. In Hayes-Roth, F., Waterman, D.A. and Lenat, D.B. (eds), Building Expert Systems, Addison Wesley, p127-167.

Buchanan, B.G. and Shortliffe, E.H. (1984). Rule Based Expert Systems, The MYCIN Experiments of the Stanford Heuristic Programming Project. Addison-Wesley.

Bundy, A., Byrd, L., Liger, G., Mellish, C. and Palmer, M. (1979). Solving Machine Problems Using Meta Level Inference. In D.Michie (ed), Expert Systems in the Microelectronic Age, Edinburgh University Press, Edinburgh.

Bylander, T. and Chandrasekaran, B. (1987). Generic Tasks for Knowledge-Based Reasoning: The "Right" Level of Abstraction for Knowledge Acquisition. International Journal Man-Machine Studies, Vol 26, p231-243.

Byrne (1991). GNU Smalltalk User's guide. Free Software Foundation, Inc.

Caviedes, J.E. (1987). Expert Systems Maintenance: Post-Implementation Support. Proceedings IEEE MONTECH 87, New York, p21-24.

Chandrasekaran, B. (1985). Generic Tasks on Knowledge Based Reasoning: Characterisation and Designing expert Systems at the "Right" Level of Abstraction. Proceedings of the IEEE 2nd Conference on Artificial Intelligence Applications, p294-300.

Chang, C.L., Combs, J.B. and Stachowitz, R.A. (1990). A Report on the Expert Systems Validation Associate (EVA). Experts Systems with Applications, Vol 1, No 3, p219-230.

Chard, R. A. 1990). The Problems of Software Maintenance and the Potential of Software Tools. NCC, The National centre for Information Technology, Manchester.

Charles, E. (1991) Checking Knowledge Bases for Inconsistencies and Other Anomalies. Workshop Notes from the Ninth National Conference in Artificial Intelligence, AAAI-91, Knowledge-Based Systems Verification, Validation and Testing, 17 July, Anaheim CA.

Childress, R.L. and Valtorta, M. (1991). EVA and the Verification of Expert Systems Written in OPS5. Workshop Notes from the Ninth National Conference in Artificial Intelligence, AAAI-91, Knowledge-Based Systems Verification, Validation and Testing, 17 July, Anaheim CA.

Clancey, W.J. (1985). Heuristic Classification. Artificial Intelligence, Vol 20, p289-350.

Clocksin, W.F. and Mellish, C.S. (1984). Programming in PROLOG, Second Edition. Springer-Verlag.

Codd, E.F. (1970). A Relational Model of Data for Large Shared Data Banks. Communications, ACM, Vol 13, p377-387.

Coenen, F. (1992). A Methodology for the Maintenance of Knowledge Based Systems. In Niku-Lari (Ed.). EXPSYS9292. IITT-International, Gournay sur Marne, France, p191-196.

Coenen, F. and Bench-Capon, T.B.C (1991). A Graphical Interactive Tool for KBS Maintenance. In Karagiannis, D. (ed). Database and Expert Systems Applications Springer-Verlag, p166-171.

Coenen, F. and Bench-Capon, T.J.M. (1992a). Maintenance and Maintainability in Regulation Based KBS. ICL Technical Journal, May, p67-84.

Coenen, F. and Bench-Capon, T.J.M. (1992b). KBS Maintenance Validation using Simulation. In Grierson, D.E., Rzevski, G. and Adey, R.A. (eds), Applications of Artificial Intelligence in Engineering VII, Computational Mechanics Publications and Elsevier Applied Science, p215-228.

Compton, P., Horn, K., Quinlan, J., Lazarus, L. and Ho. K. (1988). Maintaining an Expert System. Fourth Australian Conference on Applications of Expert Systems, p110-129.

Compton, P. and Jansen, R. (1988) Knowledge in Context: A Strategy for Expert System Maintenance. Proceedings, AI88, Australian Joint Artificial Intelligence Conference, Springer-Verlag, p292-306.

Compton, P. Srinivasan, A., Edwards, G., Malor, R. and Lazarus, L. (1991). Knowledge Base Maintenance Without a Knowledge Engineer. in Liebowitz, J. (ed), Expert Systems World Congress Proceedings, Pergamon Press, Vol 1. p668-675.

Constantine, M.M. and Ulvila, J.W. (1990) Testing Knowledge-Based Systems: The State of the Practice and Suggestions for Improvement. Expert Systems with Applications, Vol 1. No 3, p237-248.

Constantine, L.L. and Yourdon, E. (1979). Structured Design. Prentice-Hall.

Cragen, B.J. and Steudel, H.J. (1987). A Decision-Table-based Processor for Checking Completeness and Consistency in Rule-Based Expert Systems. International Journal of Man-Machine Studies, Vol 26, p633-648.

Craw, S. and Sleeman, D. (1990). Automating the Refinement of Knowledge-Based Systems. Proceedings ECAI 90, Stockholm, August 6-10, p167-172.

Cuda, T.V. and Dolan, C.P. (1991). Tool Aided, Non-Formal Knowledge Verification. Knowledge-Based Systems Verification, Validation and Testing Workshop Notes from the 9th National Conference on Artificial Intelligence, AAAI-91, 17 July.

Culbert, C. and Savely, R. (1988). Expert system verification and validation. Paper presented at the First AAAI Workshop on Validation and Testing of Knowledge Based Systems, Palo Alto, CA.

Cutts, G. (1991). Structured System Analysis and Design Methodology. Blackwell Scientific, 2nd Edition.

Davis, R. (1984). Interactive Transfer of Expertise. In Buchanan, B.G. and Shortliffe, E.H. (eds), Rule-Based Expert Systems: The MYCIN Experiments of the Stanford Heuristic Programming Project, Addison-Wesley, p171-205.

de Kleer, J. (1986) An Assumption-Based TMS. Artificial Intelligence 28, p127-162.

DeMarco, T. (1979). Structured Analysis and System Specification. Prentice-Hall.

De Millo, R.A., McCraken, W.M., Martin, R.J. and Passafiume, J.F. (1987). Software Testing and Evaluation. The Benjamin-Cummings Publishing Co. Inc.

Delfs, H. and Winkelmann, K (1991). TOROS-HYPER: A Tool for the Integration of Hyper Documents into Knowledge-Based Systems. In Karagiannis, D. (ed). Database and Expert System Applications Springer-Verlag, p275-280.

Diaper, D. (ed) (1989). Knowledge Elicitation Principles, Techniques and Applications. Ellis Horwood.

Diederich, J. and Linster, M. (1989). Knowledge-Based Knowledge Elicitation. In Guide, G. and Tasso, C. (eds) (1989). Topics in Expert System Design: Methodologies and Tools. North-Holland, p322-350.

Diederich, J., Ruhmann, I. and May, W. (1987). KRITON: A Knowledge Acquisition Tool for Expert Systems. International Journal of Man Machine Studies, Vol 26, p29-40.

Ducassé, M. and Emde, A. (1988). Opium+, a Meta-debugger for PROLOG. Proceedings ECAI, Munich, 1-5 August, p272-277.

Duffin, P. (ed) (1988). KBS in Government 88. Blenheim Online, Pinner.

Feldman, S. (1979). MAKE - A Program for Maintaining Computer Programs. Software - Practice and Experience, 9, p255-265.

Fickas, S. (1987). Supporting the Programmer of a Rule Based Language. Expert Systems, Vol 4, No 2, p74-87.

Fidelak, M. and Victor, F. (1989). Verification of Production Systems. Proceedings of the International Conference on Computing and Information (ICCI 89), Elsevier, p371-378.

Fieschi, M. (1990). Towards Validation of Expert Systems as Medical Decision Aids. International Journal of Bio-Medical Computing, Vol 26, No 1-2, p93-108.

Finlay, P.N., Forsey. G.J. and Wilson, J.M. (1988). The Validation of Expert Systems: Contrasts with Traditional Methods. Journal of Operational Research Society, Vol 39, No 10, p933-938.

Forder, J.M. and Taylor, A.D. (1991). The Local Office System. In Bench-Capon, T.J.M. (ed), Knowledge Based Systems for Legal Applications. Academic Press.

Futatsugi, K., Coguen, J.A., Jouannaud, J.P. and Meseguer, J. (1985). Principals of OBJ2. Proceedings 12th ACM symposium on Principals of Programming Languages, New-Orleans, p52-56.

Gane, C. and Sarson, T. (1979). Structured System Analysis: Tools and Techniques. Prentice Hall.

Gashing, J. (1979). Preliminary Performance Analysis of the Prospector Consultant System for Mineral Exploration. Proceedings of 6th International Joint Conference on Artificial Intelligence, Morgan Kaufman, p308-310.

Geissman, J. (1988). Verification and Validation for Expert Systems: A Practical Methodology. Proceedings, 4th Annual Artificial Intelligence and Advanced Computer Technology Conference, p344-51.

General Research Corporation (1985). TIMM User's Manual. General Research Corporation, Santa Barbara, California.

Genrich, H.J. and Lautenbach, K. (1981). System Modelling with High Level Petri Nets. Theoretical Computer Science, Vol 13, p109-136.

Gilb, T. (1979). A Comment on the Definition of Reliability. ACM Software Engineering Notes, Vol 4, No 3, July.

Ginsberg, A. (1987). A New Approach to Checking Knowledge Bases for Inconsistency and Redundancy. Proceedings 3rd Annual Conference Expert Systems in Government, IEEE, p102-111.

Ginsberg, A. (1988). Knowledge Base Reduction: A New Approach to Checking Knowledge Bases for Inconsistency and Redundancy. In Proc 7th National Conference on AI (AAAI88), August 1988, St Paul MN, vol 2, p585-589.

Ginsberg, A. and Weiss, S. (1985). SEEK 2: A Generalised Approach to Automatic Knowledge Base Refinement. Proceedings IJCAI, p367-374.

Gladden, G. (1982), Stop the Life-Cycle - I want to get off. ACM Software Engineering Notes, Vol 7, No 2, p35-9.

Goldberg, A. and Robson, D. (1983). SMALLTALK-80: The Language and its Implementation. Addison-Wesley

Green, C.J. and Keyes, M.M. (1987). Verification and Validation of Expert Systems. WESTEX 87, Proceedings of the Western Conference on Expert Systems, p38-43.

Grisoni, M. (1987). The Validation of Knowledge-Based Systems. IEE Colloquium on Testing Expert Systems, London, p4/1-6.

Grover, M.D. (1983). A Pragmatic Knowledge Acquisition Methodology. Proccedings International Joint Conference on Artificial Intelligence, p436-438.

Hart, P.E., Duda, R.O. and Einaudi, M.T. (1978). PROSPECTOR -- A Computer-Based Consultation System for Mineral Exploitation. Mathematical Geology, Vol 10, No 5, p589-610.

Hayes, I. (ed) (1987). Specification Case Studies. Prentice Hall.

Hayes, P.J. (1979a). The Naive Physics Manifesto. In D. Michie (ed), Expert Systems in the Microelectronic Age, Edinburgh University Press.

Hayes, P.J. (1979b). The Logic of Frames. In Metzing, D. (ed), Frame Conceptions and Text Understanding, de Gruyter.

Hicks, R.C. (1990). A Composite Methodology for Low Maintenance Expert System Development. Proceedings of the 3rd Annual Hawaii International Conference on System Sciences, Vol 3, Computer Society Press, p 293-302.

Inaba, M., Taichi, A., Sumigama, T. and Sakurai, M. (1991) Application of an expert System to a Blast Furnace Operation. In Liebowitz, J. (ed), Expert Systems World Congress Proceedings. Pergamon Press, Vol. 1, p30-37.

Irani, E.A., Matts, J.P., Hunter, D.W., Slagle, J., Kain, R.Y., Long, J.M. and the POSCH Group (1990). Automated Assistance for Maintenance of Medica Expert Systems: The Posch AI Project. Proceedings 3rd Annual IEEE Symposium on Computer Based Medical Systems, IEEE Computer Society, Los Almitos CA, p275-81.

Jackson, M.A. (1975). Principles of Program Design. Academic Press.

Jackson, M.A. (1983). System Development. Prentice-Hall.

Jacob, R.J.K. and Froscher, J.N. (1990). A Software Engineering Methodology for Rule-Based Systems. IEEE Transactions on Knowledge and Data Engineering, Vol 2, No 2, June 1990, p173-189.

Jansen, B. and Compton, P. (1989). A Data Dictionary Approach to the Maintenance of Expert Systems: The Knowledge Dictionary. Knowledge-Based Systems, Vol 2, No 1, p14-26.

Johnson, N.E. (1989). Mediating Representations in Knowledge Elicitation. In Diaper, D. (ed), Knowledge Elicitation: Principles, Techniques and Applications, Ellis Horwood, p179-194.

Johnson, R., Joly, G. and King, P. (1987). Validation and Verification in Expert System Rule Sets. IEE Colloquium on Testing Expert Systems, London, p3/1-3.

Jones, C.B. (1986). Systematic Software Development Using VDM. Prentice-Hall.

Johnson, R., Joly, G. and King, P. (1987). Validation and Verification in Expert System Rule Sets. IEE Colloquium on Testing Expert Systems, London, p3/1-3.

Kai, C. and Weston, S. (1988). Software Maintainability: Perceptions of EDP Professionals. MIS Quarterly, June 1988, Vol 12, No 2.

Kearsley, G. (1988). Validation of an Expert System: The CBT Analyst. Journal of Computer-Based Instruction, Vol 15, No 2, p61-64.

Klinker, G., Bond, C., Genelet, G. and McDermott, J. (1987). A KNACK For Knowledge Acquisition. Proceedings AAAI 87, Seatle, USA.

LaFrance, M. (1987). The Knowledge Acquisition Grid: A Method for Training Knowledge Engineers. International Journal Man-Machine Studies, Vol 26, p245-255.

Landauer, C. (1990). Correctness Principles for Rule-Based Expert Systems. Expert Systems with Applications, Vol 1, No 3, p291-317.

Lemmon, E.J. (1965). Beginning Logic. Van Nostrand Reinhold (International), Hong Kong.

Linden, T,A. (1990). A Meta-Level Software Development Model that Supports V & V for AI Software. Expert Systems with Applications, Vol 1, No 3, p271-279.

Lindsay, R., Buchanan, B.G., Feigenbaum, E.A and Lederberg, J. (1980). Applications of Artificial Intelligence for Chemical Inference: The Dendral Project. McGraw-Hill,

Long, J.A. and Neale, I.M. (1991). KBS Validation, verification and Testing with Multiple Experts. In Liebowitz, J. (ed), Expert Systems World Congress Proceedings, Pergamon Press, Vol 2, p989-996.

Lopez, B., Meseguer, P. and Plaza, E. (1990). Knowledge Based Systems Validation: A State of the Art. AI Communications, Vol 3, No 2, p58-72.

Luger, G.F. and Stubblefield, W.A. (1989). Artificial Intelligence and the Design of Expert Systems. Benjamin Cummings, Redwood City.

McCracken, D.D. and Jackson, M.A. (1982). Life Cycle Concept Considered Harmful. ACM Software Engineering Notes, Vol 7, No 2, p28-32.

McDermott, J. (1980). R1: An Expert in the Computer Systems Domain. Proccedings of AAAI-80, National Conference on Artificial Intelligence, Stanford, California, p269-271.

McDermott, J. (1982). R1: A Rule Based Configurer of Computer Systems. Artificial Intelligence, Vol 19, No 1, p39-88.

Micco, M. (1988). Acceptance Testing of Expert Systems: Issues of Verification and Validation. Proceedings, Focus on Software, ACM 18th Annual Computer Science Conference. ACM, New York, p214-217.

Minsky, M. (1975). A Framework for Representing Knowledge. In Winston, P.H. (ed), The Psychology of Computer Vision, McGraw-Hill, New York.

Mockler, R.J. and Dologite, D.G. (1992). Knowledge-Based Systems: An Introduction to Expert Systems. Macmillan Publishing Company.

Montgomery, A. (1988). GEMINI - Government Expert System Methodology Initiative. In Kelly, B. and Rector, A. (eds), Research and Development in Expert Systems IV, Cambridge University Press.

Moran, T. (1990). Five Years of Deep Knowledge: A Personal View. AISB Quarterly 74, p20-31.

Morell, L. J. (1988). Use of Metaknowledge in the Verification of Knowledge-Based Systems. Proceedings 1st International Conference of Industrial Engineering Applications of Artificial Intelligence and Expert Systems (IEA/AIE), ACM New York, p847-857.

Morris, L. (1988). Maintenance-Oriented Design of Expert Systems. ISA Transactions, Vol 28, Part 1, p23-26.

Motta, E., Eisenstadt, M., Pitman, K. and West, M. (1988). Support for Knowledge Acquisition in the Knowledge Engineer's Assistant (KEATS). Expert Systems, February, Vol 5, No 1.

Motta, E., Rajan, T., Domingue, J. and Eisenstadt, M. (1990). Methodological Foundations of KEATS, The Knowledge Engineer's Assistant. In Wielinga, B., Boose, J., Gains, B., Schreiber, G. and van Sommeren, M. (eds), Current Trends in Knowledge Acquisition, IOS Press, p257-275.

Motta, E., Rajan, T., Eisenstadt, M., (1989). Knowledge Acquisition as a Process of Model Refinement. International Journal of Man-Machine Studies.

Naur, P. and Randell, B. (eds) (1969). Software Engineering: A Report on a Conference Sponsored by the NATO Science Committee. NATO.

Neches, R., Swartout, W. and Moore, J.D. (1985). Enhanced Maintenance and Explanation of Expert Systems through Explicit Models of their Development. IEEE Transactions on Software Engineering, Vol SE-11, No 11, p1337-1351.

Nguyen, T.A. (1987). Verifying Consistency of Production Systems. Proceedings 3rd Conference on AI Applications, (IEEE) Computer Society, Kissimmee, FL, 23-27 February, 1987, p4-8.

Nguyen, T.A., Perkins, W.A., Laffey, T.J. and Pecora, D. (1985). Checking an Expert System's Knowledge Base for Consistency and Completeness. Proceedings IJCAI85, p375-378.

Nguyen, T.A., Perkins, W.A., Laffey, T.J. and Pecora, D. (1987). Knowledge Base Verification. AI Magazine, Summer, p69-75.

Nieuwenhuis, M.A. (1989). TESSEC: Een Expertsystem voor de Algemene Bijstandswet. Deventer, Kluwer.

Nwana, H.S. and Paton, R.C. (1990). Domain Characterisation through Knowledge Analysis. Proceedings AAAI 90, Knowledge Acquisition Workshop.

O'Keefe, R.M., Balci, O. and Smith, E.P. (1987). Validating Expert System Performance. IEEE Expert, Vol 2, No 4, p81-89.

O'Keefe, R.M. and Lee, S. (1990). An Integrative Model of Expert System Verification and Validation. Expert Systems With applications, Vol 1, No 3, p231-236.

O'Leary, D.E. (1991). Knowledge Acquisition Opportunities Resulting from Verification, Validation and Maintenance. In Liebowitz, J. (ed), Expert Systems World Congress Proceedings, Pergamon Press, Vol 3, p2873-2881.

O'Leary, T.J., Goul, M., Moffitt, K.E. and Radwan, A.E (1990) Validating Expert Systems. IEEE Expert, Vol 5, No 3, p51-58.

O'Leary, D.E. and O'Keefe, R (1989). Verifying and Validating Expert Systems. Tutorial at IJCAI 1989.

Oliver, A.E.M. (1987). Techniques for Expert System Testing and Validation. Proceedings 3rd International Expert Systems Conference, Learned Information, p271-276.

Orr, K.T. (1977). Structured System Development. Yourdin Press, New-York.

Parikh, G. (1986). Handbook of Software Maintenance. John Wiley & Sons.

Paton, R.C. and Nwana, H.S. (1990). Domain Characterisation Through Knowledge Analysis. Proceedings of AAAI-90 Workshop on Knowledge Acquisition, July, Boston, MA.

Paton, R.C., Nwana, H.S., Shave, M.J and Bench-Capon, T.J.M. (1991). From Real World Problems to Domain Characterisations. Proceedings of the Fifth European Knowledge Acquisition Workshop, May, Creiff, Scotland.

Pau, L.F. (1987). Prototyping, Validation and Maintenance of Knowledge Based Systems Software. Proceedings 3rd Annual Expert Systems in Government Conference, IEEE Computer Society, Washington, p248-253.

Pipard, E. (1988). Detection d'Incoherences et d'Incompletitudes dans les Bases de Regles; Le System INDE. Proceedings AVIGNON 1988, p15-33.

Politakis (1985). Empirical Analysis of Expert Systems. In Research Notes in Artificial Intelligence 6, Pitman.

Pople, H.E. (1982). Heuristic Methods for Imposing Structure on Ill Structured Problems: The Structuring of Medical Diagnosis. In Szolovits, P. (ed), Artificial Intelligence in Medicine, Westview Press, Colorado, p119-185.

Popper, K. (1963). Conjectures and Refutations. Routledge and Kegan Paul, London.

Preece, A.D. and Shinghal, R. (1991a). COVER: A Practical Tool For Verifying Rule-Based Systems. Knowledge-Based Systems Verification, Validation and Testing, Workshop Notes from the 9th National Conference on Artificial Intelligence, AAAI-91, Anaheim CA, 17 July.

Preece, A.D. and Shinghal, R. (1991b). DARC: A Procedure for Verifying Rule-Based Systems. In Liebowitz, J. (ed), Expert Systems World Congress Proceedings, Vol 2, Pergamon Press, p971-979.

Prerau, D.S., Gunderson, A.S. Reinke, R.E. and Adler, M. (1990) Maintainability Techniques in Developing Large Expert Systems. IEEE Expert, June, Vol 5, No 3, p71-79.

Pressman, R.S. (1988). Software Engineering, A Practitioners Approach. 2nd Edition. McGraw-Hill.

Radwan, A.E., Goul, M., O'Leary, T.J. and Moffitt, K. (1989). A Verification Approach for Knowledge-Based Systems. Transportation Research, Vol 23A, No 4, p287-300.

Rajan, T., Motta, E. and Eisenstadt, M. (1988). ACQUIST: A Tool for Knowledge Acquisition. In Kelly, B. and Rector, A. Research and Development in Expert Systems IV. Cambridge University Press.

Rich, E. and Knight, K. (1991). Artificial Intelligence. McGraw Hill.

Roberts, C. and Hall, L.O (1991). Exploiting Rule Organisations to Improve Correctness and Performance of Rule Based Systems. Knowledge-Based Systems Verification, Validation and Testing Workshop Notes from the 9th National Conference on Artificial Intelligence, AAAI-91, 17 July.

Robson, D. (1981). Object Oriented Software Systems. BYTE, Vol 6, No 8, p74-79.

Rochkind, M.J. (1975). The Source Code Control System. IEEE Transactions on Software Engineering, Vol SE-1, No 4, p364-370.

Roscoe, G.S. (1988). 9370 Expert System Configurater Knowledge Base Verification. Proceedings 4th International Expert Systems Conference. Learned Inf., Oxford, p159-167.

Ross, D. (1985). Applications and Extensions of SADT. IEEE Computer, Vol 18, No 4, p25-34.

Rousset, M.C. (1987). Sur La Validite des Bases des Conaissances. Proceedings 7th Journees International Avignon, p269-282.

Rousset, M.C. (1988). On The Consistency of Knowledge Bases: The COVADIS System. Proceedings ECAI, Munich, 1-5 August, p79-84.

Routen, T.W. (1989). Hierarchically Organised Formalisations. In Proceedings of the Second International Conference on AI and Law, Vancouver, ACM Press, 1989.

Routen, T.W. and Bench-Capon, T.J.M. (1991). Hierarchical Formalisations. International Journal of Man-Machine Studies, Vol 35, July, p69-93.

Royce, W.W. (1970). Managing the Development of Large Software Systems. Proceedings, WESTCON, CA, USA.

Satre, T.W. and Massey, J.G. (1991). Expert System Verification and Validation, Part I: Defining the Concepts. In Rzevski, G. and Adey, R.A. (eds), Applications of Artificial Intelligence in Engineering VI, Computational Mechanics Publications and Elsevier Applied Science, p859-872.

Schatz, H. Strahs, R. and Campbell, L. (1987). Designing an Expert System for Long-Term Maintenance. Journal of Accounting and EDP, Vol 3, No 3, p20-24.

Scheffer, P.A. and Rzepka, W.E. (1985). A Case Study of SREM. (IEEE) Computer, Vol 18, No 4, p47-54.

Sherman, D.M. (1987). A PROLOG Model of the Income Tax Act of Canada. Proceedings First International Conference on Artificial Intelligence and Law, Boston, May 1987, ACM Press, p127-136.

Sievert, G.E. and Mizell, T.A. (1985). Specification-Based Software Engineering with TAGS. (IEEE) Computer, Vol 18, No 4, p56-65.

Skingle, B. (1987). The Validation of Knowledge Based Systems. Proceedings of the International Conference on Knowledge Based Systems (KBS87), Online Publications, p27-36.

Smeaton, G.P. and Coenen, F. (1990). Developing an Intelligent Marine Navigation System. (IEE) Computing and Control Engineering Journal, Vol 1, No 2, p95-103.

Software Architecture and Engineering Inc. (1983) KES General Description Manual. Software Architecture and Engineering Inc., Arlington, VA.

Soloway, E., Bachant, J. and Jensen, K. (1987). Assessing the Maintainability of XCON-in-RIME: Coping with the Problems of a VERY Large Rule-Base. Proceedings of AAAI-87, Vol 2, p824-829.

Sommerville, I. (1989). Software Engineering, Third Edition. Addison Wesley.

Sowa, J.F. (1984). Conceptual Structures. Addison-Wesley.

Sprague, R.H. (Jr) and Carlson, E.D. (1982). Building Effective Decision Support Systems. Prentice Hall.

Stachowitz, R.A. and Chang, C.L. (1988). Verification and Validation of Expert Systems. Tutorial at AAAI-88.

Stachowitz, R.A. and Combs, J.B. (1987). Validation of Expert Systems. Proceedings of The 20th Annual Hawaii International conference on System Sciences, p686-695.

Steele, G.L. (1990) Common LISP: The Language (2nd Edition). Digital Press, Bedford MA.

Storrs, G.E. and Burton, C.P. (1989). KANT, A Knowledge Analysis Tool. ICL Technical Journal, Vol 6, No 3, May, p572-581.

Suwa, M., Scott, A.C. and Shortliffe, E.H. (1982). An approach to verifying completeness and consistency in a rule-based expert system. AI Magazine, Fall, p16-21.

Suwa, M., Scott, A.C. and Shortliffe, E.H. (1984). Completeness and Consistency in a Rule-Based System. In Buchanan, B.G. and Shortliffe, E.H. (eds), Rule-Based Expert Systems: The MYCIN Experiments of the Stanford Heuristic Programming Project, Addison-Wesley.

Svenson, J.S., Kordelaar, P.J.M., Wassink, J.G.J. and van t'Eind, G.J. (1991). Analysing Legislation with ExpertiSZe. Proceedings The Hague Conference, European Group of Public Administration.

Swanson, E.B. (1976). The Dimensions of maintenance. Proceedings of 2nd International Conference Software Engineering, October, p492-497.

Swartout, W. (1983). XPLAIN: A System for Creating and Explaining Expert Consulting Systems. Artificial Intelligence, Vol 21, No 3, p285-325.

Teichrow, D. and Hershey, E.A. (1977). PSL/PSA: A Computer Aided Technique for Structured Documentation and Analysis of Information Processing Systems. IEEE Transactions Software Engineering, SE-3, No 1, p41-48.

Threadgold, R. (1991). Controlling Database Integrity. In Rzevski, G. and Adey, R.A. (eds), Applications of Artificial Intelligence in Engineering VI, Computational Mechanics Publications and Elsevier Applied Science, p219-238.

Threadgold, R. (1992). Adapting a KBS in the Face of Change. In Grierson, D.E., Rzevski, G. and Adey, R.A. (eds), Applications of Artificial Intelligence in Engineering VII, Computational Mechanics Publications and Elsevier Applied Science, p197-214.

van Melle, W., Shortliffe, E.H. and Buchanan, B. (1984). EMYCIN: A Knowledge Engineer's Tool for Constructing Rule-Based Expert Systems. In Buchanan, B.G. and Shortliffe, E.H. (eds). Rule-Based Expert Systems, The MYCIN Experiments of the Stanford Heuristic Programming Project, Addison-Wesley.

Vanthienen, J. (1991). Knowledge Acquisition and Validation Using a Decision Table Engineering Workbench. In Liebowitz, J. (ed), Expert Systems World Congress Proceedings, Pergamon Press, Vol 3, p1861-1868.

Wasserman, A., Pircher, P.A., Shewnake, D.T. and Kersten, M.L. (1986). Developing Interactive Information Systems with the User Software Engineering Methodology. IEEE Transactions Software Engineering, SE-12, No 2, p236-345.

Watson, I.D., Shave M.J. and Moralee D.S. (1989). A Knowledge Analysis Methodology Using an Intermediate Knowledge Representation Based on Conceptual Graphs. Proceedings, 9th International Workshop on Expert Systems and their Applications (Avignon), p183-198.

Wielinga, B.J., Breuker, J.A. and van Sommeren, M.W. (1986). The KADS System, Functional Description. Esprit Project P1098 Deliverable T1.1, Department of Social Science Informatics, University of Amsterdam.

Wielinga, B.J., Schreiber, A.T. and Breuker, J.A. (1992). KADS: A Modelling Approach to Knowledge Engineering. Knowledge Acquisition (Special Issue: The KADS approach to knowledge engineering), Vol 4, No 1, March, p5-54.

Wiener, R. and Sincovec, R. (1984). Software Engineering with Modula-2 and ADA. John Wiley & Sons.

Wilensky, R. (1984). LISPcraft. W.W. Norton & Co.

Winston, P.H. (1984). Artificial Intelligence, 2nd Edition. Addison-Wesley.

Xerox (1985). Artificial Intelligence Systems: The Lisp Library Packages Manual. Xerox Corporation.

Yoon, J.P. (1989). Techniques for Data and Rule Validation in Knowledge Based Systems. COMPASS 89, Proceedings of the 4th Annual Conference on Computer Assurance System Integrity, Software Safety and Process Security, p62-70.

Young, R.M. (1987). The Role of Intermediate Representations in Knowledge Elicitation. In Moralee, D.S. (ed) (1987). Research and Development in Expert Systems IV. Cambridge University Press, p287-288.

Yourdon, E. and Constantine, L. (1978). Structured Design. Yourdon Press.

Index